Graphic Design for Board Games

Board games are increasingly recognized as an artform of their own, but their design and aesthetics are just as important as their gameplay mechanics. In this handbook, art director and graphic designer Daniel Solis offers his 20+ years of expertise in graphic design in tabletop gaming.

With a sense of humor, plenty of examples, and simple tips, *Graphic Design for Board Games* covers everything from typography to retail presence. Learn how to effectively use graphic design elements to enhance player experience. Create stunning game components, clear rulebooks, and effective game boards that will keep players engaged.

Key Features:

- Highlights unique challenges and solutions of graphic design for board games
- Includes commentary from over a dozen board game graphic designers
- Explains complex concepts with numerous visual examples
- Trains designers to incorporate heuristics, accessibility, and semiotics

Newcomers will learn introductory concepts of visual communication. Intermediate designers will find ways to anticipate common visual obstacles and improve playtest results. Experienced veterans will find insightful comments shared by fellow professionals.

Soon you'll design unforgettable gaming experiences for your players!

CRC Press Guides to Tabletop Game Design
Series Editor: Geoffrey Engelstein

Thematic Integration in Board Game Design
Sarah Shipp

Graphic Design for Board Games
Daniel Solis

Graphic Design for Board Games

Daniel Solis

CRC Press
Taylor & Francis Group
Boca Raton London New York

CRC Press is an imprint of the
Taylor & Francis Group, an **informa** business

First edition published 2025
by CRC Press
2385 NW Executive Center Drive, Suite 320, Boca Raton FL 33431

and by CRC Press
4 Park Square, Milton Park, Abingdon, Oxon, OX14 4RN

CRC Press is an imprint of Taylor & Francis Group, LLC

ISBN: 9781032592459 (hbk)
ISBN: 9781032583365 (pbk)
ISBN: 9781003453772 (ebk)

DOI: 10.1201/9781003453772

Typeset in Minion
by Newgen Publishing UK

Contents

Series Preface, vii

Acknowledgments, ix

About the Author, xi

INTRODUCTION   1

CHAPTER 1 ▪ Typography   3

CHAPTER 2 ▪ Iconography   37

CHAPTER 3 ▪ Diagrams   68

CHAPTER 4 ▪ Cards   106

CHAPTER 5 ▪ Punchouts   150

CHAPTER 6 ▪ Game Boards   187

CHAPTER 7 ▪ Rulebooks   213

CHAPTER 8 ■ Boxes and Packaging   234

CHAPTER 9 ■ Conclusion   275

INDEX, 285

Series Preface

THE HISTORY OF GAMES goes back at least 5,000 years, and game materials are routinely found in archeological digs around the world. They are an integral part of what makes us human.

And yet the scholarly study of games as a craft, tabletop games in particular, is a relatively recent development. Their study has gone hand in hand with an explosion of creativity in tabletop games, and increasing cultural penetration and acceptance in all their forms.

Because of their centrality to the human experience, it is unsurprising that the study of games touches on many spheres. Art, science, philosophy, storytelling, psychology, math, social dynamics, and system engineering are just some of the disciplines that inform and guide the design of games, and our reaction to them.

The goal of this book series is for each volume to take a tightly focused look at a single topic within this spectrum, authored by an expert in the field. The diversity of topics demands a diverse set of authors, each of whom brings their particular knowledge, experience, and perspective to the realm of game design.

It is in this spirit that we are very pleased to bring you this volume of the CRC Press Guides to Tabletop Game Design.

Geoff Engelstein
Series Editor

Acknowledgments

I T'S BEEN A WONDERFUL new challenge to put down in writing so much of what I've learned over my career. I'm sure there are still big gaps that I neglected to write down. The biggest challenge of summarizing your entire job is forgetting what you take for granted. Thankfully I've had a lot of help along the way.

This book wouldn't have even come about had Geoff Engelstein not proposed it. I've had a history of declining opportunities because I didn't feel qualified, but Geoff wouldn't allow me to let this one slip away. You have my eternal thanks for believing I'm qualified to write this.

No doubt some of my knowledge may be outdated since the world of graphic design can advance so quickly. It takes a full community of professionals supporting one another to keep up with a quickly-changing profession. I would like to thank my fellow designers who participated in the survey from which we curated the quotations throughout this book:

- Bill Bricker (90+ titles)
- Lindsay Daviau (Restoration Games)
- Kirk W Buckendorf (*Ready Set Bet, Undergrove*)
- Rory Muldoon (*Voyages, Aquamarine, Waypoints, Tinderblox, Skora*)
- Jacoby O'Connor (*Raccoon Tycoon, Mosaic*)
- Jeppe Norsker (*50 Clues*)
- Todd Sanders
- Tony Mastrangeli
- Stephanie Gustafsson (*Middara, Castles by the Sea, Rolling Heights*)
- Mike Markowitz (*Alexandros* (1991), *I Am Spartacus* (1992))
- Torben Ratzlaff (*Tiny Travels, Welcome Words*)

- Heiko Günther
- Brigette Indelicato (*War Chest, Dice Miner, Votes for Women, Zoo Vadis, The Plot Thickens*)
- Estefania Rodriguez (*PopCats Fighter*)

I'd also like to thank the many publishers who gave us permission to use their products as examples throughout this book. I appreciate you taking the time to consider this weird proposal for a textbook.

- Fred Hicks, Evil Hat Productions
- Zev Shlasinger, Play to Z
- Justin Ziran, WizKids
- Scott Gaeta, Renegade Games
- Jason Tagmire, Button Shy
- Travis Worthington, Indie Game Studios
- Mike Hummel, Studio Big, Asmodee North America
- Michael Mindes, Tasty Minstrel Games
- Olive Wesley, Izzy Iqbal, and Patrick Burksson, Null Signal Games

Very special thanks to all of my Patrons who have supported me throughout the year+ that it's taken to write this book. You've been very patient and helpful with me. In particular, I want to thank Luis Francisco for offering suggestions that really helped to fill out the book's details and clarify key points.

I'd like to thank my own mentors and early supporters who guided my first steps in graphic design. Thanks to Tara Street for being my mentor when I was a very young designer fresh out of school.

Thanks to Greg Stolze, Fred Hicks, and Cam Banks for giving me first chances to freelance professionally.

Thanks to Matt Wolfe and the Game Designers of North Carolina for being a sounding board for the various figures in this book.

Thanks to Mur Lafferty for advice on how to find a sustainable working routine.

Finally, thanks to my partner Megan Raley for everything.

About the Author

DANIEL SOLIS is an art director, graphic designer, and board game designer with over 20 years of industry experience. He has overseen the visual development of over 100 board games and accessory products, including HeroClix "Iconix" series, *Marvel: Remix, Dungeons & Dragons: Onslaught, Star Trek: Captain's Chair, Sidereal Confluence: Remastered Edition, Clash of Cultures: Monumental Edition, Jokkmokk,* and *Fantasy Realms Deluxe Edition.* As a game designer, his games include Kodama: the Tree Spirits published by Indie Games Studios and Junk Orbit published by Renegade Games Studios. His video tutorials have taught hundreds of designers how to quickly prototype their card games. He lives in North Carolina.

About the Author

Introduction

*B*OARD GAMES ARE GREAT! *At least that's what you've told your friends. Now it's time to prove it.*

After some light cajoling and several rounds of calendar-scheduling, they agreed to spend a rare free evening learning a brand new game. That means you're the emcee for the night. Before everyone arrived, you set up the board, shuffled the decks, and neatly organized pools of cardboard chits. Now all that's left is to do is actually teach the dang thing.

So here they are at the table. They mess with the chips you had neatly stacked in a particular order. They pick up the miniatures you had arranged in their starting positions. They joke about eating the colorful, candy-like tokens. Hey, at least they're interested!

Now you must keep their attention as you explain the rules. All the while reassuring that, yes, this will be a fun time.

But first, let's talk about victory points…

Does any of this sound familiar? That games teacher has the thankless task of corralling everyone's attention. Meanwhile, the new players are politely trying to grasp the game well enough to reach the promised fun-time, but worried about being clumsy or forgetful. Unfortunately, board games don't come with automatic feedback or error screens letting players know they've made a mistake. Special powers may be confused. Important

DOI: 10.1201/9781003453772-1

steps could be accidentally skipped. A game-breaking misunderstanding could spoil the whole experience.

But all is not lost! You're the graphic designer! You're the teacher's teacher and the players' invisible assistant. You put clear visual reminders of special edge cases on the game board. You arranged card text to be legible at comfortable distances. You used colors and icons on the tokens so they're visually accessible even in dim light. You formatted the rulebook to be useful both as during the step-by-step tutorial and then later as a conveniently indexed reference source. Heck, you even worked with the illustrators to draw the art to meet certain criteria.

Your efforts have removed the skill gap between the more experienced teacher and the newcomers. As the teacher explains the game, they point to clear visual references and well-prepared iconography. When players have questions, they intuitively recognize the answers without even realizing.

Good graphic design is so effective at smoothing out the gameplay that it's hardly even noticeable. It makes novice players feel more fluent, more quickly. It makes the teacher's job easier. With luck, all this good will can give the game a better reputation, supporting further sales and making business more feasible for the publisher and designer.

This book presents some best practices and lessons I've learned over my years as a graphic designer in the board game industry. I'll cover everything inside and outside the box as thoroughly as possible. We'll begin with the essential foundations of good typography and the unusual visual demands of a typical modern board game. From there, we'll discuss the most common internal components like cards, boards, and tokens. I've also asked other graphic designers in the industry to share their insights, which will be sprinkled throughout.

I've tried to include LOTS of visual references and actual game images. You can read this cover to cover or skip directly to the particular task you're working on right now. Up to you! Soon you'll be laying out the next great board game!

The Graphic Designer on a game should be a part of the playtesting [...] You will learn infinitely more about how your design is working out.

KIRK W BUCKENDORF

CHAPTER 1

Typography

INTRODUCTION TO TYPOGRAPHY

Typography is the art of using type to convey an essential meaning, translate complex ideas, and express a distinct mood. The importance of type on graphic design goes well beyond any color, image, or texture, yet it's often overlooked as an afterthought as part of the overall design.

Consider the paragraph below:

```
NULLA POSUERE SAPIEN ET IMPERDIET ALIQUAM.
PRAESENT ULLAMCORPER INTERDUM NISL UT ORNARE.
DONEC A TORTOR SAGITTIS, PLACERAT FELIS AC,
CONVALLIS ERAT. CRAS EGET ELIT SIT AMET DOLOR
FAUCIBUS IMPERDIET EU VEL EROS. MORBI JUSTO
EX, SOLLICITUDIN NON LIBERO EGET, GRAVIDA
RHONCUS ARCU. NULLAM CONDIMENTUM TEMPOR IPSUM
VITAE LUCTUS. NULLA FACILISI.
```

Some die-hard minimalists might delight in the matter-of-fact style presented here. For everyone else, it's readable for maybe a line or two, but beyond that it becomes monotonous. Any essential information would be lost in the dreary endless blocks of homogenous rectangles. While a layperson might think this paragraph is important, so it should be in all-caps

DOI: 10.1201/9781003453772-2

to visibly "shout" the text, this just renders everything equal volume of noise. The font used here is monospaced, meaning it has equal width for every character, punctuation, and space. Because it is set in all-caps, the heights of the letters are equal as well. Let's try that paragraph again without all-caps, set in a more standard sans serif font.

Nulla posuere sapien et imperdiet aliquam. *Praesent ullamcorper interdum nisl ut ornare. Donec a tortor sagittis, placerat felis ac, convallis erat.* Cras eget elit sit amet *dolor faucibus imperdiet eu vel eros. Morbi justo ex, sollicitudin non libero eget, gravida rhoncus arcu. Nullam condimentum* **tempor ipsum vitae** *luctus. Nulla facilisi.*

Silhouette is the secret of typography. A word's shape is how it is recognizable. A fluent reader doesn't read one letter at a time, but takes in each word as a distinct unit, including its unique ascenders, descenders, open spaces, swirls, and unique ornamentation. Now if certain words or key terms needed to be called out as important, they'd stand out to a much greater degree.

In the revised paragraph I've also emphasized certain passages to draw more attention. Note that "emphasis" in this case isn't just adding bolds, italics, or both. It's also controlling the *lack* of emphasis surrounding those key points so that they have something against which to stand out. I made significant space between any two points of emphasis so that they did not compete with each other.

Font, emphasis, and case formatting are all very basic tools available to anyone with Microsoft Word or Google Docs. As you begin your journey in graphic design, it's important to understand that these basic decisions should not be set to a default provided by your program. These should be intentional choices, reflecting the ideas behind your project.

Your game components might just have black text on a white background. That's certainly likely early in the prototyping stage, but even the most minimal and austere game must show signs of an intentional, considered designer at work.

Graphic designers are often brought in later in the equation but I think we have a lot to offer in how a game might develop. I'm a game designer myself and I find it valuable working on graphic, illustration and rule design concurrently.

RORY MULDOON

CONTRAST DIRECTS THE EYE

Layout is the act of directing a reader's attention from one section to the next, as smoothly as possible without the reader even noticing that they're being guided. For the purposes of this book, we'll be assuming your audience is a Western reader of English. Other languages and alphabets have their own customs that are beyond the scope of this book.

On a plain body of text with no other distractions, a reader first looks at the top-left corner of the page. Something extremely attention-grabbing may draw their eye elsewhere, as shown in Figure 1.1. Otherwise, their reading will travel from left to right along the first line of text, then come down to the next line to begin again from left to right.

Rather than fight this habit, work within it to help organize your content. Make the left page begin with one major topic, which flows briefly into the next page, immediately followed by the beginning of a whole new topic. This guideline also applies to small components like cards or tiles. Put the most critical information along the top edge of the component, closer to the top left.

To maximize legibility, you want as much contrast between the text and its background as possible. If your text is dark, you want a light background. If it's light, you want a dark background.

Of course, this creates a relatively bland layout that you might want to spice up with some textures. This is fine as long as the average contrast remains in place, so you wouldn't want to put dark text on a black-and-white striped pattern since the black text would disappear against the black stripes. If that pattern were lightened to the point where the darkest stripes were only about 10–15% tint, that would be more legible.

For extra emphasis on certain words, you can change the color of the text, but keep the white background, or you can change the background to a light shade of a different color, keeping the text black. Avoid putting dark colors against dark backgrounds, though.

For even more extreme emphasis, you can completely invert the color scheme: White text on a dark background. However, I find that certain fonts with variations in line weight don't withstand this treatment very well. The thinnest parts of their letterforms may literally disappear as the surrounding ink creeps in around the edges. For these areas, it's best to use a sans serif font that has a consistent, substantial line width like Franklin Gothic, Myriad Pro, or Trade Gothic (Figure 1.2).

Eventually you'll notice this.

Despite this being the first line...

You'll read this first because it's high contrast.

You'll probably read this next.

And perhaps you'll read this third.

FIGURE 1.1   Example of using contrast to draw attention.

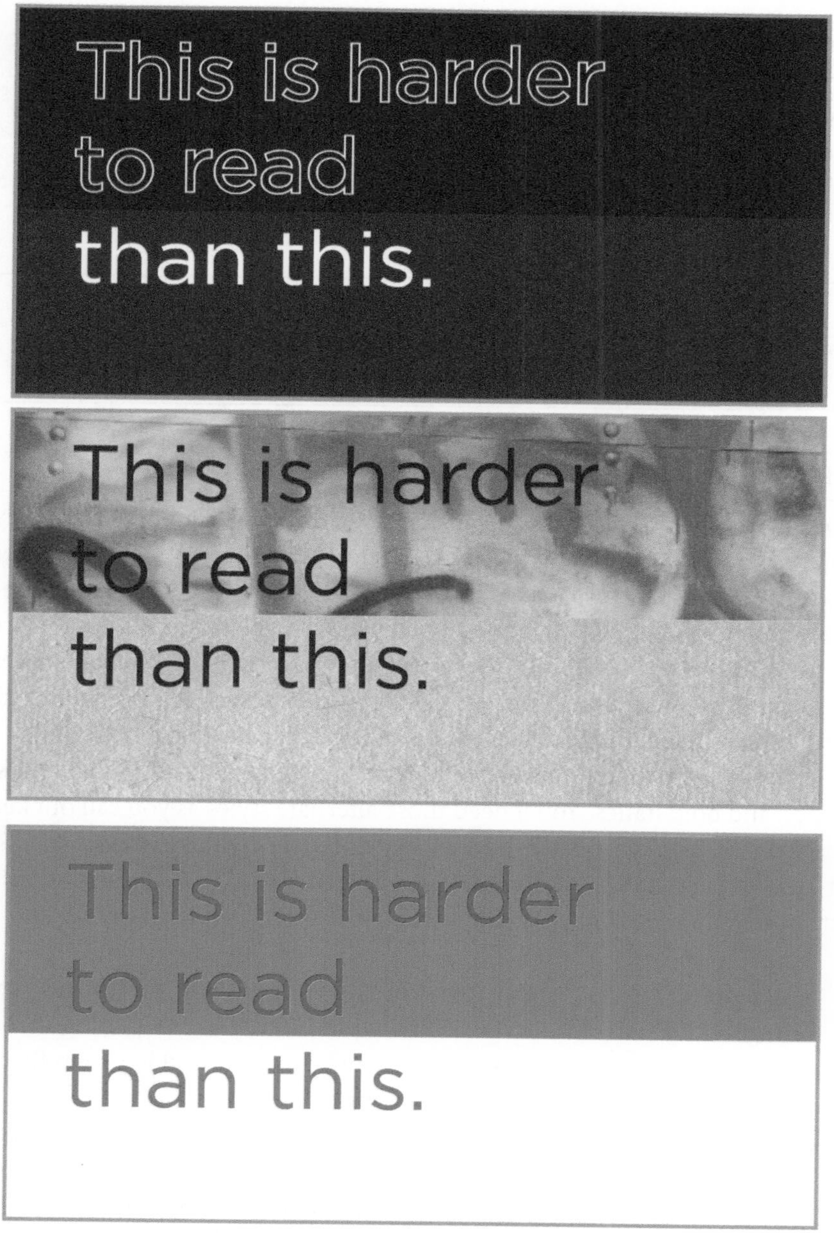

FIGURE 1.2   Three examples of poor contrast.

BOX 1.1 DROP SHADOWS WON'T FIX BAD CONTRAST

Amateur designers may notice that text is difficult to read against a certain background. However, their most common mistake is adding a stroke or drop shadow to the text. This only adds noise to the visuals and makes the text even harder to read. The solution is to improve the background, making it lighter or darker so that the text doesn't need any adulteration.

Higher contrast areas, like black and white, stand out more, while more subtle contrast areas, like tone-on-tone, recede.

LINDSAY DAVIAU

CHOOSE A BASIC FONT FOR BODY TEXT

Your game can't be played if it can't be read. The greatest barrier to entry for any tabletop game is typically its dense, jargon-filled technical rules text. A quirky font only makes that text harder to read, restricting gameplay. Though you may be tempted to convey a theme through your choice of fonts, the body text is not the place to go wild like that. (There are other opportunities, which we'll discuss later in this chapter.) For body text, it's best to be as simple as possible, even if it may seem boring.

A basic body font should have a variety of optional styles, like bolds, italics, and bold italics. You'll need those alternate styles as you call out key game terms. You may also need special glyphs like math symbols, accents, or type ornaments, typically used in bulleted lists. Here are some basic attributes of letterforms that help make them more legible (Figure 1.3).

Serifs: These are the small "feet" or other decorative extensions you might find on some letters. Most typefaces are broadly categorized into serif or sans serif fonts, but it may be more useful to group them into Humanist and Geometric categories.

Counter-Spaces: These are large entirely spaces within characters like 8, O, P, or R. These may also be partially indicated spaces in letters like the underhanging strokes in 9, and certain variations of g, 4, and y. Fonts designed for legibility, small-print, or long-distance signage usually have widely drawn counter-spaces to reduce any ambiguity between characters. Body text fonts have their own quirks, based on the aesthetic choices of the font's designer. Your goal is to ensure your

Minion

This is an example paragraph meant to show you how text flows differently for each font, given the same number of words. Each paragraph is set to 11pt and 14pt leading. Each text frame is set to the same height and width. Note how a paragraph's height and width might change as a result of the typeface's proportions. *(This is important to note so you make the best use of limited page count.)* Finally, test for specific recurring terms in your game to ensure legibility.

Garamond Premier Pro

This is an example paragraph meant to show you how text flows differently for each font, given the same number of words. Each paragraph is set to 11pt and 14pt leading. Each text frame is set to the same height and width. Note how a paragraph's height and width might change as a result of the typeface's proportions. *(This is important to note so you make the best use of limited page count.)* Finally, test for specific recurring terms in your game to ensure legibility.

Roboto

This is an example paragraph meant to show you how text flows differently for each font, given the same number of words. Each paragraph is set to 11pt and 14pt leading. Each text frame is set to the same height and width. Note how a paragraph's height and width might change as a result of the typeface's proportions. *(This is important to note so you make the best use of limited page count.)* Finally, test for specific recurring terms in your game to ensure legibility.

Trade Gothic Next LT Pro Condensed

This is an example paragraph meant to show you how text flows differently for each font, given the same number of words. Each paragraph is set to 11pt and 14pt leading. Each text frame is set to the same height and width. Note how a paragraph's height and width might change as a result of the typeface's proportions. *(This is important to note so you make the best use of limited page count.)* Finally, test for specific recurring terms in your game to ensure legibility.

Baskerville URW

This is an example paragraph meant to show you how text flows differently for each font, given the same number of words. Each paragraph is set to 11pt and 14pt leading. Each text frame is set to the same height and width. Note how a paragraph's height and width might change as a result of the typeface's proportions. *(This is important to note so you make the best use of limited page count.)* Finally, test for specific recurring terms in your game to ensure legibility.

FIGURE 1.3 Sample fonts that I typically use for body text.

letters are distinguishable from each other when read in their most common use-cases.

Ascenders and Descenders: These are parts of a letter that rise above and below the average height of the rest of the text. Ascenders and descenders are what help make long stretches of text easier to read, since they give words distinct silhouettes that can be quickly scanned. Ascenders are present in all capital letters and lowercase letters like h, f, and l. Descenders are usually present only in lowercase letters, like g, q, and p, though some fonts may add descenders to capital letters like Q or J.

Humanist Shapes: Humanist typefaces were the earliest set of letters used in printing, so they're appropriate for any game historical or fantasy setting. Being influenced by calligraphic handwriting traditions, humanist typefaces have fluid and variable stroke weights mimicking an ink pen. This may cause the thinnest strokes to disappear at small sizes or at low contrast, but the unique letterforms may help some readers distinguish characters more easily. These typefaces encompass most serif fonts like Garamond or Times, but may also include some sans serif fonts like Gill Sans or Optima.

Geometric Shapes: This cleaner aesthetic gradually rose in popularity as efficiency became more valued than idiosyncratic artisanship. These typefaces are drawn with symmetry and mathematical exactness. This may make the letters use less space on the page, but some readers find the rigid regularity difficult to read. This category encompasses sans serif fonts like Futura and Trade Gothic, but to some degree may also include serif fonts like Bodoni or Didot.

The three primary editions of *Love Letter* show how typographic considerations can change over time (Figure 1.4).

Top row: Cards from the original Japanese edition of *Love Letter* (Kanai Edition, 2012). Note the use of language-neutral diagrams embedded in the top-left corner, for ease of reference while the cards are held in hand.

Middle row: The same cards from the second edition (Seiji, 2012). This edition puts greater emphasis on the artwork and Rococo borders. The body text and headers have more script-like flourishes, meaning

FIGURE 1.4 Evolution of *Love Letter* cards. Seiji, Kanai (2012) *Love Letter*, Second Edition [Board game]. AEG.; Seiji, Kanai (2019) *Love Letter* [Board game]. Z-Man Asmodee.

the text has to be larger and sometimes get a little too close to the top and bottom borders. The row of stars along the left tell you how many copies of that card are present in the deck, but they're not integrated into the overall design.

Bottom row: The most recent edition as of publication (Seiji, 2019). This edition continues the Rococo border style, but has a more modern sense of typography. The large numeral has higher contrast against its background. The body uses a more neutral serif font, so the text area doesn't have to be as large. Lastly, the background behind the header and body text soften and lighten as they approach the center, maximizing the readability where text is most dense.

BOX 1.2 RELIABLE FONT SOURCES

Source your fonts from reliable distributors. Google Fonts are free, open source, and may be used for commercial projects. This is my first choice for any beginner designer. DaFont and FontSpace have huge collections, but filter your searches by commercial license. Adobe Fonts are included in any Creative Cloud subscription plan (as of this writing), so you can sync these fonts directly to any Adobe application.

As I get older it gets harder and harder for me to read tiny text. If you drop below an 8pt font, you're gonna leave someone struggling.

BILL BRICKER

THE "TWO ALPHABETS" RULE

You might be looking for a hard and fast rule for a "best size" of body text. Back when typography was manually set in metal blocks, "point size" was set to a consistent standard (Figure 1.5). Now a digital font's "12pt" might be quite different from another font's "12pt." While it's tempting to seek a universal size for all cases, it's best to choose a more flexible guideline.

Keep your lines of text between 1.5 and 2 lowercase alphabets long. In other words, literally type abcdefghijklmnopqrstuvwxyzabcdefghijklmnop qrstuvwxyz. If your line width hits somewhere between the second k and second z, you're in a good spot.

FIGURE 1.5   Comparison of different fonts set to the same point size.

- If you set your text to be longer than 2 alphabets, the reader's eyes may start drifting away before they reach the end of the line.
- If you have less space available, the text may feel a bit too choppy, making a disjointed reading experience.

All those caveats said, you may nevertheless want some hard sizes as a guideline. I can offer these tips:

- For most readers, body copy set to 10pt with 12pt of line spacing is adequate. (You might hear this referred to by the shorthand term "10 over 12.")
- You can enlarge the text to 12 over 15 if necessary, which starts to look more like a children's book's text. This is fine when your game is actually intended for children!
- If your text will also have small embedded icons, make sure you've accounted for enough line space to make those icons legible at small scales.

BOX 1.3 RAGGED EDGES AND RIVERS

For most body text, it's best to use left-aligned text with a "ragged right," since typical readers need a consistent starting location for each line of text. Right-aligned text will make it difficult for readers to find the next line. Avoid the use of full justification, since it will create unpredictable gaps and contiguous "rivers" of white space that interrupts the flow of reading. For similar reasons, it's best to not use hyphenation, since it might interrupt key game terms and make rules harder to parse. (I've seen key game rules be missed just because of an awkward line break.)

Print out early versions at full size and judge how well you can read them, if they have enough room to breathe, [and] what needs adjusting.

HEIKO GÜNTHER

CONSERVING SPACE

There may come a time when you have to set more text than can comfortably fit in the space available. To resolve this problem, you have a few options (Figure 1.6).

To conserve vertical space, pick a font with very short ascenders and descenders so that you can safely reduce the space between lines. You want to avoid the descenders of a line of text intersecting the ascenders of the line below it. Just one note of caution: The shorter those strokes, the less distinct the shape of the word and the less legible it becomes.

If horizontal space becomes too tight, take a close look at the average width of your font's characters. If the characters are wide, then the words will be even wider, thus limiting how many words you can fit into each line.

To conserve horizontal space, find a font with "Compressed" or "Condensed" in the name. These letters are much narrower, allowing you to fit the same number of words in as little as half the original column width. Despite those cost-saving advantages, long stretches of compressed type can be difficult to read, so reserve it for an appendix or glossary. Note: Characters that are already narrow, like 1, i, j, and l, may become harder to discern when squeezed in with a bunch of other narrowed text.

It's also important to consider the distance at which your text will be read. At the most intimate distances, like a card held privately in hand, sizes

Bernino Sans Compressed Regular
This is an example paragraph meant to show you how text flows differently for each font, given the same number of words. Each paragraph is set to 11pt and 14pt leading. Each text frame is set to the same height and width. Note how a paragraph's height and width might change as a result of the typeface's proportions. (This is important to note so you make the best use of limited page count.) Finally, test for specific recurring terms in your game to ensure legibility.

Bernino Sans Condensed Regular
This is an example paragraph meant to show you how text flows differently for each font, given the same number of words. Each paragraph is set to 11pt and 14pt leading. Each text frame is set to the same height and width. Note how a paragraph's height and width might change as a result of the typeface's proportions. (This is important to note so you make the best use of limited page count.) Finally, test for specific

Bernino Sans Regular
This is an example paragraph meant to show you how text flows differently for each font, given the same number of words. Each paragraph is set to 11pt and 14pt leading. Each text frame is set to the same height and width. Note how a paragraph's height and width might change as a result of the typeface's proportions. (This

Kepler Std Condensed Subhead
This is an example paragraph meant to show you how text flows differently for each font, given the same number of words. Each paragraph is set to 11pt and 14pt leading. Each text frame is set to the same height and width. Note how a paragraph's height and width might change as a result of the typeface's proportions. (This is important to note so you make the best use of limited page count.) Finally, test for specific recurring terms in your game to ensure legibility.

Kepler Std Regular
This is an example paragraph meant to show you how text flows differently for each font, given the same number of words. Each paragraph is set to 11pt and 14pt leading. Each text frame is set to the same height and width. Note how a paragraph's height and width might change as a result of the typeface's proportions. (This is important to note so you make the best use of limited page

Kepler Std Medium Extended
This is an example paragraph meant to show you how text flows differently for each font, given the same number of words. Each paragraph is set to 11pt and 14pt leading. Each text frame is set to the same height and width. Note how a paragraph's height and width might change as a result of the typeface's proportions. (This

FIGURE 1.6 Variable widths within a single typeface. The highlighted areas show how far the ascenders descenders deviate from the x-height.

can be as small as 10pt. Point size, 8pt is acceptable if necessary, but you get diminishing returns the more you compromise text size for text space.

Larger text is required for a table-based component, allowing players reading upside-down to still recognize labels and key locations. Set that text to at least 14 and 16 point size minimum. 24pt would be even better, if it fits naturally onto your component.

A small piece of game development advice: Set your prototype card text to 12pt and 15pt line spacing. If your card's effect is so complicated that it won't fit naturally onto the card, it's probably too complicated.

Do not look at popular CCGs as a guide for what sizes you can get away with. Often those games can use much smaller text because they have an embedded, forgiving audience. Your prototype is something brand new and hasn't earned that privilege yet.

BOX 1.4 SERIF VS. SANS SERIF

"Serifs" are the small extensions that spread out at the ends of strokes in certain letterforms. You can see these in fonts like Garamond, Minion, Baskerville, or Perpetua. These are made for easy reading across long stretches of text on a page, but can also take up quite extra room for those little extensions. "Sans Serif" fonts, like Helvetica, Open Sans, and Roboto, are more space efficient because they lack those details, which is why you typically see them in public signage, but some readers find them less comfortable to read over long stretches on the page. I find serif best for "main" body text and sans serif best for "secondary" sidebars, lists, or appendices.

I'll always start with notebooks and pencils to get a sense of how things work at scale.

RORY MULDOON

FONT SETTINGS FOR HEADERS

When I advise game designers on how to submit their manuscripts, I usually ask them to keep headers to at most three levels. Two would be even better, but usually the writers can't help themselves and indulge in that extra level of granularity.

First-level headers begin a completely new topic, like "Setting Up the Game," "How to Play," and "Game End." Here you have the most freedom to tap into your game's theme with a flavorful font, but make sure these headers are all very short. At most, one full column width, never going to two lines if you can help it. The actual size will vary based on your font choice and the average length of your header titles, but I generally aim for double the size of my body copy font.

Second-level headers are subtopics within a major section. For example, within "How to Play" you might have second-level headers like "Playing a Card," "Moving a Pawn," or "Gathering Resources." Make these headers a simpler font, like a bold version of the body copy font. Keep them about double the size of body copy and follow the same single-line size restriction as first-level headers. You can make them stand out even more by setting them to be ALL CAPS, though it might look like "shouting" if used too much.

Third-level headers are extremely brief sub-subtopics. Usually I would only set up headers like this if the game designer likes to insert frequent sidebars throughout the text, which require their own header titles. Usually I make these the same font and size as the body copy, but bold and/or ALL CAPS.

Other Headings: Avoid Heading 4 and beyond. Anything beyond three levels of header makes the visual hierarchy cluttered. That said, if you're opening a whole other type of content, like an Appendix or a lengthy example of play, it might be worthwhile to set up a whole new set of Headings 1, 2, and 3, specifically for those sections, separate from the three headings you're using in the main text.

When choosing a header font for the highest-level titles, you want to have as much contrast with the body text as you can. If the body is serif, the header is sans serif. If body text is light, you want bold headers. For top-level headers, I usually at least double the body font size as well.

In the example Figure 1.7, you can see how the top-level header is dramatically different from the body text. Each level of header gets incrementally closer to matching the body text. This creates an intuitive downstream sense of organization as each sub-topic gets progressively more specialized.

Level 1 Header	**Level 1 Header**
This is body copy. Lorem ipsum dolor sit amet, consectetur adipiscing elit. Cras volutpat justo eu nunc lobortis ornare. Nulla quis erat pellentesque, varius eros posuere, sem.	This is body copy. Lorem ipsum dolor sit amet, consectetur adipiscing elit. Cras volutpat justo eu nunc lobortis ornare. Nulla quis erat pellentesque, varius eros posuere, sem.
Level 2 Header	**Level 2 Header**
In in diam vel massa laoreet faucibus. Etiam quis nulla nec tortor porttitor tempor. Fusce finibus libero. Aliquam eget semper nulla. Donec sodales odio sodales sagittis. Donec accumsan purus leo, at sollicitudin elit pellentesque ut.	In in diam vel massa laoreet faucibus. Etiam quis nulla nec tortor porttitor tempor. Fusce finibus libero. Aliquam eget semper nulla. Donec sodales odio sodales sagittis. Donec accumsan purus leo, at sollicitudin elit pellentesque ut.
Level 3 Header	**Level 3 Header**
Suspendisse feugiat, libero ut efficitur efficitur, orci ipsum sagittis velit, id tincidunt sem leo at elit. Integer semper quis odio ultricies malesuada.	Suspendisse feugiat, libero ut efficitur efficitur, orci ipsum sagittis velit, id tincidunt sem leo at elit. Integer semper quis odio ultricies malesuada.

FIGURE 1.7   Examples of three levels of headers interspersed with body text.

BOX 1.5 STROKES AND OUTLINES AROUND TEXT

If you must use strokes or outlines around your text, note some of the quirks of how your program treats those effects. Photoshop's Outline layer effect can't make sharp, clean corners around text. Illustrator's Stroke function does make sharp corners, but you have to check that the outline only extends outside the letterform, not within it. (Extending into the letterform makes it look thinner and harder to read.)

Think about font size. Text that is right in front of the player can be slightly smaller than if it needs to be read from across the table.

LINDSAY DAVIAU

LISTS

There's a certain school of technical writing that loves writing in lists. I'm honestly not sure where this habit comes from, but I see it in enough rulebook drafts that it's a big problem when I get a manuscript formatted entirely as nested lists with no headers or titles at all. When used properly, lists are great for drawing attention to key sequences, options, or small subtopics. However, if the whole document is a list, then it all blurs together.

When you write a list use the actual list functions available in your writing app. Every writing app should have that functionality. Do not artificially make a list with manual line breaks and spaces. These won't work in an actual layout and just make life harder for your graphic designer (Figure 1.8).

Here is when and how to use lists most effectively:

Lists as Sequences: These are things like a specific order to actions taken in a turn. They should be ordered with letters, numbers, or even roman numerals. Here is a simple example from a card game:

1. Draw a Card
2. Acquire Resources
3. Play a Card

This is an explicit order of operations, with a clear sequence.

Lists as Options: These are things that can be done in any order, up to the player's choice. These should be presented with non-alphanumeric glyphs, like circles or triangles. Here is a simple example from a tactical combat game:

- Deploy a Unit
- Move a Unit
- Attack with Units

Because this list uses the same bullet style, it's more like a menu of possibilities, not necessarily assumed to be in a particular sequence.

Lists with Sub-Orders: These are listed items with conditional prerequisites or multiple outcomes where it's important to list them out in a certain hierarchy, without implying a certain order of operations. Here you can continue using non-alphanumeric glyphs as long as the indentations are used consistently.

- Deploy a Unit
  - You must have sufficient resources to select this option.

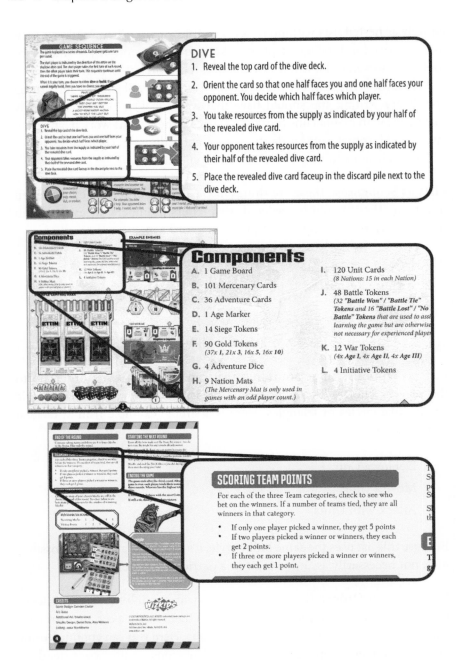

FIGURE 1.8 Examples of numbered, lettered, and bulleted lists. Top: *Seastead.* Middle: *Ettin.* Bottom: *Atlantic Robot League.*

- Deploying to a hostile zone costs double the normal number of resources.
- Move a Unit
  - You may move a unit North, South, East, or West. It may not be moved diagonally.
  - Moving one space is free. Any further movement costs fuel.
  - When your unit shares a space with an enemy unit, that space is considered a hostile zone.
- Attack with Units:
  - An enemy unit loses health equal to your unit's strength.
  - If a unit has 0 or less health, it is removed from the board at the end of the current turn.

Lists as Inline Headers: If you've already used your allotted three levels of headers, but you still think it's worthwhile to give a sub-section its own small title, you can use bolded terms followed by a colon. That gives the paragraphs a clear prefacing label. I mainly use these for glossary definitions or similar index references. You can see an example of this in the three "Lists as ..." paragraphs in this section.

BOX 1.6 OUTDENTS AND INDENTS

A layout program gives you granular control of list formatting, allowing you to set the "indent," the distance at which an edge is inset relative to the rest of the text. Layout programs also let you control the indent of the first line alone. Normally this is used to add an initial extra space at the first line. However, you can set this first-line indent to a negative number, thus creating an "outdent." I adjust these settings so I can control how much space lies between the left margin, the list glyph, and the left edge of the text.

Understand the strengths and weaknesses of each program and tool. Don't layout rules in Illustrator and don't do illustration in Indesign.

JACOBY O'CONNOR

LINE SPACING AND PARAGRAPH SPACING

When I look at a page, I like to imagine what that page "sounds" like by its first impression. If it's all an uninterrupted wall of text, it sounds like a monotonous lecture. I would rather have the page sound like a lively conversation with your favorite teacher. I want to offer opportunities for a reader to catch their breath, interject, and consider the concepts they've just learned.

Let's take a look at the example layout in Figure 1.9. The first page shows examples of two extremes. The top half has lines too close to each other, creating a dense block that would be difficult to read. The second half has lines that are spaced too far apart, which makes the whole page seem awkwardly paced. The two extremes on the same page make the whole look unconsidered and chaotic. The reader would not be able to get a predictable reading rhythm.

The second page is more evenly paced. The spacing between paragraphs is about 1.5× the space between each line of body text. This 1.5× ratio is my usual rule of thumb for paragraph spacing. (If the line spacing is set to 12pt, the paragraph spacing would be +6pt, or 18pt in total.) This is usually sufficient to avoid any intersections between ascenders and descenders. Larger spacing has diminishing returns though. I don't make the paragraph spacing larger than that because it doesn't help the flow any more than 1.5× and it would also cost that much more space on the page that I might need.

Now note the spacing around headers. In the second page, I make the space-before a full 2× the line spacing and reduce the space-after to a standard line height. (If the line spacing was set to 12pt, the space before the header would be 24pt and the space after would be 12pt.) The overall cost of room on the page is the same as a standard paragraph, but the extra gap prepares the reader to expect that a whole new subject is about to begin.

BOX 1.7 DOUBLE-SPACING AFTER SENTENCES

Major style guides once mandated adding an extra space after each sentence. Now, both APA and MLA recommend against using that extra space because modern digital typography automatically proportions spaces after sentences to create an optimal reading experience. Nevertheless, there are generations of instructors that have never shaken this habit and have also drilled this habit into their pupils. If you're submitting your manuscript for layout, you should be aware that one of the first things I do is literally search for any instance of two spaces and replace them with one space. I repeat that process until only single-spaces remain. Sorry, instructors!

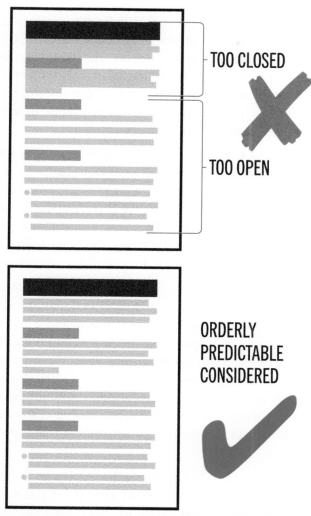

FIGURE 1.9 The top page has inconsistent spacing. The bottom page does have different spacing for headers, lists, and body copy, but they're all internally consistent.

Negative space is a good thing! Don't jam your text right up to the edges of the holding shape that it's in.

LINDSAY DAVIAU

Give elements and text more space if possible.

TORBEN RATZLAFF

PROBLEM CHARACTERS

Some typefaces don't have enough distinguishing features between certain characters, especially between their numbers. The usual culprits are sans serif, modernist, or futuristic fonts that have removed so many distinctive features of their characters that they become indiscernible from each other. This is especially problematic for components that might have to be read upside-down or at odd angles (Figure 1.10).

Distinguishing 7 and 1: 7 should have an exaggerated angle, with a wide stance that significantly extends its top bar. It may also be handy to have a small crossbar across the mid-section, though this is often only present in "handwritten" style fonts. To contrast the 7, you can use a 1 so abstract that it just becomes a skinny vertical line. Just be careful, this wouldn't be near a capital I or lowercase l, since those may also be mistaken for a 1. My preferred option is a 1 that has a short, downward sloping top stroke and a strong serif at the base.

Distinguishing 6 and 9: Always add a directional indicator to 6 and 9 so the difference is clear. If there is room, add a complete line underneath the numeral. If space is limited, a strong bold dot should suffice. There is an especially creative solution in the original edition of the card game Pairs by James Ernest. The "six" card is written as a word, turned 90° so it takes up about the same amount of space as a single numeral. I thought this was clever, but may raise some eyebrows among traditionalists or just confuse players, so use this approach with caution.

Distinguishing O and 0: Most fonts render the letter "o" and "O" as rounded, wide characters while number zero is set tall and narrow. Those distinctions may be too subtle for your use-case, so you can add a slash to the zero, making a "null" character. You might instead add a small dot to the center of the zero, as long as it's clearly not an "8."

Distinguishing Z, 2, 3, and 5: Make sure your font exaggerates the sharpest corners and rounded curves. The Z should be wide with severe angles, perhaps a crossbar. The 2 should have a generous upper curve to contrast the Z's harsh points. 3 and 5 each have a rounded lower section facing the same

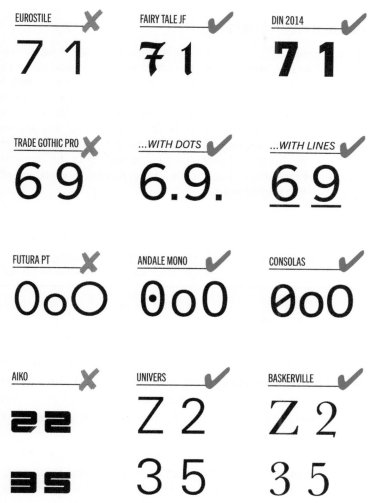

FIGURE 1.10 Top row: Add distinguishing features to 7 so it looks more distinct from 1, like a steeper angle, a crossbar, or longer top bar. Second row: Add lines or dots to the bottom of any instance of 6 or 9 when they might be seen upside-down, like on a token. Third row: If your game needs a number zero, be sure it looks distinct from the letter O, such as with a dot, a crossbar, or a distinctly narrower profile. Fourth row: Highly thematic fonts can sometimes compromise legibility for style, so make sure the context makes their intent clear.

direction, so ideally your font will adjust the heights or thickness of these sections to make them distinct. In addition, make sure the 5's angular top half is very squared off.

BOX 1.8 OLDSTYLE FIGURES

The oldest traditional typefaces use numerals more like letters, with ascenders, descenders, and variable horizontal spacing depending on the width of the numeral. There are many modern fonts that harken back to that typographic tradition, but it's not always an appearance you want for your text. If you're using an OpenType font, you may have the option to enable "Tabular Lining" for your numerals. The way to access this function varies by program, but is usually easy to find with a quick Help Search. "Tabular" keeps the horizontal spacing equal, regardless of the numeral's width. "Lining" keeps the vertical height of the numerals equal, usually something close to a capital letter.

[When play testing], it is important to know what future players will experience in order for you to know what you have to fix.

ESTEFANIA RODRIGUEZ

USING DISPLAY FONTS

"Display" is a very broad category of typeface and fonts intended for large sizes like banners, titles, and posters. They're great for those short punchy situations, but not appropriate for long spans of body text. They have idiosyncratic characters that can look repetitive and unnatural if seen too often. This is especially apparent when the font is meant to resemble a real person's handwriting (Figure 1.11).

Hand-drawn fonts are very tempting for their organic appearance and distinctive air of authenticity, but therein lies their biggest weakness. Any repeated letters immediately mark any handwritten font as artificial. For example, the W, O, and D, in WOODWIND would all look identical if set in a typical handwritten font. It looks unprofessional, as if you just grabbed something online and let the default font settings dictate your design.

If you truly intend to give handwriting a realistic appearance, I strongly recommend actually writing the letters in real life instead of using a font. If you must use a font, modify the repeated letters so they look more organic to the overall title. If the font is meant to look grungy and corroded, change how the identical letters have been degraded. They should have different patterns of nicks and cuts around their edges.

Welcome home

welcome home

Welcome home

Welcome home

Welcome home

welcome home

FIGURE 1.11   Display fonts can express a tone of voice. Here the same message is repeated in the fonts Mrs Eaves, ChauncyPro-Bold, Amador, Emily Austin, Nexa Rust Script, and Moby. Note how each example gives the message a tone of friendliness, prestige, or foreboding. The text hasn't changed, just the font.

That said, you might be able to find a handwritten font that includes a feature called "contextual alternates." This feature adjusts the appearance of commonly grouped characters like "st," "ing," and "oo." Even for letters that are not grouped together, well-built fonts will offer alternate glyphs for other individual letters. Fonts with this feature are rarely free, but they're worth the purchase to support the font's creator.

If you can't find a readymade grungy font that works for you, there's always the option to take an existing "clean" font and distress it yourself. The advantage here is that you know you're working from a strong basis for legibility. From there, you can search for "grunge textures" and use them to mask out chunks of letterforms. As you go through this process, be careful to keep the tops of your letters mostly intact. Usually those are the most recognizable parts of a line of text, which helps retain their readability.

Hand-drawn and grungy letters can certainly make a visually pleasing design if used with care and intent.

BOX 1.9 CONTRASTING GRUNGE WITH CLEAN

The caution I expressed earlier about contrasting light vs. dark also applies to grunge vs. clean. If you put your distressed typography on an equally distressed background, you risk making the entire text unreadable. Put your grunge text on a relatively simple background. (Or if you have a distressed background, make sure your text is basic enough that it retains its own legibility.)

The font choices and color palettes are so different for, say, *Return to Dark Tower* compared to *Thunder Road: Vendetta*. The theme sets the tone for everything we design.

LINDSAY DAVIAU

HOW TO APPROACH CULTURAL TYPOGRAPHY

Many game themes are set in real-world cultures and historical periods, or at least set in fantasy worlds that are inspired by them. Cultural sensitivity is important and worthy of further discussion with all project members, but it's beyond the scope of this book (Figure 1.12).

I bring it up to point out an area where even the most experienced graphic designer might fall prey to laziness. If someone asks why you picked a font, or color, or border, you want to give a knowledgeable answer with full command of the facts. Do not rely on tired stereotypes and harmful caricatures.

A graphic designer or art director finds out why the game's designer has chosen a theme for their game. Perhaps there's some deeper connection to a narrative that can be built around. If you're unlucky, the game designer just picked a theme based on superficial appearances and popular stereotypes. (I wish that were not so common.)

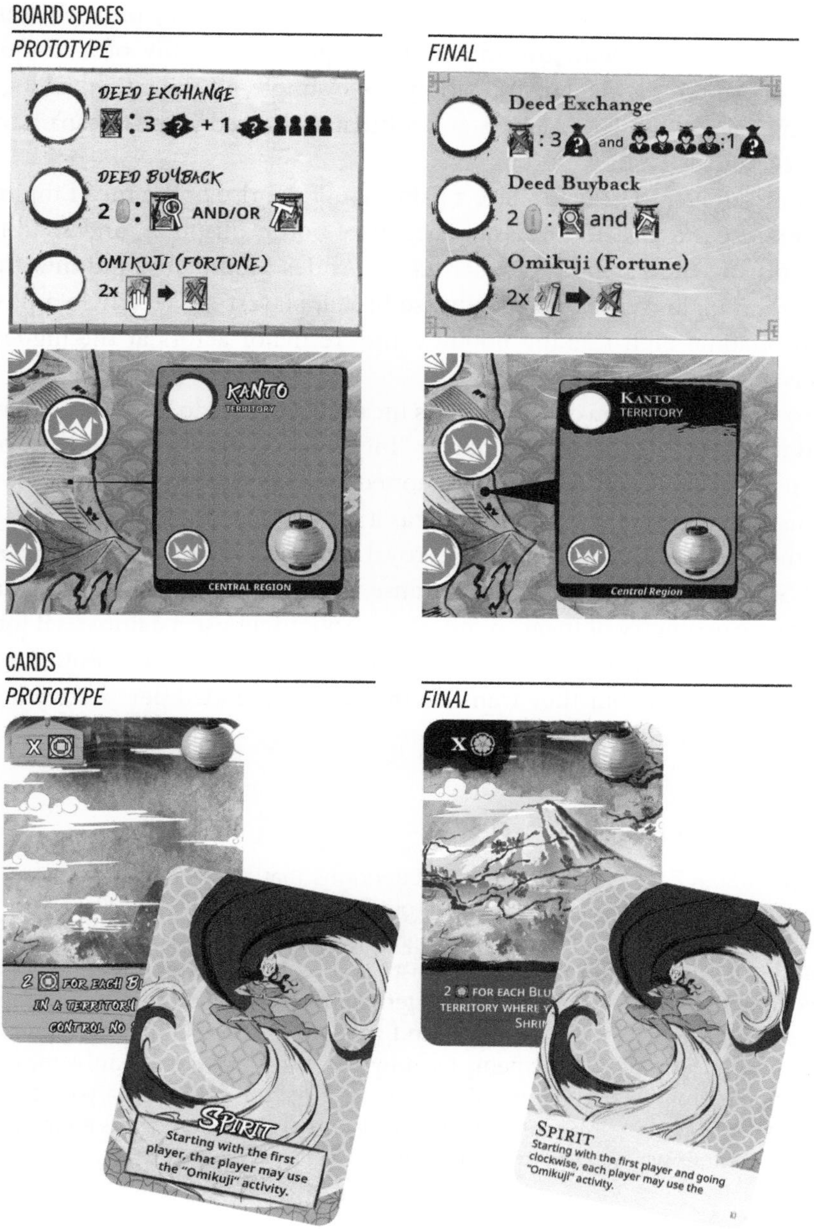

BOARD SPACES

PROTOTYPE

FINAL

CARDS

PROTOTYPE

FINAL

FIGURE 1.12 Typography changes in *Jinja*, from the original prototype to the final design. We changed the all-caps inkbrush font to Mrs Eaves, which still expresses a sense of elegance and refinement. We also changed backgrounds and contrast so we would not need to use strokes around any text.

Whatever the game designer's intent, do not default to the most obvious visual associations with the theme. Every game is worthy of a unique approach and individual investigation. For example, a Viking themed logo doesn't have to use runic letters and a Russian themed game doesn't have to use an inverted R.

For example, let's say we have a game about the rise of the Inca Empire. Players expand agriculture crops, negotiate border disputes, and solidify a hold from the Pacific shore, across the Andes Mountains, and into the Amazon jungle. With a perspective so broad, players are clearly in a position of some high-ranking nobility. They're major actors at the highest levels of statecraft.

So what font do you choose for this Inca game? First, do NOT just download whatever you find in a search for "Inca font." (The Inca had actually no written alphabet, only a system of knotted strings called "quipu.")

Instead, consider the player's role as a powerful noble. Find a font that the modern audience would view as royal and monumental. You might use Gill Sans Ultra Black for a logo because it has clean geometric lines that evoke the geometry of Incan architecture. You might use a dainty serif font like Mrs Eaves for headers because it has an upper-class aura. Both fonts are anachronistic, but they translate the game's intended perspective in a way players intuitively understand.

BOX 1.10 "CHOP SUEY" FONTS

"Chop Suey" fonts are the stroked letterforms that have been a mainstay on restaurant signs, menus, and take-out boxes since the late 1800s. These have no connection to any real typographical tradition. They're an ad hoc orientalist impression of "the Far East" that Chinatowns adopted out of economic necessity to appeal to Western tourists. These fonts have an ugly history in propaganda, caricature, and general Sinophobia. Nevertheless, I still see these design elements used by American and European games, without commentary or irony. (I've been guilty of this myself as a younger oblivious designer.) All I can say is that you should avoid these fonts entirely. Find another way to convey the theme.

Any graphic designer knows revisions and feedback are part of the process. And because tabletop games are so interactive, there will be a lot of opinions on how things should be done. Sometimes you will even get conflicting opinions. It's your job to separate out the good feedback from the edge cases.

TONY MASTRANGELI

TYPOGRAPHY GRIDS

You might be familiar with the idea of a grid as it appears on a chess-board or spreadsheet. In graphic design the "typographic grid" is more like a waffle. There are individual cells in the grid, but with sizable gaps between those cells. Once a layout is complete, you should not see the grid at all, only its invisible structure guiding the size and placement of your content.

Typographic grid are a scaffold to organize body text, headers, diagrams, art, tables, and charts so they're all well-proportioned in relation to the page, card, game board, or tile. This makes your content easier to read and gives a subliminal sense of calm accessibility.

To build your grid, imagine your blank game component with a 3mm margin around every edge. For larger components like game boards, that margin might be as large as 15mm. Within that margin, divide the space into multiple columns. For pages, you might go as large as 8 columns. For game boards, it can be 12 columns or more. For smaller components, like tiles and cards, it might have to just be 2 or 3 columns. There should be a minimum 3mm gap between these columns, though for larger uses like pages and boards, I go as large as 10mm.

The width of those columns can be guided by my aforementioned rule of thumb about text length. Avoid lines of text being longer than two lowercase alphabets. You can define your typographic grid's column widths around that constraint.

Optionally, you can mandate a universal baseline height as part of your typographic grid. This ensures that elements of your component align to the same increments of text height. Personally, I don't get that strict with my grids unless I have so much content that I need an iron grip man-dating perfectly aligned order. It's great for a sense of visual harmony, but harmony isn't necessarily what I want to convey depending on the game's theme.

In Figure 1.13, you'll see how grids give you a foundation from which you can deviate then return to at will. It's a playground for your creativity. Experiment and practice with your own typographic grid and you can make your own stunning layouts!

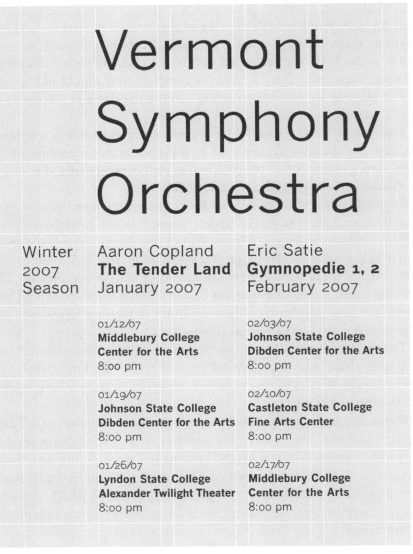

Vermont Symphony Orchestra

Winter 2007 Season	Aaron Copland **The Tender Land** January 2007	Eric Satie **Gymnopedie 1, 2** February 2007
	01/12/07 **Middlebury College Center for the Arts** 8:00 pm	02/03/07 **Johnson State College Dibden Center for the Arts** 8:00 pm
	01/19/07 **Johnson State College Dibden Center for the Arts** 8:00 pm	02/10/07 **Castleton State College Fine Arts Center** 8:00 pm
	01/26/07 **Lyndon State College Alexander Twilight Theater** 8:00 pm	02/17/07 **Middlebury College Center for the Arts** 8:00 pm

FIGURE 1.13   Illustration of multi-column grid. The white lines indicate the margins of each cell within the grid. Content is aligned to these grids to give it an implicit sense of organization and readability.

BOX 1.11 PAGE NUMBERS

Place your page numbers in the far-bottom corners of the page so they're easy to reference at a glance. Size them around 12pt or larger, with sharp contrasts against the background so they are easy to read. Maintain at least 5mm clearance all around the number, so it's safely away from the edge of the page and won't intersect with the body text or graphics. Choose a basic, plain font with easily recognized numerals. Remember to account for the space necessary for two digits, not just one, especially if your chosen font is especially wide.

You can learn a lot by studying layout and typography from the masters. Grid Systems by Josef Müller-Brockmann is a great book if you can get hold of it.

RORY MULDOON

SPACING MULTIPLE COLUMNS

For a small book like the one you're holding now, about 6″×9″, you'll probably find the width just large enough to follow my "2 alphabets" guideline. That means it would be a single-column layout.

If you're setting a rulebook on a page size larger than 6″×9″, you may find that the width of your text column exceeds two alphabets. In such a case, it's time to split the page into multiple columns.

In Figure 1.14, compare example (a) with example (b). Both pages are set to the same dimensions with the same font settings, but example (a) fits much less content on the page. Every paragraph commits a full page-width, regardless of the actual number of words on that line. Example (b) divides the page into two columns, allowing for greater information density without any loss of legibility. It also adds a little more room for more text, should it be necessary.

I recommend about 1cm of "gutter" space in between the columns to ensure they do not get muddled with each other. You'll see narrower gutters on periodicals, magazines, and newspapers, but rulebooks are technical documents with their own necessary affordances. Your typical rulebook reader is already harried enough searching for a key rule without having to scan through what looks like a dictionary page.

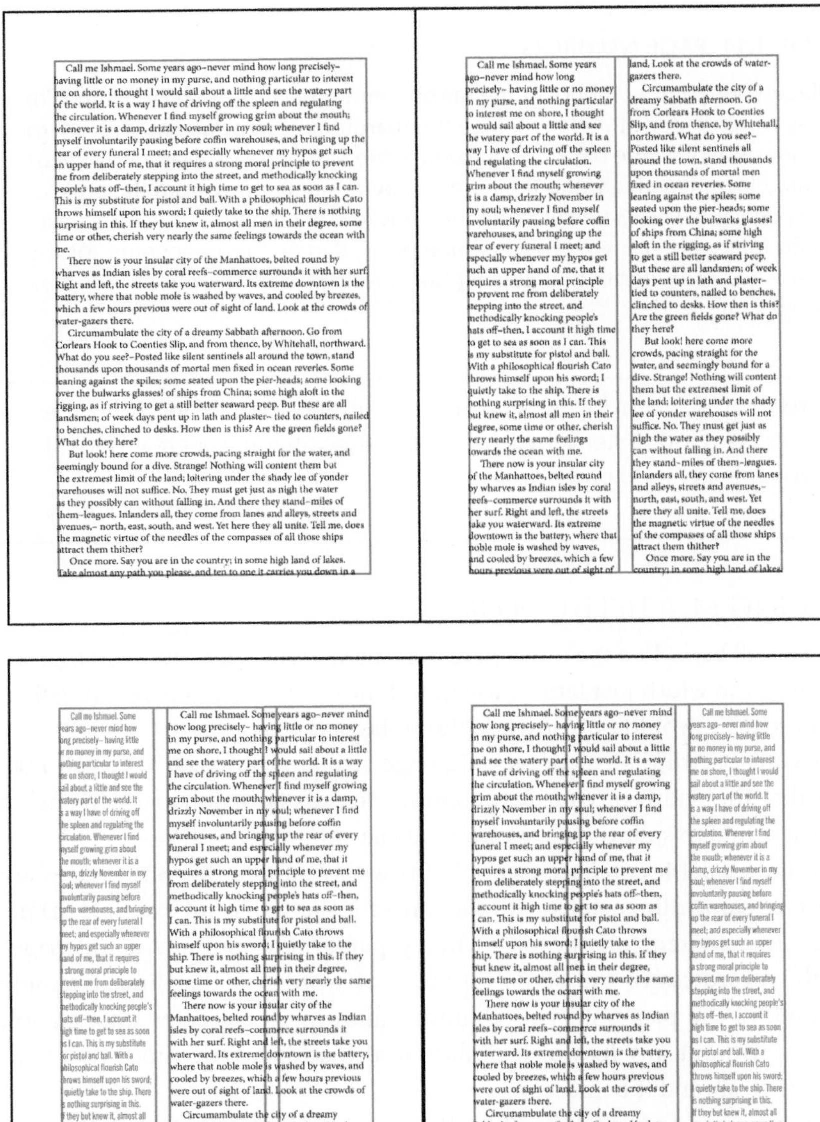

FIGURE 1.14 Comparing the text density of three different column layouts using the same length of text and same font settings.

BOX 1.12 ALTERNATE WIDTH COLUMNS

Some rulebooks will devote two-thirds of a page to a single "main column" of rules text. The remaining third is a narrower side column of shorter text that summarizes the main rules for quick reference. It's a clever solution to equally satisfy those learning the game from scratch and experienced players who just need a quick refresher, but it can result in an overall longer rulebook. It may also be confusing for new players unaccustomed to this duplicated information.

Square rulebooks often work best with 3 columns to layout text.
STEPHANIE GUSTAFSSON

SUMMARY OF TYPOGRAPHY

In 2012, the nuclear research center, CERN, announced that they had discovered strong evidence for the long-theorized "God Particle," the Higgs Boson. During their slide presentation showing their extensive testing and thoroughly considered lab results, one might have noticed that their text was set entirely in the font Comic Sans.

Comic Sans is a free font included in Microsoft products since the mid-90s and quickly became the dominant font for a "casual" vibe. I won't go into the long, mostly silly arguments between aesthetes, pragmatists, utilitarians, and pot-stirrers. The gist is that because it's free, it gets used a lot, and some in the graphic design community get sick of seeing it every-where, especially where another choice might have seemed more appro-priate. Group A is annoyed. Group B gets annoyed that Group B expresses annoyance. Thus, a cycle of internet arguments perpetuates ad infinitum.

So when CERN announced a major achievement, it's understandable that Comic Sans might have been seen as a curious choice. Surely some-thing more formal would be warranted. In truth, we don't know why CERN chose Comic Sans. It might have just been a default in a PowerPoint slide template. Perhaps someone on the team learned that Comic Sans has idio-syncratic details that makes it more legible to readers with dyslexia. Comic Sans is also very friendly, perhaps making these ground-breaking discov-eries seem a little more approachable.

Then again, it's still particle physics. Perhaps no typography choice might have made the findings any more understandable.

All this is to say, even if you make no choices in your typography, a choice will be *inferred* by your readers. Be prepared with an answer if someone asks these questions.

Summary Questions

- Who is your target reader for this text?
- How is their eyesight?
- What is their literacy level?
- Will they be expected to read any text aloud?
- How much text is there in the whole game?
- How should this text be formatted to best serve that reader?
- What environmental challenges must be overcome to make this text readable?
- How does this affect your choices for headers and body copy?
- Have you given the text sufficient contrast to be legible?
- Do the font choices fit the mood and theme of the game?
- Have you structured your line lengths to avoid tiring the reader?
- Is there sufficient balance of empty space?

CHAPTER **2**

Iconography

INTRODUCTION TO ICONS

Iconography is both an academic study and a professional practice. I'd love to just jump straight into giving you a library of icons you can use in your projects. It's more useful to understand how neutral symbols are imbued by individual experience, historical context, and cultural impressions to take on greater utility. But first, let's talk about Mr. Burns.

Specifically, *Mr. Burns, a Post-Electric Play*, by Anne Washburn. I saw a performance of this play at the now-closed Manbites Dog Theater in 2015. The play begins after an undefined apocalyptic event. In the first act, recent doomsday survivors share a campfire and reminisce about the *Simpsons* episode "Cape Feare." In the second act, set decades later, a troupe of actors makes a living by re-enacting the Simpsons canon, resulting in some characters and events being blurred together. In the final act, set hundreds of years later, the performers take on serious religious overtones depicting a heroic Bart dueling demonic melding of Sideshow Bob with Montgomery Burns.

What I remember most is the costumes of the third act. The whole cast now wears masks similar to those used in Ancient Greek theater. Each character holds props that are very loosely based on the character's original appearance. Bart wears a golden crown with sharp points, based on his original high-top hairstyle. Marge wears a tall blue headdress similar to a papal miter. She carries a golden sphere with a red circle in the center, all that visually remains of baby Maggie. Cartooning is already a practice of distillation, but seeing these further refinements into religious iconography was a lot of fun.

I didn't expect to find such a rich example of iconography in a live stage play, but there we were with a fairly accurate summary of how complex images get codified into icons. Until relatively recently, iconography has been an art history discipline. Researchers analyzed images to find which subjects are present in a work, how they are depicted individually or composed as a group, and which elements are independent of one artist's style. Often this was focused on the study of classical works, where artists depict commonly recognized religious or mythical scenes.

Now, iconography has greatly broadened to include more general study of signs as any form of communication. Those signs may come from any source, be it a religious mural or banal yard sign. Consider the icons of certain movie genres. For example, what are the "icons" that signify a Western film? Cowboy hats, horses, vast horizons, sunsets, revolvers. What are the icons that signify a sci-fi film? Spaceships, aliens, advanced technology, planets. What happens when those icons blend into each other's genres? What does a cowboy hat signify when worn on the bridge of a starship? What does a laser pistol imply when wielded by duelists on a dirt road at high noon?

Iconography as a practice takes new and existing symbols, then adds a new context to communicate new meaning. Consider the capital letter A. By itself, it doesn't spark a lot of emotional response or convey a singular inherent meaning. When you paint it in red and enclose it in a rough circle, you get a commonly used symbol for anarchism. Paint it in white on the forehead of a blue helmet, you get a symbol for Captain America. Draw an extra crossbar across the middle, you'll get a symbol of a defunct Argentine currency (₳).

Where this is pertinent for board games: If you're lucky, you can find new original glyphs or symbols that you can define for your game. More often, you'll be co-opting and recombining extant symbols to represent rather complicated mechanical concepts. In either case, this chapter aims to give you a quick overview of past and current iconography in board games.

VISUAL LANGUAGES IN BOARD GAMES

"Visual language" includes artwork, graphic design, typography, icons, and all other visible elements of the game and how they interact with each other. (This is separate from the written language of the game.) Executed well, all the visual elements of your game coordinate with each other to make the interface almost invisible, letting players learn and enjoy your game as quickly as possible. In other words, it is intuitive (Figure 2.1).

I usually bristle at the word "intuitive," since it's not an objective metric. There isn't a slider I can move toward "more intuitive." Some will gain fluency in a visual language faster than others. It's my job to make sure that no one is left out of the fun because they found the game unreadable. Intuition is fundamentally subjective and idiosyncratic, even if players don't realize it. A player may say "these visuals are intuitive," but they really mean "I, Myself, Personally, found these visuals intuitive." Graphic designers must unpack the gnarly concept of "intuition" and articulate what the user may not be able to do themselves. I find intuitive visual language usually has three elements:

Consistency: A visual cue appears in recurring contexts, meaning the same thing. In Magic: the Gathering, a curved arrow icon means the verb "to tap" or "turn this card sideways, so something happens." Note that this icon is ONLY used in the context of a prerequisite for an effect. The icon is not used for the status of being "tapped" or "untapped." It's not even used when the game effect tells you to tap other cards!

Accessible: Your visual language is only as intuitive as it is accessible. The use of distinguishable colors, patterns, shapes, fonts, and other visual effects can help players intuitively understand the game. If you're using numbers to represent expense, quantity, strength, and other attributes, you'd want each of those cases to be visually distinct in some way for ease of reference.

Precedented: It's fine to attempt an innovative new approach to visual language, but you should be prepared to concede some ground to players' expectations. In a game about growing fruits in a medieval European village, your goods might be symbolized by an apple, banana, and avocado because they look very different from each other. However, some players may raise an eyebrow at tropical fruits being grown in Northern Europe.

No game exists in a vacuum. Other games have established visual norms that you're working around or against with your own particular visual language. Even the player's native written language influences how well they

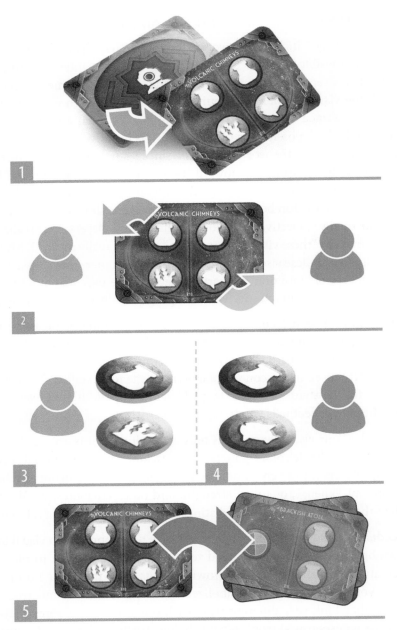

FIGURE 2.1 *Seastead* (2020). This diagram illustrates the multi-step process of the "Dive" action in the game. On your turn, you reveal the top card of the deck. You rotate it so one side faces your opponent and the other side faces yourself. You and your opponent collect the resources indicated on your respective halves of the card. Then you discard the card, ending your turn.

understand your visual language. (If you put expenses on the left side and results on the right, a reader of right-to-left language might reverse your intent.) I've even had players misinterpret my iconography because I wasn't aware some punctuation has defined meanings in computer programming or mathematics!

BOX 2.1 CONSISTENT TERMINOLOGY

The first step to consistent visual language is consistent written language. Game terms are not interchangeable. Don't call a component a "unit" on page 1, a "troop" on page 2, and then "unit" again on page 3.

If a number on a card is called "value" or "rank" or "strength," stick to that term throughout the rulebook. Once you've established a game term, make sure that term is exclusive to that concept.

For example, defining the terms "round" or "area" or "set" is especially valuable since they're used in different ways by different games. Ask your editor and proofreaders to look for these ambiguities. They are often easy to miss when you're too close to the text.

It is through design that we transform concepts into objects, that we give a shape to things we only imagine before.

HEIKO GÜNTHER

WHY USE SYMBOLS?

The board game publishing business typically has razor-thin margins. As a method of recouping costs, publishers often pursue localization contracts for international audiences. A licensor in Brazil can import the latest German board game while minimizing their overhead expenses that the German publisher incurred. The one cost the Brazilian publisher does have to handle is translating the game's text into their local languages and dialects (Figure 2.2).

To make a game as enticing for localization as possible, many publishers try to make their game components as language-neutral as possible. In their ideal world, all the cards, tokens, boards, and other bits wouldn't have a single word on them. That restricts any translation costs to the rulebook and box alone. Ideally, the importing publisher would be able to use the exact same components as the original edition of the game, only swapping the rulebook and box for their local market.

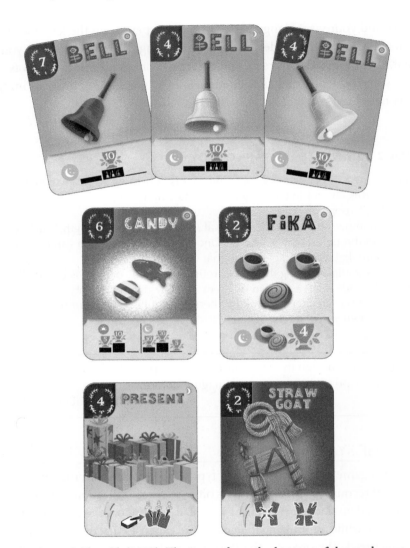

FIGURE 2.2 *Jokkmokk* (2023). The icons along the bottom of the card represent methods of scoring or executing special actions. Bells are scored at the end of the game, indicated by the moon icon: You score 10 points if you have the most complete set of all three types of bells. Candy is scored mid-game, indicated by the sunset, and at the end of the game: Players earn various point values depending on if they have the most, second-most, or third-most candy. Fika is scored at the end of the game: You score 4 points for each pair of one coffee and one bun. Presents are resolved immediately upon gaining them, indicated by the lightning bolt: You draw one card per player from the deck and give one card to each player. Straw Goat: Each player submits one card from their collection to a pool, and then each player drafts one card from that pool.

This diffuses costs to multiple parties, thus allowing a larger print run that becomes more efficient thanks to economics of scale. Printing a small quantity costs more per-unit than a large quantity. Thanks to those reduced per-unit costs, the original publisher makes a quicker profit. With luck, the game is a hit worldwide, making profits for all involved.

Why mention this in a book about graphic design? Because all these financial constraints lead to "language-neutral" symbology being very common in board games: cards, tiles, and boards using pictograms to convey intricate game effects. When done well, this makes the game easier to parse at a glance. When done poorly, it just makes the game equally befuddling for speakers of any language.

The original edition of *Bang!* (Sciarra, 2002) mostly used icons to represent its limited set of in-game actions. However, some card effects were so nuanced that it resorted to using a "book" icon, which meant the player had to refer to the rulebook for a complete explanation. At the time *Bang!* was first published, customers might have tolerated that crutch, but modern customers expect a more elegant solution.

Point Salad, *Sushi Go*, and *Bohnanza* are typical examples of using iconography to represent set collection mechanisms. In *Point Salad* and *Sushi Go*, you earn variable amounts of points for collecting certain sets of cards. In *Bohnanza*, the points strictly escalate from 1 to 4 points, but the amount of cards necessary to reach those scores varies by the type of card.

Race for the Galaxy is an extreme example of using iconography for almost all game effects. Though it has a consistent internal grammar to its symbols, there's a significant learning curve when first playing the game because it is so dense. This is further hindered by its use of low-contrast pastels and colorblind-inaccessible colors.

This chapter introduces some basic concepts of symbolic language, when to best use iconography, and how to design those symbols to be as effective as possible.

BOX 2.2 HYBRID APPROACH TO ICONS

Lords of Waterdeep takes a hybrid approach to visual language. Icons are used to represent the most common game resources: cards, cubes, pawns, points, and money. In other words, they only use icons for nouns. (Verbs and descriptors are presented in plain text in the rare case as they are necessary for more nuanced game effects.)

> I will ask people what they think my icon says. It's important not
> to prepare people so they can have as many fresh eyes as possible.
>   ESTEFANIA RODRIGUEZ

ABSTRACTION VS. REPRESENTATION

Over the centuries, a whole menagerie of Chess pieces have come and gone
from local variants of the game. In the original Indian game of Chaturanga,
you would have fielded an Elephant instead of a Bishop and a Raja instead
of a King. Playing Shogi in Japan, you'd have Generals and Lances. Playing
Xiangqi in China, you'd have Chariots and Cannons. Wherever chess
spread, its metaphors adapted to the local customs and frame of reference
(Figure 2.3).

Learning the modern game of Chess, you simply have to remember
vaguely that the king is important, but not powerful; that the "horse" or
"knight" is especially mobile compared to the other pieces; that the "castle"
or "rook" moves in straight lines because … well, just because.

Therein is a disconnect between what the game-piece represents (an
armored soldier on a horse) and how it's been abstracted into game
rules (moving in an L shape). This is also disregarding how far removed
the representations are from modern life. (I've never met a knight
myself, but I'd be curious to take a stroll with one and see how they
actually move.)

In 2013, Catalyst Games' *The Duke* used wooden tiles with grids and
shapes to illustrate each piece's unique movement (Figure 2.4). A circle is
a standard move, like a Chess Pawn or King. A triangle is a "sliding" move
like a Chess Bishop or Rook. If a shape is hollow, that indicates a jumping
movement, like a Chess Knight. This language forgoes all metaphor, opting
to use pure geometry to explain the rules of the game.

The Duke's tiles could have been published as an utterly abstract set
of tiles. The tiles would be self-expressive, language-neutral, unbound
by any historical associations and cultural context. However, each tile
still has a name printed on the tile, which is written in English. Each also
has a simple pictogram of a handheld weapon. "Assassin" is represented
by a curved blade, "Bowman" by a bow and arrow, "Wizard" by a magic
wand. By conceding to a degree of representation, The Duke achieves
three goals.

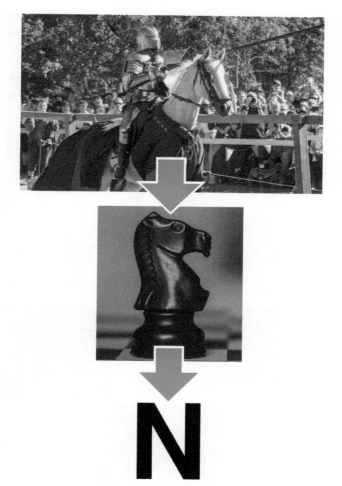

FIGURE 2.3 An example of a board game's components represented with increasing levels of abstraction. Top: A photo of what a chess knight represents. Middle: Opposing chess knight pieces. Bottom: The letter N, used to represent the piece in chess notation.

1. **Verbal Shorthand**: A name makes the game easier to discuss. Rather than say "the tile that moves one space diagonally or two spaces forward," you can say "Footman."

2. **Mechanical Metaphor**: The name loosely explains how a tile behaves. For example, a "Bowman" can attack at a distance without moving.

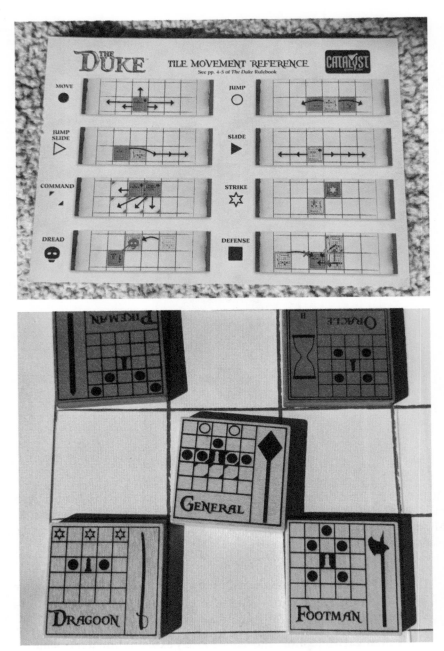

FIGURE 2.4 Components from *The Duke* (2013) (Catalyst Games).

3. **Orientation**: Your own tiles must be oriented in a particular direction facing your opponent. By placing the name along the bottom, players can easily tell the correct orientation.

As you develop the visual language of your own game, you must decide how much abstraction your players will tolerate. At what point does abstraction stop helping and instead become a barrier to entry?

BOX 2.3 NOTATION

Chess of course has its own "icon" system using algebraic notation to record each player's turn. This code is extremely compressed and can take some time for players to become fluent. Experienced players can visualize an entire game just reading the logs. Annotators can even add commentary, with question marks for bad moves and exclamation to commend a good move.

Poor graphic design can undermine the experience of a mechanically good game. Good graphic design can elevate good games into great products.

RORY MULDOON

WHEN TO USE ICONS

Using icons instead of certain words offers several advantages. Replacing an often-used game term with an icon can conserve valuable space on small components like tiles or cards. An icon may be recognized from any orientation and by any literacy level, making the game more accessible. And of course, icons can simply add aesthetic value to your board game, making the overall gameplay experience more pleasant (Figure 2.5).

You should design your icons with certain principles in mind:

Clarity: Icons should be designed with their typical scaling in mind. It does no good to design a highly detailed icon when it will be displayed at 5mm. The icons should be unambiguous at small or large scales. The game will not always be played in the perfect development conditions, so the

FIGURE 2.5 *Clash of Cultures: Monumental Edition* (2021). Text on the cards integrates small icons representing various resources, components, and conditional attributes.

icons must be sturdy enough to be partially obscured, viewed in dim light, or recognized out of context.

Standardization: Following a cohesive set of rules for your icons' appearance makes it easier for players to internalize how they're used in your game. Each choice of shape, orientation, and color should be backed by a specific meaning throughout the icon family. If a subset of icons shares certain characteristics, that must be done with intent, not by accident, or else it leads to confusion.

Intuition: Your icon design should work hand-in-hand with the game's themes to help tie together its metaphors and mechanisms. Consider your average player's history with other games in the same category and what precedents you can use as a visual shorthand in your icon designs. You must determine when a representation icon works better than an abstract icon.

Recognition: A good set of icons makes each one distinct enough that they can be immediately recalled as easily as a letter or number. If icons bear any similarities, it should be with intent, to communicate some other concepts like "all these icons are basic resources" vs. "all of these other icons are rare goods."

Fatigue: Game designers and developers vastly overestimate the intuitive nature of their iconography. They're simply too close to the game for an objective view. Until a player achieves fluency, understanding each icon takes effort. That effort is on top of learning the game itself, but the average player won't recognize the difference. The effort to learn the game is the same as learning the iconography, and either one can make a negative impression.

As you develop your iconography, try not to get defensive when you get feedback that it's not as clear as you had thought. Take the feedback and consider how to optimize them for better clarity and ease of use. Consider accessibility concerns like color recognition, language barriers, and general experience with board games. All these weigh on the success or failure of any set of icons.

BOX 2.4 VECTOR FILE FORMATS

When you draw in a program like Photoshop, you're brushing individual pixels into the canvas to create a "bitmap" image. By contrast, vector editing programs like Adobe Illustrator or Inkscape use geometric points, polygons, and fills to draw their images. These programs will create "vector" files like .eps or .svg formats. Vector's main advantage is that these images can be scaled to any size without causing losing image quality. The second advantage is that vector files may be used as glyphs to create a customized icon font. Before investing in a vector editing program, try using sites like game-icons.net to browse, customize, and download vector files that have already been created.

How players understand the game, its rules and what to do is all informed by the game's graphic design.

TORBEN RATZLAFF

DESIGN IN BLACK-AND-WHITE FIRST

Designers now have the luxury of designing with every color and soft element in the world, but this was not always the case (Figure 2.6). In the early days of professional graphic design, creators had to consider the constraints of rough inks, pulpy paper, and very small print sizes. An icon would have to be equally legible in tiny fax letterhead, a blurry tattoo, and low-resolution TV broadcast. That's why generations of designers learned to create visual marks in black-and-white first. If it worked as a pure silhouette, it would survive the worst treatment the world could throw at it.

While your game icons don't have to go through such a crucible, it's still useful to begin with those tight black-and-white constraints to ensure your icons are as legible as possible. Your impulse might be to jump straight into colors, but this can be a distraction that sidetracks the entire design process. For the sake of simplifying the design process, it's best to start from the most basic version of your icons before adding more variables that need to be independently tested.

Depending on your components, you may not always have the option of printing an icon with all the high-end rendering that you prefer. For

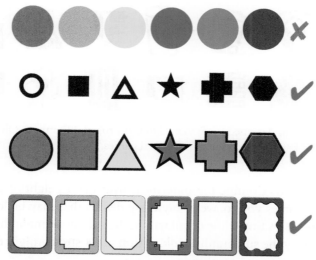

FIGURE 2.6 This shows the challenges of designing with color from the beginning. Top Row: Using the same shape in different colors is insufficient to distinguish them at a glance. Second Row: Designing black shapes without color helps ensure that each icon is distinct before applying color. Third Row: Adding color as a secondary attribute helps further reinforce the differences between the icons. Bottom Row: Card borders can also be tied to each color, helping them stay distinct.

example, dice faces are typically engraved and painted with the same color on every face. If you have a different icon on every face, can they be recognized from any orientation, even if they're the same color? You can be confident that they work if you've designed in black-and-white from the beginning.

To be clear, this isn't advocating for minimalism for its own sake. You will eventually add other elements to support the readability of your icons, like color or texture (Figure 2.7). However, the distinctive identity must be evident in the first place. A black square, black circle, and black triangle are more distinct from each other than a red circle, a blue circle, and a yellow circle. If the icon can't be recognized by its silhouette alone, adding color and detail won't help it.

Here are three tips for designing in black-and-white:

Design Small: If your icons must be legible at small scales, avoid creating any open spaces within the icon's silhouette, since those spaces may

FIGURE 2.7   Icons designed for *System Gateway* project. (Thanks to Olive Wesley, Izzy Iqbal, and Patrick Burksson at nullsignal.games.)

disappear entirely. Confine the outermost width and height of your icon to 1cm. This forces you to avoid any fussy details that may be lost in the printing process. A tiny white detail within the silhouette might literally be flooded away by the surrounding ink. A thin black stroke might disappear if it's below typical print resolution.

Test Often: As you design your icon set, take a step back and blur your eyes to see if they still retain their legibility. (For me, I just have to take off my eyeglasses for the ultimate vision test!) Print your icons on your home printer. Show the icons to other people who aren't familiar with your project to ensure that the uninitiated player would be able to discern and recognize them.

Rotate and Flip: Your icons may be seen from any skewed angle if it's on game boards, tiles, cards, or dice. It's important that they still retain their identity from any orientation. A triangle pointing up is basically the same as a triangle pointing down, so those two icons would not be distinct enough to pass this test. Note: Make sure your icon does not accidentally look like something else when viewed upside-down. You don't want to accidentally make a rude image!

BOX 2.5 GRAYSCALE

As a middle-step before attempting color, you might add some grayscale gradients to your icons. Just be careful not to rely too strongly on this as an identifying feature. The lightest shades placed on the edge of an icon may disappear and break the silhouette you've worked so hard to design.

Good design makes the rules and mechanics more intuitive to learn.
STEPHANIE GUSTAFSSON

Revisions and feedback are part of the process. [...] Sometimes you will even get conflicting opinions. It's your job to separate out the good feedback from the edge cases.

TONY MASTRANGELI

SUBDIVIDING ICONS INTO GROUPS

There may be times when you need to have a subset of icons that are conceptually related to each other, like distinguishing basic resources from advanced resources. In those cases, I recommend using a very simple outer shape or outline around the icon for each subset.

In *Super-Skill Pinball*, players use a marker to fill in dice icons on a dry-erase game board, thus scoring points. These marks may be erased at certain moments, thus making them available for scoring again. We needed a visual reminder that distinguished each of these dice icons from each other and we could not use colors, since those were already connected to another game concept (Figure 2.8). So each of the dice icons is surrounded by a certain type of outline.

- A solid outline means that these icons are part of a set. When that set is complete, the marks are erased.
- A dashed outline means that the marks remain until the end of the round, at which time the marks are erased.
- A double-outline means that these marks remain until the end of the game and may never be erased.

Here are some more reasons you might visually categorize a set of icons:

Degrees of Refinement: Use an outer shape to surround certain resource icons. The number of sides increases to represent the refinement of that resource. Basic resources may be icons alone, without an outer border. "Level 1" refinement is represented by a circle, "Level 2" by a triangle, "Level 3" by a square, and so on.

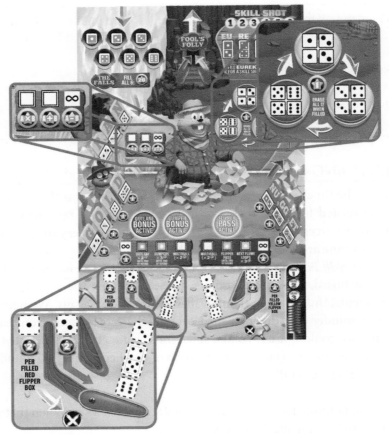

FIGURE 2.8   Dice icons in *Super-Skill Pinball.*

Reference Components: The outer shape can represent the physical appearance of your game components. For example, if an effect allows you to increase the income of a resource, it might be surrounded by a square, which corresponds to a cube on your personal income track. If an effect merely grants you one unit of that resource, it might be surrounded by a circle, corresponding to a round resource token.

Gain and Spend: The outer shape can represent acquiring or spending the noted icon. For example, the icon alone merely represents the resource as a standalone concept, like a dollar. Surrounding it in an "X" shape represents spending that dollar. Surrounding it in a smooth rounded square means

FIGURE 2.9   Elemental icons from *Gates of Mara*.

gaining that resource. (Note that it's often simpler to just add a "+" or "-" beside an icon to represent earning and spending.)

Wild Icons: Your game might have sub-groups for example resources that may be spent vs. assets that remain static or only grow over time. The icons within a category should have a shared attribute. In *Gates of Mara*, four elements of fire, air, earth, and water are all rough circles. When an effect asks for "any element," that icon shows all four icons within a single circle. This makes it clear that the quantity is still 1 but the actual element is up to the player. See Figure 2.9.

By the time you need to group icons into various subcategories like this, take it as a warning that you might be going too far in converting all of your game concepts into icons. Sometimes it's better to just use plain text rather than wrack your brain to create 100 easily distinguished icons.

BOX 2.6 ILLUSTRATED ICONS

You may see some games that use artwork for their icons for a more naturalistic touch. This is fine as long as the fundamental silhouettes of the icons are established and maintained. Icons may be illustrated by hand, with the organic details of a pencil-sketch that fits the game's setting. However, the shapes must remain very clearly defined, with sharp contrasts against their backgrounds. Make them easily read even in dim light or in grayscale (Figure 2.10).

Small icons and text that looks good on screen may not translate as well to print.

RORY MULDOON

FIGURE 2.10   Cards in Arf!

MAKING COLORS ACCESSIBLE

Colorblindness is often cited as a reason to choose accessible colors, but accessibility actually helps all players engage with your game. Color perception problems can happen to anybody, thanks to poor lighting or even printing errors. Efforts to solve for colorblindness help all players (Figure 2.11).

When you must assign colors to a set of components, there is one rule to follow first: **Within a group of colored components, you may use *either* Red, or Green, or Brown. Pick one.**

For more detail, here is some advice for how to use and pair colors within the same set of components.

- **Black with White**: Excellent for two-player games. This maximizes contrast.
- **Red with Blue**: Easy to discern even in adverse conditions. Both colors can group with black or white. Make sure the tints are relatively light, since some shades of blue and red can be dark enough that they look black. Do not group Red with Green.

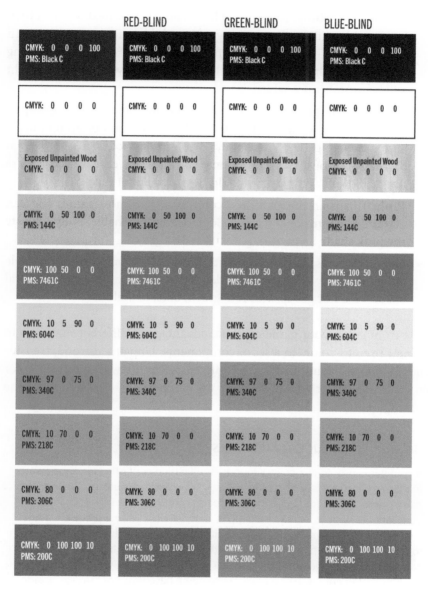

FIGURE 2.11 How typical color palettes appear to different types of color-blindness. Note how red/green/brown are effectively identical.

- **Cyan or Sky Blue**: Do not group with yellow, white, or gray. Cyans may group with blue if significantly lighter, but only if all other options are exhausted.

- **Green with Yellow**: These might look a little putrid next to each other, so use with caution. Green can group with blue. Red can group with yellow. Do not group green with red or brown. Be careful grouping yellow with white, since even the most lemon-yellow shade might still be mistaken for white.
- **Purple or Indigo**: These colors blend red and blue, so don't group in the same category with either red or blue. Also do not group purple and indigo together since they're so similar to each other. Even following all of these precautions, you must be careful that they're not tinted so dark that they could be mistaken for black.
- **Pink**: This is an underutilized color option in most games and can certainly help make any game feel more approachable. Fully saturate the pink shade if you group it with red or gray.
- **Grays, Browns, Earthtones, and Pastels**: These are the least reliable colors because colorblindness defaults most colors to these general shades. Do not group with red, green, blue, or yellow.

Aside from color, your game can take advantage of different materials to add new pseudo-colors to a set of components. Unpainted wood, translucent plastic, and shiny metal are easily recognizable without using color *per se*. Screen printing illustrations on components also helps tell the pieces apart.

BOX 2.7 TRANSLUCENT MATERIALS

If your game uses translucent components, like dice or plastic cubes, be aware that severely restricts your color options. You must account not just for the components' pigment, but whatever background colors might change the component's appearance. For example, a translucent yellow piece on a blue surface will appear green. It's best to limit the colors of translucent components to three primary pigments: red, blue, and yellow. Note that translucent plastics can also have unique embedded details and finishes, so a white piece might have a pearlescent finish or a black piece might have wisps of "smoke" inside.

Good design emphasizes the gameplay and makes the rules easier to remember and follow.

LINDSAY DAVIAU (RESTORATION GAMES)

DOUBLE-CODING COLORS

Instead of using colors alone, it's best to "double-code" each color with a correlated visual cue, like an embedded icon. Usually this is done in the service of colorblind or otherwise visually impaired players, but it helps *all* players navigate your game more easily.

Figure 2.12 shows a fan of cards using only colors, without double-coding. Without additional visual support, these colors could easily be confused for each other. By adding a small icon within each colored circle, it's easier to parse each card-type at a glance, even in the corner alone. Putting a large, distinct geometric shape in the corner of the card makes it easier to recognize them at a glance.

You can also lean on pre-existing color associations when coding each color. For example, let's say your game needed different fruits. You can pick a different color and fruit pairing: a Red strawberry (with visible seeds), a slice of Orange (with visible lines of pith), a Green pear (with stem), a blueberry, a purple eggplant.

Taking this one step further, you could give each card-type a unique border, with its own distinct details in the corners and textures along the edge.

As you develop your icons and borders, always pay special attention on how you distinguish red and green. Make sure their non-color features are as different as possible, since they're the most likely to be confused for each other. If red is round, make green sharp. If red is striped, make green dotted. If red uses a filled icon, consider giving green a hollow outlined icon.

BOX 2.8 10 ABSTRACT ICON-COLOR-PATTERN PAIRINGS

If your game doesn't have a particular theme and you just need some guaranteed way to distinguish up to different colors, make sure your red and green icons are as different as possible. If one is round, the other is sharp. If one is filled, the other is hollow. Similarly, make your blue and yellow icons different. Also make your grey icon very different from purple, black, or dark blue icons (Figure 2.13).

Be consistent and clear with your design language. If you assign a certain meaning (value, rule) to a graphic, color, layout or style it has to be consistent overall. The design should also be intuitive and explain as much as possible by itself. Also think about implementing redundancy, especially for colors (combine them with shapes).

STEPHANIE GUSTAFSSON

FIGURE 2.12 *Trickster: Fantasy, Trickster: Symbiosis, Trickster: Starship* (2015). Each Trickster deck has cards in seven different colors featuring seven different characters. Each combination is unique, for a total of 49 cards. Because the decks may be shuffled together, I wanted to keep the color codes consistent and abstract across the series. Note how I took care to make the icons for red different from green and blue different from yellow. This was to help colorblind accessibility.

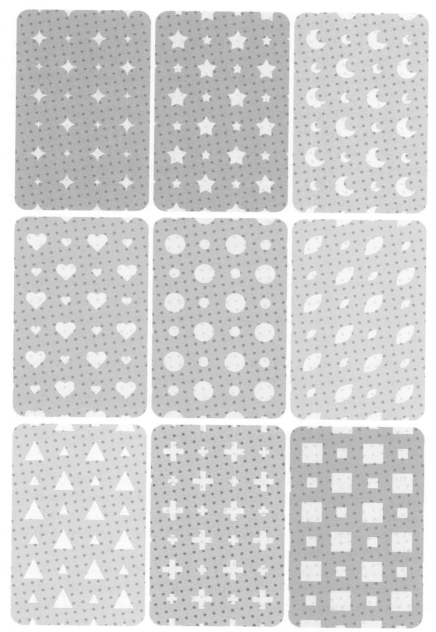

FIGURE 2.13   Patterned backgrounds using colors and shapes.

KEYWORD LIGATURES AS ICONS

Ligatures are special glyphs that merge together two or more commonly grouped letters, like "st" or "fi." Some fonts have ligatures as hidden glyphs that must be activated with a certain sequence of letters or characters, so "fi" automatically changes to the ligature glyph. You can take advantage of this feature to make custom fonts that insert icons into the flow of text as easily as typing a keyword (Figure 2.14).

You can make a custom font that makes an icon replace a certain sequence of characters. For example, you can write the word APPLE, then select that word and change the font to a custom font you've created. That font has been set up to treat APPLE as a ligature, replacing it with a glyph: an icon of an apple. Here are some tips for making the best keywords:

Unique: The keyword should be something that would not normally occur in the course of normal writing. For example, if you have an icon for the word "mage," you want to avoid the icon appearing accidentally in the word "damage," "image," or "magenta." To avoid any accidental use, you might use capitals that don't normally appear in text, like MAGE.

Memorable: Abbreviated keywords might make logical sense in the moment, can be very easy to forget or mistype. For example, keywords <icon_A> are too opaque. Months into a project, it's easy to forget what "A" stands for. In addition, brackets like <> are easy to mistype as () or []. Avoid multiple special characters in your keywords. ATTACK or APPLE are better.

Literal: Some designers may use thematic keywords like "strength" for an icon of a sword or "defense" for an icon of a shield because those are the terms used in the game. This is up to personal taste, but I've had more success with keywords that literally say what the icon is, so I'd use SWORD and SHIELD as my keywords.

In each of these examples, you may have noticed that I use all-caps for my recommended keywords. This comes from years of personal experience watching developers accidentally bound to some early technical mistakes. I recommend using plain words written in all-caps, like APPLE, SWORD, and MAGE, because they are easy to spell, will rarely occur in normal text, and they accurately represent what the icon looks like. Here's an example of what a game effect might look like in plain text.

MEMO TO DEVELOPERS
ICON STYLE GUIDE

This game uses a custom font to automatically insert icons anywhere within the flow of text. To ensure proper functionality, download and install the latest version of the font at this link. The left column shows each of the icons. The middle column shows the keyword to prompt the icon. These keywords are case-sensitive, so make sure they are capitalized and spelled correctly.

TECH

ABILITIES
These tags represent skills and actions that each character might possess. Note that they're all in circles. Any new abilities added to the game will also be in circles.

INTEL

STRENGTH

AGILITY

FLIGHT

RANGE

URBAN

LOCATIONS
These tags are applies to certain cards when they're tied to a certain place or region. This definition can be very broad, but all these icons are in the map pointer shape.

SPACE

TIME

COSMIC

MUTANT

CONDITIONS
Extra conditions on a character or location. These are in a spiky shape.

RADIATION

MISCELLANEOUS
When we need a unique tag that doesn't fit any other category, it has no outer shape.

STONE

MAGIC

FIGURE 2.14 A typical document I would create in the beginning of a project so all collaborators know the keywords for icons to appear in text.

Spend 2 APPLE: Place a MAGE on the board equipped with a SWORD. It has ATTACK 2 until end of turn.

You should write a full document with all the keywords you plan to use for the game and share that document with your collaborators. That makes it easy for all participants to spellcheck their work and ensure the icon font works as intended.

BOX 2.9 FONT CREATION TOOLS

As of this writing, my favorite free icon font creation tool is IcoMoon <icomoon.io>. It's a browser-based desktop app that offers thousands of its own icons to get you started and allows you to upload your own flat monochrome SVG icons. My favorite paid icon font creator is FontSelf Maker <fontself.com>, a plugin for Adobe Illustrator that allows multicolor icons.

Graphic design is as crucial to a game as the game design and mechanics.

JACOBY O'CONNOR

CASE STUDY: *TRICKSTER: CHAMPIONS OF TIME*

I self-published the original edition of Trickster in 2012. It would later be picked up by a traditional publisher and re-released as Trickster: Champions of Time. You can see some of the icons used in that new edition in Figure 2.15.

Each character allows the player to do a game effect when they play the card. Generally these effects move cards between different "zones" of play, such as a player's hand of cards, the deck, the discard pile, and so on. I represented the discard pile with a flat "trash can" icon, which I thought would be universally understood. I represented a player's hand with a literal hand icon. I represented a player's personal collection of acquired cards with a "house" icon, which I admit has an odd thematic element that might be discordant with themes like fantasy and science-fiction, but it was easily recognized and looked different from the other icons.

The card effects often specified ownership of a certain zone, like "your hand" or "an opponent's hand." I used hollow shapes to represent "you"

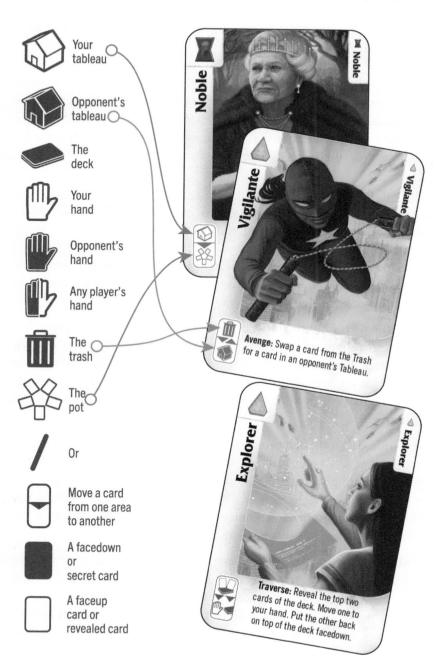

Your tableau

Opponent's tableau

The deck

Your hand

Opponent's hand

Any player's hand

The trash

The pot

Or

Move a card from one area to another

A facedown or secret card

A faceup card or revealed card

Noble

Vigilante

Avenge: Swap a card from the Trash for a card in an opponent's Tableau.

Explorer

Traverse: Reveal the top two cards of the deck. Move one to your hand. Put the other back on top of the deck facedown.

FIGURE 2.15 Cards and icon reference from *Trickster: Champions of Time* (2017).

and filled shapes to represent "opponent," thus a hollow hand meant "your hand of cards."

I assigned a distinct shape to each suit/color and made sure the icons only appeared on a plain white background. I made sure that red and green suits had identifiable shapes that wouldn't be confused for each other. I took similar measures for the yellow and blue icons, since I didn't want them to be confused for green either. I also changed the background texture for each suit so it would have a different watermarked pattern.

SUMMARY OF ICONOGRAPHY

These finicky little symbols and glyphs can cause a disproportionate amount of angst while you're designing a game's layout. So much meaning and strict legal interpretation is bundled up into these tiny pictures that they feel like they'll collapse under their own density. Just remember you're not alone in the project, you have developers, playtesters, players, and years of past games from which you can draw advice.

Analyze the text: Find the most commonly used nouns in the game. See how icons can supplement or substitute those words to aid faster fluency. Find opportunities to make certain concepts clearer by visually tying them to physical game components. Look for any cards or boards that are overly stuffed with text, which might be eased by the use of more space efficient icons instead.

Start simple: The most detailed and colorful your icon, the harder it will be to recognize at small scales and far distances. Begin with basic geometric shapes with plain black fills and no strokes. As you add more details, consider how this helps the icon look different from the rest. Sometimes you *should* give icons a similar appearance if they're part of a related group, but they should still be easily distinguished from each other.

Organize the library: Once you have a set of icons, share that with the rest of your development team and ask for their input. Make sure they understand which keywords are correlated with which icons. See if the icons can withstand all the future developments they have in mind for later expansions or promo items. Plan ahead for possibly making a custom font out of this icon library, cleaning up your files so they're easy to import into a font creation app.

Summary Questions

- How do you see current games use glyphs and diagrams?
- What are the key recurring nouns in your game?
- What symbols will you use to represent each of those nouns?
- How do you represent interactions between these nouns?
- How are movement, conversion, and transaction visually distinct?
- Are you using similar symbols to represent different concepts, like arrows?
- How do you note ownership, such as "your cards" vs. "opponent's cards"?
- What diagrams and glyphs are you co-opting from other games?
- When you do so, is your usage the same or different enough to be confused?
- What measures are you taking to avoid icons being misinterpreted?
- Are you creating original glyphs for this game?
- If so, have you checked that those glyphs are devoid of existing meaning for your audience?
- What visually links glyphs that are part of the same group or category, like resources?

CHAPTER 3

Diagrams

INTRODUCTION TO DIAGRAMS

Comics have taught me a lot about designing diagrams for board games (Figure 3.1). Both games and comics are a 2-D medium that must depict 4-D content. Both must show time, movement, cause, effect, and even branching choices, all without the benefit of video or sound effects. Thankfully modern comics have over a century of visual vernacular that I have learned to adopt for my own diagrams.

I treat a diagram like a miniature comic strip showing a sequence of game events. "Sequence" is the operative word there. The most common mistake I see from beginner designers is when they try to fit too much content into a single panel. Usually this is because a section of text has been written as one solid paragraph, so the new designer feels compelled to do the same visually. Let's take this dense rules paragraph for a fictional game:

On your turn, you may play one card from your hand. Then you must advance your pawn along the track clockwise, landing it on the nearest space showing that card's symbol. You may "jump" over other occupied spaces, but you may not land on an occupied space. If the nearest space

DOI: 10.1201/9781003453772-4

is occupied, you may not play that card. After moving, you may repeat this process, following the same rules. You may continue playing cards and moving your pawn as long as you have unique cards to play. You may not play the same symbol twice in one turn. At the end of your turn, discard any played cards then draw cards from the deck until you have five cards in hand.

It would be a mistake to try to fit all of that content into a single-panel diagram. How do you show the legal actions as well as the illegal actions in one image? It's better to divide that paragraph into smaller chunks and reorganize it into a series of panels.

> Figure 3.1(a)—A hand of cards, with one "apple" card raised and highlighted by an obvious starburst.

> Figure 3.1(b)—A wide view of the entire game board, an arrow indicating the active pawn's movement going over occupied spaces. A zoomed-in close-up of the next "apple" space.

> Figure 3.1(c)—This shows three more moments, each in their own narrow panel. Each panel shows a different card and the pawn moving to that corresponding space. The gutters are angled to indicate that these moments occur in a direct sequence.

> Figure 3.1(d)—Four played cards going from a hand into a discard pile.

> Figure 3.1(e)—Four cards going from the deck into a hand.

> Figure 3.1(f)—These panels have a "hazard" border and a "ban" symbol in the corner, to indicate that these actions are prohibited. The first panel shows a sequence of cards with the same symbol. The second panel shows the pawn moving onto an occupied space.

In this chapter, I offer some tips and notes of caution on how to best execute diagrams in your game. You may recognize some practices from other games you've seen or played. However, I can't speak to what another graphic designer was thinking when they made their own visuals. I can only explain my own thought processes, my experience, and my usual rationale. Have some sympathy for the harried designer next time you see a confusing diagram in a rulebook. It's hard to tell what compromises were made for time, size, color, material, localization contracts, or any number of other unseen factors.

FIGURE 3.1   Example diagram for a fictional board game.

THE PURPOSE OF DIAGRAMS

If icons are the "words" of a visual language, diagrams are the "sentences." Diagrams are complete statements with subject, object, and intent. By combining images, glyphs, and numbers in carefully constructed sequences, you can communicate game mechanisms to readers of any language.

However, there are always diminishing returns beyond a certain degree. The more you try to encode text into a diagram, the greater the risk you create opaque hieroglyphics that rely on a separate written glossary to decode, which may defeat the purpose of the diagram in the first place.

That said, it's good to know what that purpose is to begin with.

Overview of Play: It's common for the back of a rulebook or a small supplementary card to show the entirety of a game in one at-a-glance summary. This can show how components are set up, what a typical turn looks like, what triggers the end of the game, and how a winner is determined. I often include very simplified overview diagrams on the back of a game box, condensing the key game actions into three distinct panels and captions.

User Interface (UI): We adopt this term from digital menu design in apps and websites. However, digital media has the benefit of being able to minimize optional menus when they're not in use. For print media, most of our interface is visible all the time, even when most of it isn't relevant in that particular moment. A good design lets players see what they need to see, but also allows them to easily filter out anything else. You'll see these diagrams on player aid cards, privacy screens, or on game boards showing legal spaces.

Examples of Play: A good rulebook frequently intersperses instructional text with written examples supplemented by clear visual diagrams. As in the diagram from the introduction, this diagram may just show the steps of a turn along with some typical prohibitions. Examples of play may also be written and illustrated in a more narrative format, with fictional players each making choices and taking their own actions.

In-Game Effects: Your game board may have certain spaces with unique effects. Rather than writing out those effects in text, where it may be difficult to localize, you can use diagrams as a more convenient method of explaining that effect. Usually this involves gaining some kind of resource or being allowed to execute a special action. In many cases, these also require an expenditure of resources or a prerequisite game-state, which effectively makes these "cause and effect" diagrams.

In Figure 3.2, we see some diagrams used for different purposes:

Figure 3.2(a)—The player board from *Heat: Pedal to the Metal* uses the top row to remind players of each phase of play during a round. The gold rings indicate steps that are done simultaneously while the rest are done in turn-order. The middle card space reminds players what to do if that space is empty, causing their race car to "spin out."

Figure 3.2(b)—The wooden tiles from *The Duke* use an icon system of stars, circles, rings, and brackets to explain how they move on a board. With this visual language, a single tile can be very dense with nuanced movement and attack abilities, yet still be clearly legible across a table or viewed by an opponent upside-down.

Figure 3.2(c)—The cards from *Santorini* use diagrams to explain each player's one unique ability they can use during play. These use a much more illustrative and directly representational art style which suits the game, but still reads clearly.

Figure 3.2(d)—The cards in *Holmes: Sherlock & Mycroft* are actually worker placement spaces that players will activate. Each card is a different character from the Sherlock Holmes stories, each with their own effect when you visit them. Here, arrows are used to represent cause and effect, rather than literal movement.

Figure 3.2(e)—The tiles in *Quacks of Quedlinberg* remind players what each ingredient in the game does at various points during play. There are so many different ingredients with such nuanced effects, that the designers have opted to use *both* plain text and illustrative diagrams to explain the full context of each effect.

Figure 3.2(f)—The ship cards from *Junk Orbit* also use text and diagrams together to fully explain each ship's special ability. The cards also use flavor text with subtle pop culture references to note what inspired

FIGURE 3.2 Examples of diagrams in practice. *Heat: Pedal to the Metal* (2022), *The Duke* (2013), *Santorini* (2016), *Holmes: Sherlock & Mycroft* (2015), *Quacks of Quedlinberg* (2018), *Junk Orbit* (2018).

this ability and build an intuitive understanding of the intended effect. Remember, language-neutral diagrams and text are not mutually exclusive, they can help each other.

Knowing *why* you're making a diagram helps you determine whether that diagram is successful in its purpose. Does the UI convey information as needed? Does the example of play correctly illustrate the rules? Are in-game effects clearly understood in the course of play? Is the overview comprehensive enough that players don't have to thumb through the rulebook? Ask those kinds of questions as you design and you'll make a very effective diagram.

The theme, the mechanics and gameplay could be amazing, but if you don't have the right graphic design skills to express to players how to play then you won't be able to play correctly. Period.

ESTEFANIA RODRIGUEZ

Most people are more than happy to give you feedback or advice on something, introduce you to someone they know, or share an opportunity.

BRIGETTE INDELICATO

USING FRAMES IN DIAGRAMS

For a single action or effect, you likely don't need any outer boundary surrounding the diagram. At most, you might need some dividing line to delineate the beginning or end of a diagram from other visuals on a game component. For example, a line underneath a card name and a line above some flavor text, with a diagram sandwiched in between.

For more complex diagrams that need to be further subdivided for clarity, you can surround each chunk of information with a simple frame. The frame and its content are what I will refer to as a "panel," to borrow a term from comics. The short amount of empty space in between panels is called the "gutter."

In comics, a panel is a single drawing in a sequence of drawings, with each panel usually depicting a single moment in time. The gutter between each panel may represent a passage of seconds, hours, or centuries. For board games, the panels serve a similar function, but the amount of time compression may vary depending on how much space is available. With a full empty rulebook page, you can unpack an entire turn into very granular

FIGURE 3.3   Example of turn order.

steps. Most of the time, space is not so readily available, and you may need to compress more information into a single frame, or use the gutters to convey their own information. However, shaping the panels can convey information as well:

Figure 3.3—Turn Order: This diagram shows rectangular rows of panels, each with one player. Within the rectangle, the gaps between panels are shaped like chevrons, directing the eye from left to right. The ends of the rectangle are flat, to convey that this entire sequence is one full unit of time in the game. Each subsequent row shows the players one position earlier in the turn order. This method is also great for games where players move tokens along progressive one-way tracks.

Figure 3.4—Phase Structure: This diagram shows distinct phases of gameplay. The first phase has players reveal a secret card simultaneously. All player icons are shown in the same panel, thus representing the sim-ultaneity of this moment. The second phase is resolved in a turn order determined by the player's revealed cards. Player icons are now re-arranged, each in their own "chevron" style panel to show that this phase is resolved in a specific order.

FIGURE 3.4   Example of phase structure.

FIGURE 3.5   Example of figurative window.

FIGURE 3.6   Example of non-temporal panels.

Figure 3.5—Close-Ups and **Windows**: Use these panels when circumstances don't allow the reader to easily pertinent details of a game component. For example, if the diagram shows a broad overview of the game in-progress which doesn't let a reader easily see the small details of a certain component. In this example, the turn order is determined at random by pulling player chits from a bag. The diagram needs to show which tiles are within an opaque bag, so I drew a dotted oval over the bag that lets the reader peek inside. There is not a literal hole in the bag in real life, but readers understand from the dotted line and semi-transparency that we're seeing through a figurative window for the sake of the explanation.

Figure 3.6—Non-Temporal Diagrams: These diagrams do not show a passage of time, but relationships between subjects. The first shows a fully competitive game. The second shows a co-operative game where all players work against the game's "bot" player. The third shows a team-based game where three players work against an opposing team of three other players. Note that the panel shapes here are not mere rectangles, but used angled gaps or displaced sub-sections to help communicate the relationships between the players.

Remember that players actively participate in the diagram's interpretation at the table. In all of these examples, styling the frames and shaping the gutters around panels is as important as the contents of each panel. The gutters are a liminal space that a reader must mentally fill in to understand your intent.

Play with your designs printed out in prototypes, and observe the other players and take in all feedback from it.

KIRK W BUCKENDORF

ALPHANUMERIC CHARACTERS IN DIAGRAMS

Though a diagram is language-neutral, you may need to use letters or numbers somewhere amidst the pictograms. If so, make them large, bold, and consistent throughout all diagrams within the game. Consistency in this case means that your letters and numbers always have the same appearance for their use-case. Numbers representing quantities look different from numbers representing sequences. Letters used as tags look different from letters representing options available within a turn.

Here are some possible reasons you might need to use letters or numbers in your diagrams.

Reading Order: Board game diagrams tend to convey rather abstract information, so you may find it necessary to literally number each panel so the reader knows your intended order. This is also helpful if panels are widely spaced from each other across a page. Keep those numbers small, simple, and out of the way in the top-left corner of a panel. If your panel only shows one moment of time, such as an initial game setup, you may need to tag elements within the frame, so readers understand the order of actions that led to that game-state.

Quantity of Units: You will eventually need to show multiple countable units of some game element. It's tempting to avoid digits and just duplicate an icon as necessary. (Three apples literally represented by [apple] [apple] [apple].) If you take this option, remember to add extra space within long strings of the same icon, dividing them into sets of 5. That will make it easier for readers to count those icons at a glance. However, if your game regularly needs 5 or more icons at once, you may have to relent and just use a digit with an icon. (Three apples represented by 3[apple]. The latter option takes less space and allows you to enlarge the individual icons.

Phases or Stages: If your game has multiple phases of play in a sequence that must be represented visually, the industry standard is typically to label them with Roman numerals. I personally have mixed feelings about Roman numerals, as they're less familiar to the general audience than a board game hobbyist expects. To make sure they're different from any other use of letters/numbers and try not to go beyond a range of I–V, preferably I–III.

The example in Figure 3.7 shows the conversion rates of different resources as time progresses through the game. The phases are arranged from left to right, indicated by a roman numeral. The quantities of resources are always depicted by duplicating the icons. The point values earned for spending those resources is always depicted as an Arabic numeral within a star shape, to help distinguish points from liquid assets like resources.

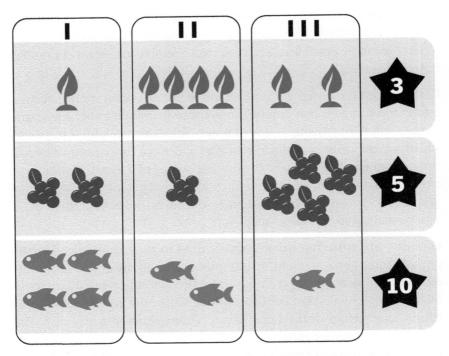

FIGURE 3.7   Examples of using alphanumeric characters in diagrams.

Information presented in a clear and intuitive way has a big impact on the ease of understanding and subsequently enjoying the game.

BRIGETTE INDELICATO

PUNCTUATION IN ICONS

Your diagrams may need to use punctuation characters to communicate some critical information, like when an action is affected by random events or if players have a choice to make. For all of these uses, try to keep your typographic choices clear and simple, so they don't get cluttered with other more pictorial elements in your diagram. Think of these as operators within an equation.

Randomness vs. Choice: If your game has both randomness and choices possible within the same game concept, then let "!" represent randomness and "?" represent choice. For example, your game might distinguish drawing a random card from the deck rather than choosing one from a visible display.

Use "!" and "?" for these cases, respectively. Use a card icon with an "!" inside to represent a random card. Use a card icon with "?" inside to represent a chosen card. Conveniently, this also lets you use the very fun interrobang glyph "‽" when you need to represent both options in one icon. Note that you should clearly define how you're using these punctuation because it's just as common for "?" to represent "mystery" rather than "choice."

Figure 3.8(a) shows an example of how you can visually define three sets of related card icons. The first shows a blank card, meaning you may draw a card from the deck or from the faceup display. A card with an asterisk means you may only draw from the display. A card with an exclamation mark means you must draw from the deck.

Transactions: It's very common to convert or exchange items in a board game. I like to use a colon ":" as a representation of that transaction, as shown in Figure 3.8(b). You may spend a banana to gain an apple.

Options: Your game may give players various sub-options within a broader action. For example, if you spend $1 and have a choice from five different items that are for sale. You may use a slash "/" or vertical bar "|" to divide the different items available. Figure 3.8(c) says "you may spend 1 apple to gain your choice of 1 banana or 2 oranges."

One-Time or Ongoing: For most games, there will be a baseline rule like "all effects can only be used once" or "all effects can be used as many times as you are able." You can assume that players will understand this baseline and they don't need a visual reminder of this rule on every diagram. However, there may be effects that break those rules. Effects like "only once per turn" can be expressed by (1×). Note that the "×" in this case is a multiplication symbol, which looks slightly different than a standard letter "x." For effects that have no limit on the number of times they may be done, you can use an infinity symbol "∞" or a cycling circle icon.

In Figure 3.8(d), the left diagram means "gain 1 air resource once per turn" while the right means "you always have 1 air resource."

Equal or Different: At times, a game effect may require that you deal with sets of identical items or all-different items, without determining what those items must be. You often see this in games where players need an option to convert some raw materials into a rarer item, like "spend any three identical basic goods to gain one luxury." In these cases, use an equal sign "=" or unequal sign "≠".

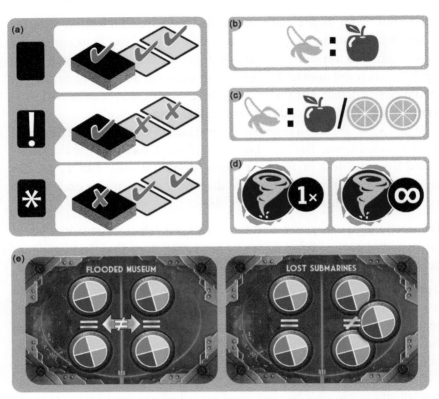

FIGURE 3.8 Examples of punctuation characters in diagrams. (a) Three card icons for drawing cards, each signifying subtle constraints on player choice. (b) A transaction of one banana for one apple. (c) A transaction of one banana for either one apple or two oranges. (d) On the left, "gain one air resource once per turn." On the right, "you always have 1 air resource.

Figure 3.8(e) shows two cards from *Seastead*. In this two-player game, one player reveals one of these cards and turns it to show which player gains which resources. By the end of the game, these more advanced cards appear which don't define the resources individually. Instead, Flooded Museum says each player must gain a pair of identical resources, but the players may not take the same resources as each other. Lost Submarines says one player gets an identical pair of resources and the other gains three unique resources, but there is no further restriction on the players' choices.

If the components are unreadable the game will be unplayable. I have seen many good game designs ruined by bad graphics.

MIKE MARKOWITZ

USING THEME IN DIAGRAMS

While it's important to understand the fundamental elements and structure of a diagram, you should also keep in mind the theme of the game so that the diagram doesn't feel too dissonant. If your diagrams are too abstract and geometric, they may just look like furniture assembly instructions. That might be fine if the game itself is otherwise abstract, but it doesn't help the players buy into the overall experience of gameplay. Use the game's theme to suggest how you might style the frames of your diagrams, which fonts to use for characters, and the general appearance of your icons.

The top example shows a generic diagram for the "relative movement" mechanism. This example is based on the game *Get Bit*, in which players are bidding to avoid being in the back of the line where the shark can bite them (Figure 3.9). This diagram shows five players bidding for a numbered position in a line. The highest bidders move to the front of the line. The lowest bidders move to the back. The player in last place loses a heart because they're closest to the shark.

The second diagram is the same information, but uses a science-fiction theme. My "futuristic" graphic design crutch is to use 45° angles. In this case, you can see them in the corners and edges of the panels. The font is changed to Aviano, which has a more digital aesthetic with straight strokes and geometric details. The heart icon is replaced with a lost tank of air and the shark is replaced with an alien.

FIGURE 3.9   Examples of relative movement, based on *Get Bit* (2007).

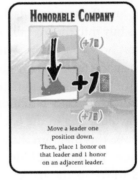

FIGURE 3.10　Diagrams from *Shogunate*.

The third diagram is again the same information, but with a fantasy theme. Here the panels have a distressed edge, resembling torn paper or textiles. The font is changed to Adobe Handwriting Ernie, which has a more humanist aesthetic. The heart icon is replaced with a flame, presumably being breathed by the dragon which has replaced the shark.

Case Study: *Shogunate*

The game *Shogunate* is set in Feudal Japan (Figure 3.10). There is a column of Clan Leader cards in the center of the play area. Each player is secretly loyal to two of these Leaders. Clan Leaders qualify for points based on their relative position in this column. At the end of the game, players reveal their loyalties and gain points earned by their Clan Leaders.

During the game, each player has action cards that manipulate the order of Clan Leaders within the column. As a prototype, these action cards had been designed with only text on them, but I really felt like they would be useful for all players if there was some visual illustration of each move. The tricky thing was that there were very subtle differences between some of the effects.

- **Path of the Arrow** has the simplest movement effect, "move one position up." I used a simple black arrow. I styled that arrow as if it were painted with a thick inkbrush. With that precedent established, I was able to iterate on this basic language.

- **Flowing Upstream** gives you a choice of moving a chosen leader one or two positions. I represented the optional second movement with a blue arrow, overlapped by the initial black arrow.

- **Cloaked in Shadows** lets you move a chosen leader to any position. In this diagram, I inverted the colors of the diagram so it's white with a black stroke. Inside the arrow I added asterisks, representing the "any" option, both up and down.

- **Dishonor** sends a Clan Leader directly to the bottom of a column. I used an arrow touching a horizontal line to imply "bottom" or the "end."

- **Honorable Company** had an interesting dilemma because it moves AND shows an increase in value. Sometimes I like to use an arrow to represent an increase or decrease of values, but in this case I opted to restrict arrows to represent movement alone. That left using a "+" to represent the added value. I used parentheses to note that secondary effect only targeted one neighbor, not both.

The game's theme [...] defines the outside knowledge players project on the game, its rules, and graphics. When done right you can use this to your advantage and let the theme do some work for you.

TORBEN RATZLAFF

DEPICTING MOVEMENT

Often you'll need to illustrate a rule in action with some kind of diagram. The challenge is depicting the passage of game-time within an efficient use of space. As a simple case, let's show the movement of a game piece. You must decide how you will show "this is where the piece began its movement" and "this is where the piece ends its movement." You're trying to show a clear before/after or cause/effect.

Let's say you were assigned to create a language-neutral diagram for a roll-and-move game like so:

"Roll one die. You may move your pawn along any path. You must move that exact number of spaces. You may not stop early or turn back during this movement."

Or if you had to show the movement of a Chess Knight based on the following text:

"A chess knight moves in an 'L' shaped pattern. It moves two squares horizontally or vertically, then moves one square perpendicular to the first movement. The knight does not stop at any intervening space between its origin or destination, thus allowing it to 'jump' over other pieces on the board. If your knight lands on a space occupied by your opponent's piece, you capture that piece and remove it from the board."

In either case, you need a diagram alongside that rules paragraph to help clarify the intent of those rules. Here are some methods of showing that movement.

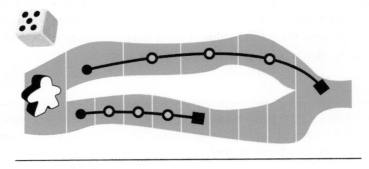

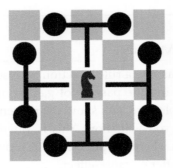

FIGURE 3.11   Depicting movement as paths.

Path: You may draw an arrow or path from the subject's original position to its end position. If using this method, it's important that the path has a distinct appearance from the play area, so it does not look like a literal game component. Try to not intersect paths since that will make it difficult to discern their direction (Figure 3.11).

Ghost: The subject's original position is set to a lighter shade or transparency than its endpoint, giving it a "ghosted" appearance. This may be exaggerated with speed lines or blur effects, as if the subject moved so fast it left behind an afterimage. In Figure 3.12, I show the subject's original position drawn with a dashed or dotted line, which maintains a very readable contrast on the page.

Tag: It may be more important to highlight where a piece is allowed to move relative to its original position, rather than the movement itself. In Figure 3.13, I use checkmarks for permitted positions (empty spaces and those occupied by opponents). I use Xs for prohibited positions (spaces occupied by friendly pieces), thus conveying the movement options AND more nuanced rules.

FIGURE 3.12   Depicting movement as ghosts.

FIGURE 3.13   Depicting movement with tags.

These methods are not mutually exclusive, they're merely tools available to you. You might combine them in a single diagram or opt to use each one separately where they're most effective.

Be open-minded to the thoughts and experiences of others playing a game.

ESTEFANIA RODRIGUEZ

IN-GAME ACTIONS

Let's make a diagram for a very simple in-game action (Figure 3.14).

Figure 3.14(a)—The effect text is written in second-person declarative tense, so "you" is implicit. To be very clear, it could be written as "*You* take 2 Apples from one opponent." For most games, you won't

(a) ~~You~~ take 2 Apples from ~~one opponent.~~

(b) take ~~2 Apples~~ from

(c) ~~take~~ ~~from~~

(d)

Gain 1 Apple or 1 Banana.

(e)

Spend 1 Apple to increase your Strength.

FIGURE 3.14 Diagrams for in-game actions.

need an icon for "you," but let's assume that this game does need that extra clarity. So you need two "person" icons, one for "you" and one for "opponent." In this example, you have two "person" icons. "You" has arms raised, a solid color and no outline. "Opponent" has arms lowered, a black outline, and a dartboard for a head to indicate that this one opponent is being targeted.

Figure 3.14(b)—Presumably, you've already made icons for your game's most commonly used nouns. If you're lucky, your nouns are actual items, like food or water, which can be represented by symbols of the real things. For more abstract concepts, like prestige, energy, or actions, try simple flat shapes like stars, lightning bolts, or hearts. If the game has fictional resources like "Unobtainium" or "Magic," then make the symbol resemble the corresponding game **component** as much as possible. For this case, you can show the apple icon twice and delete the "2" from the diagram.

Figure 3.14(c)—The only remaining text is the verb "take" and the conjunction "from." It's helpful to look at the effect from a very high-level perspective and translate the game effect into different "zones" of the game area. In this case, the effect is really saying "2 Apple moves from Zone A (an opponent's supply) to Zone B (your supply)." The transfer of resources can be represented by a large arrow going from left (the opponent's icon) to right (the "you" icon). Within that arrow, you show the two icons for Apple. Thus you have a complete diagram for this game effect that can be easily recognized at most scales.

Here are some more examples of common effects and how they might be diagrammed.

Figure 3.14(d)—"Gain 1 Apple or 1 Banana." While this is still technically a transfer of resources from one game zone (the general supply) to another (your supply), using an arrow and making an icon for the general supply may make the diagram rather cluttered. In most cases, players will understand that these simple effects presumably affect themselves alone. You can show "+" an icon for the apple and banana. You can represent "or" with a diagonal slash "/"

Figure 3.14(e)—"Spend 1 Apple to increase your Strength." This transactional style of effect is very common in games. It's implicitly an

Players may be entitled to perform a Suit Action at various times during the game. Each suit in the deck has a different Suit Action associated with it. Here is what each player does when they perform a Suit Action in each of the suits:

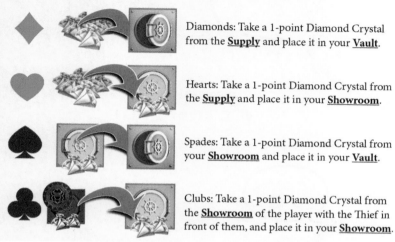

Diamonds: Take a 1-point Diamond Crystal from the **Supply** and place it in your **Vault**.

Hearts: Take a 1-point Diamond Crystal from the **Supply** and place it in your **Showroom**.

Spades: Take a 1-point Diamond Crystal from your **Showroom** and place it in your **Vault**.

Clubs: Take a 1-point Diamond Crystal from the **Showroom** of the player with the Thief in front of them, and place it in your **Showroom**.

FIGURE 3.15   Diagram of four possible actions from *Diamonds* (2014).

"if/then" statement. In other words "If you choose to lose 1 apple, you increase your Strength by one increment." Most games use ":" to divide the "if" and "then" portions of a diagram. Let's also presume this game has a "Strength Track" rather than Strength tokens. In that case, it's useful to depict "increase" as a different symbol from "gain." In this case, upward-pointing chevrons imply an upward movement of along the strength track.

Figure 3.15 is an excerpt from the rulebook for *Diamonds*. Each suit of a standard card deck lets you move diamonds among different vaults as shown. Note how the arrow in each example goes over or under the vault icon to indicate whether it's publicly accessible.

Figure 3.16 is an example of the "Extortion" phase of *Senators*, in which a player sets a price for their opponents' goods. Note how each step of play focuses on one point of time, using transparency to attract or avoid attention when most pertinent. The colors of arrows are color-coded to match the acting players. Inactive players are about 25% opacity, like the white player in the second panel or the pink player in the third panel. When the green player makes an offer, it's depicted as a comic-style speech bubble.

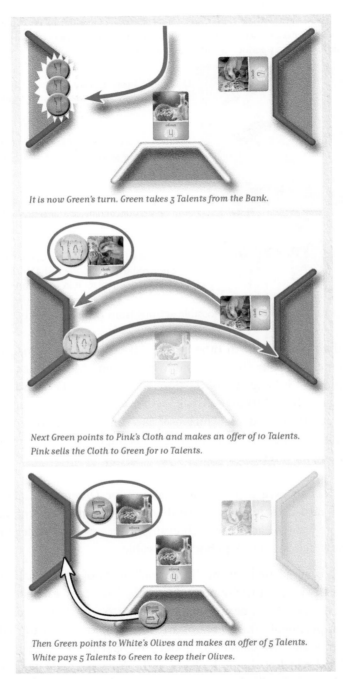

It is now Green's turn. Green takes 3 Talents from the Bank.

Next Green points to Pink's Cloth and makes an offer of 10 Talents.
Pink sells the Cloth to Green for 10 Talents.

Then Green points to White's Olives and makes an offer of 5 Talents.
White pays 5 Talents to Green to keep their Olives.

FIGURE 3.16   Diagram of a multi-step in-game action from *Senators* (2017).

I was lucky to be a graphic designer first and learn to apply it to games. I would suggest if you are a gamer, learn graphic design; if you are a graphic designer, play games.

JACOBY O'CONNOR

SHOWING PLAYERS IN DIAGRAMS

Mostly I avoid showing actual real-world players within a diagram since their meaning may become muddled with in-game roles ("mayor," "farmer," "assassin") or individual character components (different types of pawns). If it is necessary to depict players, I try to make them theme-agnostic so they're clearly outside the world presented by the game's fiction. They don't have to be shown at a literal table, but they should clearly not be cowboys, astronauts, or knights.

Presumably, these diagrams would have to show players executing in-game actions and interacting with each other. So the player icons must be detailed enough to be distinguished but not enough to distract from the rest of the diagram. You don't want idiosyncratic details distracting from the intent of the diagram.

I personally have a huge collection of player icons that I made a few years ago inspired by the on-screen graphics from Korean reality show *The Genius*. (You can download these icons from patreon.com/danielsolis). In my icon set, I made a set of "paper doll" silhouettes and added different details for their clothing, facial details, and clothing. However, I didn't add eyes, noses, or mouths. I also avoided giving them specific gender coding if possible. My intent is that they would remain anonymous while being individually distinguishable.

When I made diagrams for *Building Blocks of Game Design*, I selected a cast of players and used them throughout the book. Each one was a unique permutation of details, with no overlap between them. They are usually limb-less unless an action requires that they show the act of pointing or selecting an item in the game.

Figure 3.17:

Figure 3.17(a)—Competitive Games: This diagram introduces the cast of players, each with their own fashion to make them distinct, but anonymous. Each player is in their own panel in a radial arrangement

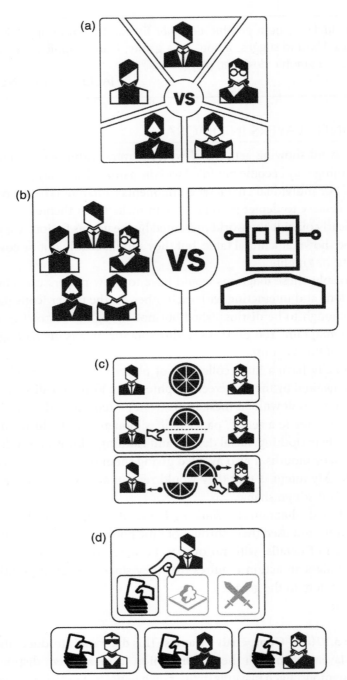

FIGURE 3.17 Uses of player icons in diagrams from *Building Blocks of Tabletop* Games.

to avoid implying a sequence or order to their position. The "vs." in the center reinforces their mutually competitive relationship.

Figure 3.17(b)—Cooperative Games: This diagram puts the cast together on one side, in their own panel on the left. To the right is a new character, a robot representing the automated challenges presented by the game. In this sense, the players are together in a team, working against a common opponent.

Figure 3.17(c)—I split, you choose: The first panel sets the "stage," a slice of orange and two players who want it. The second panel gives the left player a hand and uses a dotted line to show that the orange has been split into half exactly. The third panel now gives the right player a hand, showing which half that player selects to keep. The unchosen half goes to the player on the left, indicated by arrows.

Figure 3.17(d)—Follow: The large panel on top shows the active player selecting from three options: Either draw a card from the top of the deck, place a meeple on a space, or attack another player. This player has chosen the first option, indicated by their hand and that the other options are grayed out to 50% transparency. The three smaller panels then show the other players each doing the same action as the active player in order. Unlike the active player, they do not have a choice, they must simply follow the leader.

The cards in Figure 3.18 show special game conditions that may occur during a game of *Among Thieves*. In the game, players participate in heists governed by a Heistmaster. Players flip a double-sided coin to indicate whether they will be honorable or dishonorable, which has an outcome in how the loot gets distributed. The card titled *Crooked Mayor* sets a precedent of "all players" being represented by simple geometric figures without further distinguishing features. *Misjudged* targets the Heistmaster of the round specifically, who is represented by a brain icon. *Rainy Day Fund* targets heist participants, who are depicted as a cartoon robber. *While The Cat's Away* targets heist participants who opted to be dishonorable, as noted by which side of their coin is flipped up.

Making something bigger on a page doesn't mean it's easier to see/read. Give assets room to breath.

ESTEFANIA RODRIGUEZ

FIGURE 3.18   Cards from *Among Thieves* (2019).

SHOWING CONDITIONAL AND OPTIONAL STEPS

You may need to make a diagram of a sequence of events with multiple possible outcomes, like rolling dice to determine the results of an attack. Your diagram may instead have to show the results of player choices, like in a push-your-luck game. In either case, a strictly linear format has to bend a little bit to accommodate these branching possibilities. These diagrams move away from "comics" format to "flowchart" format.

Keep it Simple: These types of diagrams are particularly ornery to organize, so don't get too fancy with your panel structure or detailed with the imagery. Only show the minimum visuals necessary to get the ideas across. The diagram will already be communicating complex information, so there's no need to make each panel of the diagram complex as well.

Flow Top to Bottom: It's most natural for readers to begin at the top of a diagram and work their way down, like going down a waterfall. You can use angled panels or simple arrows to reinforce this natural habit, but most readers will do it intuitively. If necessary for space constraints, you can make smaller sub-sequences that flow horizontally, but those should always go from left to right. (Note: Other regions may naturally read from right to left, so know your audience before making a decision here.)

Clear Start and End: Avoid paths that bend, circle, or otherwise break the natural reading order. This only complicates the diagram and gets in the way of reader comprehension. Avoid intersecting arrows or lines. If they must intersect, avoid implying that spot is a junction or node by making one of the overlapping lines distinct from the other.

The diagrams in Figure 3.19 depict different styles of conditional game events.

Figure 3.19(a)—Variable Turn Order: The diagram on the left shows an open, chaotic auction without restrictions. The jumble of speech bubbles overlaps each other to depict simultaneous negotiation. The diagram on the right shows an English auction, beginning with an auctioneer offering an opening bid, followed by successively higher bids, culminating in a winning high bid. Each bid is presented in a vertical line, reading from top to bottom. The speech bubbles each point to the bidder. I made sure one bidder bid multiple times, to show this was allowed. I also made sure not to imply any turn order.

Figure 3.19(b)—Delayed Purchase: This diagram shows the act of buying a resource, but that resource not coming into play until later in the game. The first panel shows the player buying an apple. The second panel shows the apple moving into a separate zone bordered by a wavy line with a sand timer. The third panel shows that the sand timer is now exhausted, thus allowing the apple to move into a player's bag.

Figure 3.19(c)—Hidden Movement: Where in the world are you? You have secretly placed your pawn in Africa. The other two players are trying to guess where you are. This diagram shows a world map that is simple enough to be a tiny size, but doesn't look like random shapes. Because this diagram is in grayscale, each continent is depicted in a different fill pattern of stripes, polka dots, and so on. The other

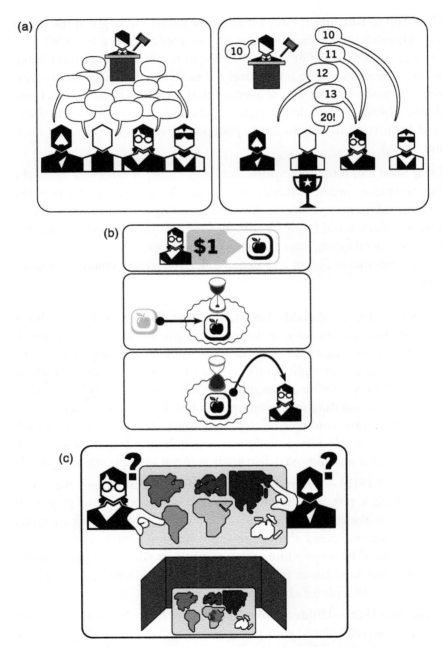

FIGURE 3.19 Diagram visualizing steps that are contingent on other events or choices.

players raise one card each guessing your location. The player on the right is correct, so they get a trophy icon beside them.

Figures 3.20 and 3.21 are excerpts from the rulebook of *Colosseum*, one of my early rulebook designs when I was still learning the craft.

PHASE 1:
INVESTING

In this phase each player can make ONE of the following investments:

- Buy a new Event Program
- Buy an Arena Expansion
- Purchase a Season Ticket
- Construct an Emperor's Loge.

There are special Event Asset tokens that allow you to make a second investment when expended, and you may also spend two Emperor Medals to make an additional investment. These are the *only* ways you are allowed to make more than one investment in a single turn.

BUYING A NEW EVENT PROGRAM

At the beginning of the game each player received 2 Event Programs. Larger programs can be purchased during the Investment phase.

The Event Programs provide the information needed to create an event, including Ⓐ its cost in coins that must be paid to the bank in order to purchase it; Ⓑ the size of the arena required to put on the performance, Ⓒ the type and number of assets required to produce it, Ⓓ and the potential number of additional spectators it could attract when performed, depending on how complete the performance is.

EXPANDING YOUR ARENA

To produce some of the more ambitious events, you must invest to expand your arena. To do this, pay 10 value in coins to the bank, take one Arena Expansion piece, and immediately place it where one of your semi-circular Arena pieces is, sliding the Arena pieces one space away from the other to accommodate the expansion. You may expand in either direction.

At the start of the game each arena occupies 2 squares on the route. After the first expansion an arena encloses 3 squares. An arena can be expanded a second and final time to include 4 squares. If there is a noble in your arena during your expansion, it remains on the same cobblestone space on the board.

PURCHASING SEASON TICKETS

You may also invest by purchasing a Season Ticket which provides 5 additional spectators for each subsequent event you produce.

To purchase a Season Ticket, pay 10 value in coins to the bank, and place the Season Ticket beside your arena.

Any number of Season Tickets may be added to your arena over the course of the game, however as with all investment purchases, only one may be purchased each round. If there are no more Season Tickets remaining, you may not purchase any more.

CONSTRUCTING THE EMPEROR'S LOGE

Having distinguished guests in your arena is always an honor. Constructing an Emperor's Loge will increase the chances of attracting these luminaries to your events. To construct an Emperor's Loge pay the value of 5 coins to the bank and add it to your arena. From now on you may roll 2 dice, instead of 1, when producing events. The results may be added together, or used as two separate rolls, however you can not gain more than one Emperor's Medal in any given turn via moving nobles. An arena can only have a maximum of 1 Emperor's Loge.

5

FIGURE 3.20   Diagram of bartering in *Colosseum* (2019).

FIGURE 3.21 Diagrams for the four possible investment actions in *Colosseum* (2019).

"Phase 1: Investing" wasn't written with an explicit gameplay example to illustrate, so I paired each paragraph with a diagram. I inserted letter tags within the flow of rules text where necessary to clarify certain details.

My hope was that players would still be able to use these diagrams as a shorthand when they needed a refresher in what to do during this phase. In hindsight, I should have divided the diagrams into completely distinct frames so that these didn't look like four different actions done in a sequence.

"Phase 3: Trading Event Asset Tokens" also didn't have a gameplay example provided, so I did my best to illustrate a typical turn. I used Jacqui Davis' illustrations of larger-than-life historical characters to represent two parties in a negotiation. I used speech bubbles with game components to represent the freeform bartering that occurs during this phase. As in Phase 1, I inserted letter tags into the flow of the text to draw attention to certain areas of the gameplay. In hindsight, I didn't need to *also* depict players around the table, since that just clutters the diagram.

It's better to over-communicate than not communicate enough.
BRIGETTE INDELICATO

PLAYER AIDS

A good player reference should make the game as smooth as possible for the *newest* players (Figure 3.22). That means:

- Help the returning player teach the game to new players.
- Give those new players a reminder of key points during their first game.
- Equip those players to become teachers for the *next* group of newcomers.

Below are helpful uses for a player aid. In all cases, use the same game terms as in the rulebook to make cross-reference as easy as possible. It's also good to include page references to the rulebook.

Setup: This is only referenced at the beginning of the game, so it should be separate from any other in-game reference material. Either put it on the back side of a reference sheet or an entirely separate sheet. Summarize any modular choices, like campaign scenarios, and changes based on player count or player order, like starting resources.

FIGURE 3.22 Player screen in *Publish or Perish: Wiñay Kawsay*, reference sheets in *Free Radicals*, and reminder diagrams in *Princes of Florence*.

Turns and Rounds: If it's short enough, put this information where players can always see it, like on a personal board, upright privacy screen, or a conveniently sized reference card. Be as comprehensive as possible, since this is the spine of all other reference content. List every phase, step of a round, optional actions, and keep them in proper order. For example, if Step 1 of a turn is to draw a card from the top of the deck, don't just say "Draw." Write that full sentence. "Step 1: Draw a card from the top of the deck into your hand." If there is a hand limit, remember to include that too. "End of turn: Discard down to 7 cards. This reference is so important, it's worthwhile to make a copy for every player, even if it might increase some nominal production costs. The benefit is worth it.

Endgame Triggers and Final Scoring: While this information is important for guiding players' strategies over the course of the game, it often only needs a few general reminders before it "sticks." As such, this is good to keep on a score pad or as a small box on the central game board. You can also put it on the back side of the turn reference card.

Global Rules: Ideally, all critical rules would be integrated into the flow of the Turn Reference when they are most pertinent. Ask the game designer and developer about recurring questions from playtesters. "Can you deliver, then move?" "Do you draw card at the start or end of a turn?" "Are coins worth points at the end of the game?" Some rules are of such global importance that they deserve to be spotlighted along. For example, "All players should be silent during the game" makes a huge impact on the play experience. Make such a reminder impossible to miss.

Icon and Diagram Reference: Show every icon in the game alongside its name. Group these icons by kind, so all the "Resource" icons are in one group, "Skill" icons are in another, and so on. If your game uses a few recurring diagrams, such as worker placement spaces on a game board, your reference text should explain each of them thoroughly in plain text *without* the use of icons. Include images and names for common game components, like pawns and tokens. Usually this reference is so long that it needs to be a full sheet of paper, often on the back side of the rulebook.

Component Anatomy: Knowing what every part of a card or tile is called may be useful for your game, but it's usually best to restrict this content to the rulebook. Only put it on the reference component if critical to gameplay.

Frankly, most games will only be played once or twice. It is an elite few games that develop a deep community who would need anything more than these clear and quick refreshers. That's not to diminish the aid's importance, only to narrow your focus and set a realistic benchmark for success. Invest your time in helping the newest player come to grips with the game.

Be consistent and clear with your design language. If you assign a certain meaning (value, rule) to a graphic, color, layout or style it has to be consistent overall.

TORBEN RATZLAFF

SUMMARY OF DIAGRAMS

My favorite attraction of BGG.con is the hallway full of dexterity games, set up for open play on tall bistro tables. Each game comes with a small placard explaining the rules, but mostly the games are pretty self-explanatory after watching people play for a few seconds. For the most part it's "don't let this stack of objects topple" or "aim an awkward projectile at a target," with some clever variations along the way.

What I love is how naturally people understand the premise of each game. With barely any tutorial, people are playing, laughing, and hollering. It's a great time. That said, I'm quick to move on to the next game, then the next, sharing my favorites with friends as they pass through the hall. Few of them keep my attention longer than a few minutes in one sitting. A more substantial strategy board game is what fully commits my focus, but those are rarely as innately understandable.

My goal is to make any board game I lay out to be as intuitive as those light dexterity games. I love it when players can sit down and infer the basic gameplay from symbols, components, and general context. 100% accessibility is not always achievable, and those efforts may not always be successful, but the goal is a noble one.

Summary Questions

- Where do you see language-neutral diagrams outside of games? I.e., furniture assembly instructions, airplane safety guides, and model kits.

- In those examples, which are most successful at communicating their information?
- What techniques are those diagrams using that you can borrow for your game?
- How accessible is your game under conditions of limited visibility, low light or colorblindness?
- Where do you find text in your game components?
- How are you using font, size, bold, italic, and other typographic attributes to convey meaning?
- How can text be supplemented or replaced by a language-neutral solution?
- What are the basic actions of your board game?
- Are your diagrams too densely packed with detail? How can they be simplified?
- How are you signifying common expressions like "or," "and," "equal," and so on?
- How are you using frames and backgrounds around diagrams to convey further meaning?
- Is your usage of visual elements internally consistent across all diagrams in the game?
- Are there some game concepts where plain text would be more practical than glyphs and diagrams?
- How are you testing the accessibility of your diagrams?
- How and when do your testers misinterpret your diagrams?
- Does their misunderstanding suggest new ways of expressing a different concept?
- Have you written the basic rules you're following in your diagrams, so you can refer back to that when someone else has a question?

CHAPTER 4

Cards

THREE PRINCIPLES OF CARD DESIGN

I spend most of this chapter getting in the weeds of print production and manufacturing. That's just where I spent most of my time in my career, so that's where I have the most information to share. However, if you're just getting started designing cards, you don't have to worry about all that just yet. There are three main principles of card design to remember as you design your card. These are not "rules" per se, just useful concepts to keep in mind.

Figure 4.1(a)—Visibility: *Make the most important information easily visible.* If your cards are held in hand, stacked, splayed, or tucked, consider the areas that are going to be most visible at that moment. Check corners and edges in particular, since those will most likely be hidden by a thumb or other components. You can use this to your advantage by hiding information that may only be relevant in special circumstances or edge cases.

Figure 4.1(b)—Hierarchy: *Arrange information from the most important to least important.* List all of the elements on a card and make a decision about which is most important. (Don't be precious and say everything is important.) For example, a card title comes up a lot so you probably want that closer to the top and a visible corner. A card cost may be relevant as

 DOI: 10.1201/9781003453772-5

FIGURE 4.1   (a) Visibility of cards from *Ettin* (2020), (b) hierarchy of cards from *Ettin* (2020), and (c) brevity of cards from *Ettin* (2020).

FIGURE 4.1   (Continued)

well, that is conditional to your specific game. If you have to pay for a card each time you play it, then it's very important. If you only pay for the card once, then you can afford to tuck it away in a more hidden area.

Figure 4.1(c)—Brevity: *Abbreviate common phrases with keywords or icons.* When your game has many cards, you have to be efficient with how much text you fit onto each card. More content means that the font has to be smaller and/or more compressed, making it harder to read. Looking for other solutions helps keep the card approachable and fun to play. Discuss with your game developers whether lengthy and recurring game terms can be condensed into shorter keywords or even use icons. For example, "Rotate this card 90°" can be condensed to the keyword "tap" or "exhaust." This is such a common action in card games, most just replace the entire clause with one simple icon that takes a fraction of the space.

You might be able to cite a few long-standing successful card games that violate one or more of these principles. Some may place critical information at inconvenient spots, or arrange information in an unintuitive order, or squeeze in paragraphs of information into tiny fine print.

Bear in mind that many of those venerable titles were first published before best practices had been established, so they're doing their best to retain their identity while still serving a more sophisticated audience. Established games also have the luxury of a built-in player base that can tolerate the quirks of their favorite hobby. (In fact, some very belligerent veterans may protest any attempt to streamline or improve their game's visuals.)

Your new game doesn't have such a luxury. Instead, it has the *advantage* of learning from the mistakes of all those prior games. You can risk breaking any of these principles at your discretion, but it's worthwhile to know the nature of that risk so you can make an informed decision. Make it clear to any player that you willfully *chose* to break these "rules" of design.

A CARD'S PURPOSE

Cards are a remarkably versatile tool, but that versatility can make it difficult to measure a successful design. It's easy to take cards for granted, and thus be surprised how difficult it is to design them well. I find it helpful to first determine the card's general purpose.

Playing cards are the traditional card deck and variations thereof. Any text is limited to simple numbers or letters, usually presented in a symmetrical composition. In Western style decks, there are 13 ranks in four different suits, possibly with one or two "joker" cards. These cards bear the names and appearances of social classes or royalty, but have almost entirely been decoupled from any actual theming in their artwork. This has allowed their appearance to be modified to fit any number of topics.

Word cards are used once and then ignored. They are common in games like Werewolf, Apples to Apples, or Just One. It simply tells you the role you play or the word you're trying to guess. Any visuals or artwork on these cards isn't strictly necessary, only serving to make the component look more interesting than a plain index card. (Figure 4.2a: Category and Word cards from *Blob Party*.)

Paragraph cards have a full body of text, usually between 50 and 100 words depending on the typography styling. These are commonly used in Event decks that cause some unpredictable in-game effects between turns. Trivia games squeeze in multiple questions on one side of the card with the answers on the other side. Narrative campaign games

FIGURE 4.2 Cards from *Blob Party*, *Tales of the Arthurian Knights*, *Bird Bucks*, *Shapers of Gaia*, and *Ettin*.

convey key story beats with these cards, asking players to read the cards aloud. However, as with the One-Word cards, these are usually used once and then ignored. (Figure 4.2(b): Quest card from *Tales of the Arthurian Knights*.)

Commodity cards represent a core currency in the game that frequently moves between a deck, a player's hand, a central supply, or a discard pile. These are used as train colors in Ticket to Ride, building resources in Catan, or trading goods in Jaipur. These can also represent literal money in the game. Commodity card designs usually fill the entire front with artwork representing that resource, making it recognizable from any distance. It rarely has any text beyond a simple suit or rank on the corners. (Figure 4.2(c): Money card from *Bird Bucks*.)

Action cards are the reliable and overburdened workhorse of most board games, representing effects a player initiates and resolves. These designs are used in collectible card games, deckbuilding games, or more complex Euro-style board games. Usually they are about half text (the actual game effect being resolved) and half art (an illustration depicting the in-world appearance of that effect). They can also include secondary information like costs to play, attribute tags, point values, and more. They're as likely to be needed in hand or kept on the table, making them a thorny design challenge. (Figure 4.2(d): Unit card from *Ettin*.)

Ongoing cards are usually kept on the table. They represent long-term effects that players will regularly need to reference and so must remain on the table, visible to all players. If they remain in a neutral space between all players, they usually represent a global status modifier (weather, fate, history) or a mutable aspect of the game space (modular locations, market demands, end-of-round scoring conditions). If in front of a specific player, they usually represent permanent upgrades, special equipment, or unique abilities. (Figure 4.2(d): Faction card from *Shapers of Gaia*, representing actions available to a player during the game.)

Cards will be gripped in hand, placed on tables, turned, discarded, read aloud, and pored over carefully. In all cases, the graphic design is crucial to letting that card facilitate a fun and memorable play experience. Tailoring your card design to match the card's purpose will benefit your game immensely.

BOX 4.1 *SYSTEM GATEWAY* REDESIGN

The card game *Android: Netrunner* went out of print in 2018. Not content to let it fade away, a community of enthusiastic fans organized as a group called Null Signal Games to keep the game alive with new fan-made cards.

While the mechanisms and game rules could continue to live on, none of the original visual expressions could be republished legally since they were intellectual property of the various licensors. That meant Null Signal Games would have to make all card designs, symbols, and artwork from scratch. They revised the graphic design with cleaner layouts and improved readability of card text, including a new set of glyphs representing frequent game mechanisms. The new designs allowed more space for card text and easier initiation for new players (Figure 4.3).

In the example cards, note how information is embedded in the shapes of the frames, the position of art vs. text, and the integration of a library of customized glyphs.

Each type of card has its own particular arrangement that, with practice, builds fluency within the player base. This is a complex game, but the graphic design team has done a commendable job making key game information as readily apparent as possible to ease the burden of learning the systems.

(The *System Gateway* project and Null Signal Games continue to release new card sets at nullsignal.games.)

The layout of a card can influence greatly how they might be held in a player's hand, how a tableau looks and functions on the table, or even from an accessibility standpoint—whether the necessary information is easily readable.

BRIGETTE INDELICATO

CARD SIZING

The standard US Poker card is 2.5″ wide and 3.5″ tall (Figure 4.4). It's so ubiquitous that even international manufacturers keep it as a stock size. Still, it's best to avoid using relative terms. Many factories list what they claim are industry standard sizes for "poker" or "mini card" or "tarot," despite having slightly different dimensions from each other. Communicate with your factory as early as possible so you don't accidentally make your cards the wrong size. Always give your dimensions in absolute numbers, usually millimeters.

FIGURE 4.3   Cards from System Gateway (2022) Null Signal Games.

The different dimensions for different card sizes are based on how a large printer sheet can be partitioned and cut into smaller cards. The fronts are arranged in a grid on one side and the corresponding backs are printed on the other side. The size of your card will determine how many cards can

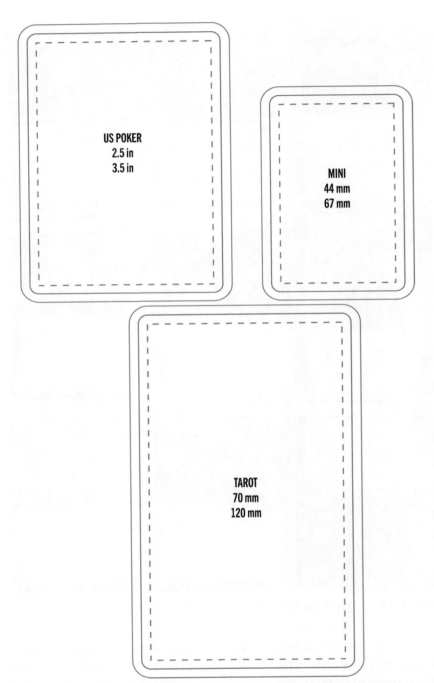

FIGURE 4.4 Actual size comparison of US Poker, Mini, and Tarot cards, along with necessary bleeds and interior safe margins.

fit onto a sheet, and thus whether you incur extra costs when one whole sheet is spent for a few extra cards in your game.

Cards are usually not cut edge-to-edge. If that were the case, one card's graphics may accidentally be visible along the edge of another card. The slightest lateral or rotational misalignments between the front and back may be noticeable when the cards are cut out, resulting in card graphics that appear 1–2mm off-center from the intended design. Instead, each card is spaced about 6mm from each other, allowing you to create a design that goes all the way to the edge without worry.

Ask your factory representative how many sheets your card list currently requires and whether it might be printed more efficiently with a smaller quantity or a different size. This may require you to cut a few cards from your deck, so be prepared for that possibility. If you're unsure where to begin sizing, use the dimensions listed below. Just be aware your factory may request slight differences.

US Poker: Exactly 63.5×88.9mm, but sometimes rounded to 63×88mm. The most common card size you'll likely need. It's small enough for the average player to hold in hand, but large enough for substantial information density. Importantly, this size fits in most common card sleeve sizes, which is a paramount concern among a dedicated segment of the board game audience.

Mini: 44×67mm. In theory this is meant to be about half the size of a poker card, but it doesn't always come to that exactly. These cards are great if you expect players to have small hands or you want to avoid crowding the game space too much. You can't fit much information on these cards, so they may not be the right choice for a deck builder or collectible card game. They're great for commodities and currency though.

Tarot: 70×120. These are a little too large for most players to hold comfortably in hand as a fan. They're best when your game has some global randomized events. The card size allows you to use large text and icons, making them very legible across the table for all players. They also allow much more text, so you can fit narrative paragraphs without making the reader squint at fine print.

BOX 4.2 IRREGULAR SIZED CARDS

Many other sizes are available, like squares, hexagons, and 2:1 rectangles for tile-based games. Again, it's best to discuss the specs for your cards with your factory early so there are no late surprise expenses.

Use standard sizes for cards to make it easier for those who sleeve.
STEPHANIE GUSTAFSSON (MIDDARA, CASTLES
BY THE SEA, ROLLING HEIGHTS)

AVOIDING PRODUCTION ERRORS

Here are some examples of what a card looks like when it hasn't been designed to tolerate the most common mis-registration errors that can occur during production.

This is a very typical collectible card design with text and borders, without bleeds (Figure 4.5).

FIGURE 4.5 The card on the left has content too far outside the safe zone. The card on the right keeps content within the safe zone.

FIGURE 4.6 The art on the left has not been drawn with enough margin to accommodate a 3mm interior margin and a 3mm exterior bleed. The art on the right has plenty of space around the edge. Note how the top of the head does not encroach into the upper safe zone.

Bad: The border and card title sit outside the 3mm safe zone. Due to a printing error, the top edge of the border is entirely cut off and the bottom-right corner has a big gulf between it and the trim line.

Good: Text and interior borders are at least 3mm away from the trim line, allowing it to tolerate a slight offset without looking unprofessional.

This is a "borderless" card with full artwork across the entire front (Figure 4.6).

Bad: The artwork did not have enough of a bleed, so the error makes a white line visible across the edges along the right and bottom. The portrait wasn't illustrated to account for the safe zone, so the top of the forehead is being cropped.

Good: The artwork extends to a 3mm "bleed" beyond the trim line. The important parts of the artwork are composed to be within the safe zone so they won't be cut off, even if slightly misaligned during production.

This card design has a fancy border that bleeds to the edge (Figure 4.7).

FIGURE 4.7   The card on the left has not extended its textures and border elements all the way to the bleed line. The card on the right is formatted with proper 3mm bleed beyond all trim lines.

Bad: The border wasn't set up thick enough. It doesn't have enough bleed, so a white line is visible when miscut. The inner edge of the border is outside the safe zone, making the border noticeably thinner along the top edge compared to the bottom right.

Good: The border details extend 3mm beyond the trim line. The inner edge of the border rests within the 3mm safe zone.

Breaking any of these rules risks very costly reprints that can delay release schedules and erase profit margins. A professional printer will warn you if you haven't followed these guidelines, because they don't want to waste their own resources and time either.

If you insist on accepting the risk, the costs for reprints will fall on your budget, possibly making the entire project unprofitable. A few millimeters is not worth it!

BOX 4.3 EXPANSIONS AND SPECIAL INDICATORS

If you plan to release expansions or additional modules for your game over time, it's helpful to include a special mark on the card front somewhere. Make sure that detail is small, simple, and in an easily sorted location. Usually this means putting it along a valuable edge that could be used for more important gameplay information. Avoid making the mistake of putting it so far outside the safe zone that it gets cropped away entirely. A small square, circle, star, triangle, or other geometric shape is sufficient to suit this purpose and can be set to be small enough to not be a distraction.

Are [cards] going to be laid out on the table, or will they be in players hands? If they're in hand, what information will players need to see in the upper left corner? Do they need to work right-side up and upside-down?

LINDSAY DAVIAU (RESTORATION GAMES)

PLANNING LAYERS

Any reasonable layout program has a "Layers" function that allows you to stack graphical elements in a certain order. This helps you organize parts of your design independently of each other. A layer's contents are obstructed by any objects on the layer above it. By using cropped graphics and image file formats that support transparency, you can create some very interesting card designs that look like the professionals! It's important to plan those layers ahead of time though, so you can make your graphics support that accordingly.

Here's an example card design and each of its layers from top to bottom (Figure 4.8):

A. **Game Content:** I always want this content in the uppermost foreground. I never want artwork or other graphics to intervene on this information since it is critical for gameplay and legal protocol. This is primarily the body text, legal fine print, and any backgrounds necessary to make that text legible. Note that it also includes the large numbers along the edge of the card as those are also important for gameplay.

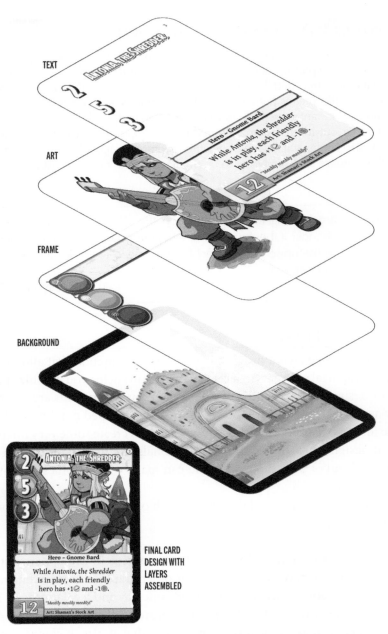

FIGURE 4.8 Example card from a collectible card game. The diagram shows how the different card elements may be organized into layers in a design program.

B. **Frame-Breaking Art**: I've commissioned my artwork to have full-body characters drawn separately from their backgrounds. That lets me put the character on its own layer, so I can have it slightly overlap some elements of the card, like the card's title and upper border. This is a "frame break" effect popular in collectible card games. Even though it looks like it's popping out of the frame, I'm still being careful that the art placement doesn't make text too hard to read or put any edge closer than 3mm to the trim line.

C. **Frames and Borders**: I've set up my frame elements in file formats that support transparency, like TIF and EPS, so they can be placed on top of any other incidental artwork beneath it. For certain designs that have a high degree of variability, I'll make separate smaller frame files for top edge, bottom edge, and so on. In this case, the card title and three stats along the side are always the same, so I've made them all one frame.

D. **Outer Bleed**: This is the background art with a ragged edge. I'm very careful to not let any notch of that edge get closer than 3mm to the actual trim line. In fact, some parts are tighter than necessary since I want to exaggerate the "frame break" effect of the character art. The bottom layer is just a full flood of ink.

Even if you don't follow this exact layer structure, I do advise keeping the text on the topmost layer so it's easy for editors and clients to highlight when the card is exported to PDF format. When text is behind an image, even a transparent part of an image, the text may not be selectable.

BOX 4.4 RANKS, SUITS, AND TAGS

If your card needs a number and an icon in the corner, make sure they're large and sharply contrasted. I tend to make numbers between 16 and 24pt. If your icons are simple geometric shapes like hearts or diamonds on a plain background, they can be as small as 5mm tall and wide. If the icons are more detailed or are on a busier background, then increase the size so they are legible, sometimes as large as 15–20mm extreme cases. It's also very common to have variable secondary icon "tags" along an edge of the card, which should also be sized like any other icon depending on its importance in gameplay. Some games have players splay their collected cards so tags are visible. Consider how much table space is needed for 2, 3, or 5 cards, all slightly offset in this manner.

What I learned in setting up graphic files for localization into 26 different languages [...] every different artist sets up files very differently, but almost universally in a way that makes it difficult for artists later in the process to work with, especially when localizing.

KIRK W BUCKENDORF

TEXT PLACEMENT

If your card requires a paragraph of effect text, the first question is where you want to place it on the card. (In all cases, let's assume you will follow the principles and guidelines described in Chapter 1 (Typography).) Different areas have their strengths and precedents to support them, so let's break them down into general zones.

Figure 4.9—Fixed height, lower-third or lower-half: This is such a common composition that you can assume it will be acceptable to most players. Decades of card games have trained the audience to assume that any text effect will be in this general area, even if it doesn't necessarily offer other gameplay advantages. It's useful for its sheer ubiquity, but you do run into problems where cards have a lot of text, forcing you to shrink to fit the frame. At the other extreme, you might have some cards with very little text, making a card that is mostly empty space. To resolve these two problems, you might try variable height text windows ...

FIGURE 4.9   Cards from *I Can't Even With These Monsters*. The text frame remains the same size regardless of how many lines of text there might be.

FIGURE 4.10 Cards from *Dice Conquest*. I wanted to flood as much of the card with artwork as possible, so I have text rise from the bottom. The cards with the least text make the most room for art.

Figure 4.10—Variable height, rising from the bottom: You may align text to the bottom of the frame, so that text rises up as high as necessary. This allows you to only take up as much room as the text demands. Note that some players prefer having a predictable location for the first line of text, so approach this option with caution. The major disadvantage is that the card's complexity is inversely proportional to the space available for its art. Simple cards with very little text get tons of real estate for illustration. More advanced cards with lots of mechanical impact get very little room for art, because so much space is dedicated to their text. This discrepancy feels off for many players, so approach this layout with some caution. It's best when cards have a more consistent amount of text.

Figure 4.11—Variable height, lowering from the top: This option is similar to the one above, but the art is no longer sandwiched between a title at the top and the card effect below. Instead, the card effect begins below the card title. This grants uninterrupted, full-bleed space on the bottom half if you wish. This layout is useful if your cards have ongoing effects in play that must be set out publicly as a reminder. The art doesn't need to be visible at all times, so you can tuck the card beneath a board or other component, leaving only the pertinent text readable.

FIGURE 4.11   Cards from *Zeppelin Attack*! The art is on the bottom half of the card and the effect text flows from the top.

FIGURE 4.12   Leader cards from *Clash of Cultures: Monumental Edition*. This game has a lot of cards and I wanted each type to be quickly discernible at a glance. For Leader cards, I put the portrait on the right and flowed text organically along the left edge. This let me customize how much space I had available for especially lengthy cards.

Figure 4.12—Column: This layout splits the card vertically down the middle, with text in a narrow column along the left or right. Depending on your choice of font, you can usually fit more text onto a side column of a card than the standard text frame. Players can also read more of the card effect while in hand. (Assuming you fan your cards in a compatible direction.) This composition also lets you tuck cards to conserve table space.

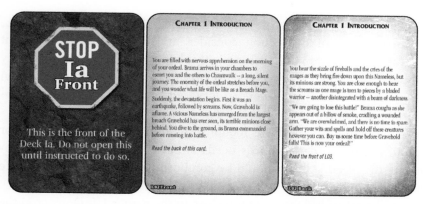

FIGURE 4.13   Story cards from *Aeon's End: Legacy*. These cards primarily deliver story beats and inform players when to stop or start reading more of the story cards. As such, I wanted the fronts and backs to have clearly different colors. The "stop" cards are also very plain and direct.

Figure 4.13—Center: This is only for cards that have no art at all, or at least minimal art that is only used as a framing device. Putting text in the center is best for quiz cards, narrative story cards, random event cards, or any other card type that just needs to be read and discarded quickly. You'll sometimes see a faint watermark icon placed behind the text as well, which is fine as long as it does not impede the text's legibility by making the background too busy.

BOX 4.5 TITLE PLACEMENT

Generally speaking, it's safe to put the card's title at the top of the card, regardless of where its paragraph sits. Sometimes you might experiment with a title along one edge, but that forces players to fan their cards a certain way and may prove unpopular.

Don't feel the need to overly design their cards. Sometimes a full bleed illustration with minimal text will speak volumes.

TONY MASTRANGELI

ART PLACEMENT AND FRAMING

For the purposes of this section, consider "art" as any form of prominent illustration or diagram that isn't explicitly plain text. Let's also put aside any subjective concerns about art direction for the time being, just focusing on the pragmatic concerns of where art is placed, how it's framed, and its production necessities.

Any art must have at least 300dpi resolution and be in CMYK color format. Art on borderless cards needs 3mm of extra content to accommodate the bleed. All art should be composed with a 3mm interior safe margin in mind.

Plan the art so it doesn't get too close to the game's UI. Don't crop the subject's heads or hands—unless it's on purpose, in which case don't make it look like an accident. Make sure key props in the art like weapons or artifacts are clearly visible in the frame. The key to composition is intent. It's okay to do some risky cropping, as long as it's clearly intentional *and* doesn't impede gameplay.

Figure 4.14(a) shows card art that has been created without these considerations. It's below 300dpi, making the image very pixelated. The left edge sits directly on the trim line instead of bleeding to the edge. Parts of the head and hands are intersecting with the card's framing elements.

Figure 4.14(b) shows a corrected version of this card, with art delivered in sharp print-ready resolution. The art has been recomposed so the left edge completely bleeds beyond the trim line, making it clear that this crop is intentional, not an accident. By contrast, the head and hands are moved so that they keep about 3mm of clearance around any of the framing elements.

Figure 4.14(c) shows some examples of variants of card frames. If you keep the same art and text placements across several cards, you can still vary the shapes of the frame that surround the art to indicate secondary mechanisms. It's one of the more subtle methods of delivering this information, so you might reserve it when you have more nuanced "sub-types" within a larger category of card. In this case, the blue color implies that these cards are all in the same broad category, but the circle or diamond border can suggest more information.

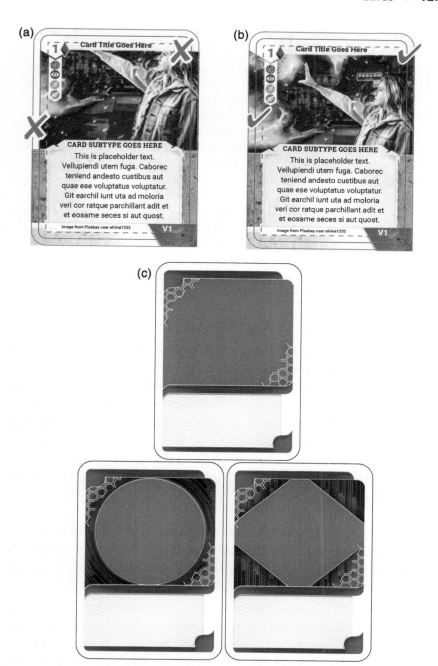

FIGURE 4.14 Examples of art positions within a card frame and how that frame may be shaped.

BOX 4.6 COMMUNICATING EFFECT IN ART

Artwork serves a practical function in play. When selecting art for a card, make sure it matches the card's mechanisms. Players may not be able to read a card's text at all times, but they'll recognize the giant dragon on the artwork. From that image, they'll remember that the dragon has certain attributes like that it flies, that it breathes fire, and that it's difficult to defeat. Even in a non-combative Euro game, the card art can depict key resources that should be easily scanned at any distance, like a pile of gold for a "Treasure" card.

The art and design is also the first thing a game is judged by without knowing any rules or gameplay, so it has to be attractive and inviting to a majority of potential players.

KIRK W BUCKENDORF

DESIGNING BORDERS AND FRAMES

Factories print several cards onto a very large sheet, separated by a 6mm gap in between each card. That allows card graphics to print all the way to the edge of the trim line. Each card's graphics extend an extra 3mm beyond the trim line to hide any mis-registrations between the front and back.

It might seem like this is only relevant if you were designing "borderless" cards that have art going across the entire card's surface, but *any* printed graphics going to the card edge must take this bleed into account, regardless of whether it's illustration or a border element. See Figure 4.15 for an example of a full-bleed border:

Figure 4.15(a)—Lines: Any distinct lines or edges should be rotated about 30-45° relative to the card edge. If your border is a rectangular frame going around the card, then its interior edge should not get closer than 3mm to the trim line.

Figure 4.15(b)—Textures: It's fine to have an illustrated border, but avoid including details that will draw the player's eye, and thus draw attention to errors. People are very aware of faces and eyes, so avoid including those in your border design. Any isolated elements, like a single dot, are more noticeable than if they're part of a texture, like a whole grid of dots, so repeat your elements until they blend into a less discernible texture.

FIGURE 4.15   Example of border design with full bleeds.

Figure 4.15(c)—Curves: Don't count on any design element hitting the edge of your card exactly. The manufacturing process is too unpredictable and such an unforgiving design only makes the inevitable mistakes much more apparent. If you have a curving element, make sure the curve arcs without distinctive corners that could hit the trim line.

Given all these pitfalls, it's common for card games to not have a full-bleed border at all. Instead, there may be a thin interior border that stops at the safe zone. Beyond the safe zone is just a flood of one flat color, usually black. If not that, then there is no printing at all, just bare paper. The "white border" design is certainly the safest to manufacture and lends a game a very classical look.

For clear typography, you'll also want to make sure no text or icons come too close to the frame, thus losing you some important space that could be used for game information. If that becomes a problem, try exploring an "incomplete" border that only runs along one edge. For example, if your border is along the bottom of the card, that allows the full available width to be used for text.

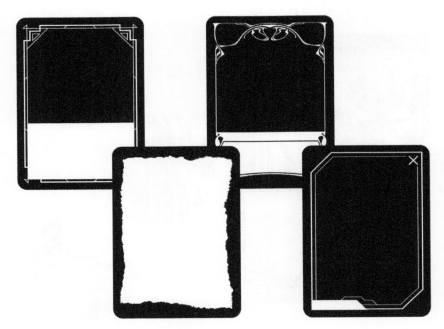

FIGURE 4.16   Examples of border styles.

BOX 4.7 BORROWING FROM HISTORY

Try exploring historical uses of borders and dividing lines for inspiration (Figure 4.16).

- Art Deco: Tightly bound geometric symmetry suggests a hubristic perfectionism.
- Art Nouveau: Curvaceous details suggest a humanist naturalism, but fill up card space.
- Grunge: Torn, ragged edges are appropriate for either ancient or dystopian themes.
- Cyberpunk: Random 45° sockets and tabs are a reliable shorthand for sci-fi settings.

If the main art is flat, cell shaded cartoon art, then your graphics should match. You don't want fully rendered, highly detailed frames when the art looks like a webcomic.

TONY MASTRANGELI

DESIGNING FOR DISTANCE

Print design generally has one major challenge compared to digital design. A digital interface can open and close "windows" as they become relevant, whereas all of your card's information is always visible. Players can be

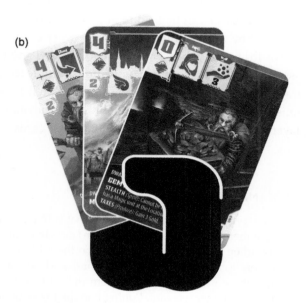

FIGURE 4.17 (a) Examples of card design viewed at various distances. Note what elements remain legible at the furthest distances. (b) Example of how card fronts are obstructed when fanned by a right-handed player.

trained when to ignore or acknowledge elements of a card, but the graphic design is what makes that easier to do.

Designing for the furthest distance is usually easiest since the answer is typically "make the thing as big as possible." When multiple players need to refer to a card on the table or in an opponent's public tableau, the text should be at least 12pt or higher. When that is impractical, plan your design to have a distinctive visual element like unique art or large icons, so players can be trained to associate a nuanced game effect with one large visual signifier.

In Figure 4.17(a), one of Dwarf Warrior's abilities is that it can fly. That effect has some intricate game interactions that are too long to write out at 12pt font size, so they're instead printed at 8pt which is still somewhat legible when held in hand. To compensate, the word "Flying" is offered as a short keyword for ease of reference and a large wing-shaped icon is visible from afar. The numbers along the bottom-right corner are mainly relevant to the card's owner, not opponents, so they can be much smaller and tucked away.

Designing for cards at a shorter distance presents more issues, even though your content can be allowed to be smaller. The issue is how players opt to hold their cards in their hand and how you can design around different habits. If your cards can be held in any orientation like a playing card, then you can get by with simple large icons at every corner.

Alas, most cards for board games are more complicated and mandate a certain "right-side up" direction so they can include multiple icons, names, artwork, a paragraph of text, and more. As a result, you'll have to force some compromises about how players hold their cards. Inevitably this will make some players grumble if it forces them to fan their cards opposite to how they prefer.

BOX 4.8 COSTS AND REWARDS

Many cards have temporarily relevant information that is important at one phase, but irrelevant thereafter. For example, the bird card in Figure 4.17(a) is part of a deckbuilding game. The card begins on the table in a public market for all players to see. To purchase the card and add it to your deck, you must pay the cost listed on the bottom right. Once the card is purchased, its cost is no longer relevant. Putting it in the lower-right corner keeps it hidden while held in hand or stacked with other cards.

How often will each piece of information on this card need to be referenced?

BRIGETTE INDELICATO

WORKING WITH CORNERS AND EDGES

The following guidelines presume a player fans their cards with the bottom card on the left and the top card on the right (Figure 4.18). If you prefer to design cards for the opposite preference, then these guidelines can simply be mirrored horizontally.

Top-Left Corner: That area is your most visible spot of the card and should have anything that is most important while held in hand. Usually this would be the cost or prerequisite to put that card into play. It might also be where you put the card's name. Even if you can't fit the entire name in that corner, just the first few letters is usually enough for a player's reference. The color of the background and distinctive shape of a border can also convey a little bit of information.

Top-Right Corner: This area is good for icons, tabs, borders, or colors that condense some secondary information that could be important either in-hand or in-play. For example, if playing this card can trigger effects of other cards in the future, you can note that with a distinctive symbol here.

Bottom-Right Corner: For most cases, this area will always be hidden while fanned. As a result, it's best for information that is only relevant during play, like in a deckbuilding game when you must buy a card before it can go into your hand. Once you've bought the card, that cost is no longer relevant, so it makes sense for it to be on the corner most likely to be hidden while in hand. In either case, this corner also competes for space with the "ability text" area of the card, so make it discrete and distinct from that area.

Left Edge: If there's any more information you think is important while held in hand, put it as close to the top as you can, hugging the left edge. This is where I usually include a column of icons or small text tags. For more complicated games, this is also where I might include "stats" like hit points, strength, and speed, but only if that information is important to read while in hand. If it's only relevant on the table, then I put that information elsewhere.

Top Edge: Most often this is where the card name would go, if that conveys important details before the card goes into play. I like to include

FIGURE 4.18 Example collectible card game with key information placed at different corners where it is most salient.

the card's full name and, if there's room, small plain text translations of the icons in the corner into readable words. The further you get toward the top-right corner, the more obstructed the card will be.

Bottom Edge: The bottom 5mm edge on the left side is best reserved for non-gameplay information that can be set in small print, like the card's serial number, deck identifier, art credit, or copyright information. This area is also good for "Star" icons representing endgame victory points, assuming those points wouldn't necessarily be relevant during play.

BOX 4.9 NON-HAND CARDS

Given all these constraints and considerations around designing for cards held in hand, it's good to remember that they're all moot if you don't intend for the cards to be in hand at all. In those cases, you have much more freedom to experiment with your layout. If a card goes straight from a deck to the discard, it can look however you want. If the deck is meant to be face-up throughout the game, revealing a new top card periodically, then the layout can be much more simple.

Play a few games with printed prototypes of the cards and tiles and watch how players read and interact with them.

KIRK W BUCKENDORF

MULTI-PURPOSE CARDS

Some games use cards to serve multiple functions during the game. For example, discarding a card could bestow some immediate resources, then you can spend those resources to play another card in front of you permanently, then you can tuck another card under that to give it ongoing bonuses. The card might even give different bonuses depending on how it's tucked, exposing one border only. By packing multiple potential tactics into a single card, it enriches each turn of the game.

At least, that's the idea. Personally, I've found multi-purpose cards to be a trap that mires ambitious novice designers in overly complicated projects. Before you attempt a game with multi-purpose cards, really interrogate your goal for the product. Does the game function just as well if you had divided-up your cards into different types, each with their specific function, rather than making all cards serve all functions?

As novel as multi-purpose cards may be to a game designer, they can be very intimidating to a novice player. Be careful you're not enamored with a design puzzle at the expense of a better overall game.

With that caveat out of the way, let's presume you do indeed want multi-purpose cards. It's helpful to divide-up your content into three categories:

Immediate: These are effects that occur once, and then the card is discarded or removed from play entirely. This information should be displayed at a rather small scale, in a location that may be easily ignored if the card is to be used in another context. Under ideal circumstances, your game is designed so that immediate effects can be symbolized by a small icon or number, so they take as little room on the card face as possible.

Ongoing: These are effects that remain persistent over several turns. To do so, the card must be placed in front of the player as part of a tableau or in the center of the play area as a global effect for all players. Most games with multi-purpose cards tend to have players tuck the cards behind boards or stack them in a staggered orientation. If this is the case for your game, then any immediate effects should be hidden so they don't distract players with too much irrelevant visual noise.

Endgame: These are effects only relevant at the end of a long phase of play or the end of the entire game. Like the Immediate effects, these should be discrete and easily ignored. Depending on how competitive you make your game, astute players will want to know where they stand in the current score tallies, which means making any endgame effects visible at all times. This may result in slower games as the game-state balloons with more information to consider over time. To avoid this, you might opt to move "endgame" cards to a separate area, hidden from anyone else but the card's owner so that opponents do not get overwhelmed by analysis paralysis.

Figure 4.19: This diagram shows a card game about managing factories' input and output. The cards have different resources on each edge and you're intended to tuck them either to the left or right of your factory. When you run the factory, the resources listed on the left are converted into the resources visible on the right. The bottom edge of the card shows an end-game condition, converting certain groups of resources into victory points. These are tucked below your factory, so your endgame conditions remain visible to all players. The top-center of the card has a set of resources that you can gain immediately by discarding the card.

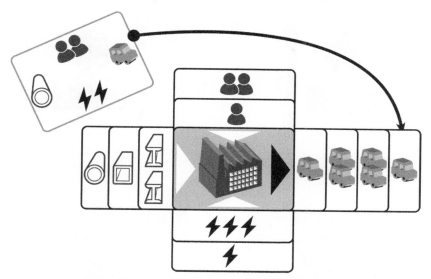

FIGURE 4.19   Example of a factory-themed game with multi-purpose cards.

You can have the most beautiful card in the world, but if no one can parse the information, it's useless.

TONY MASTRANGELI

OTHER ORIENTATIONS

Designing a card with an unusual orientation is a very useful method of completely setting that type of card apart from the rest of the deck.

Horizontal Cards: This card orientation is great if the card is not intended to stay in one player's hand. If it *is* part of a hand, players may have to tilt their head to read the card, signaling opponents key information. If that's an acceptable handicap, here are some examples to use as reference.

Figure 4.20(a): This is a Location card used in a competitive two-player card game. Each Location has a unique effect on play, so that effect text is duplicated on the edges that face each player. Even though the text is small, it's still oriented for the convenience of both players. Other critical information like the card title and the Location's value is only shown once, in the middle of the card along one long edge. This reminds players that there's an

(a)

(b)

(c)

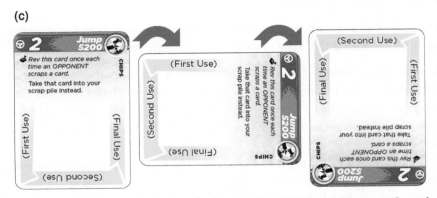

FIGURE 4.20 Examples of unorthodox card orientations: Horizontal cards, Bimodal cards, and Rotating cards.

implicit tug-of-war between them, with this Location's value at stake. Note that the card title is placed along the left edge, so that it's somewhat recognizable even if fanned with other upright cards.

Biomodal Cards: These are cards that still have a typical vertical orientation, but they are divided in half somewhere to indicate that they can "transform" under certain conditions. One-half of the card is considered the default, while the other half is the transformed state.

Figure 4.20(b): This card represents a secret identity and a superhero alter ego. The secret identity is the default orientation, with a standard header. It has a short area of text explaining the conditions by which the card may be rotated 180°. I've designed the dividing border to have a swirled, curved appearance to remind players that this is a "turning" card. I've tilted that border so that both short ends of the card have room for a complete card title header area, along with secondary tags belonging to either the default or transformed state.

Rotating Cards: These are cards that stay out in play, but may rotate orientations over time to convey different information.

Figure 4.20(c): This card effect is meant to be activated a fixed number of times. The number of activations is tracked by small pips along the corners of the card. This design uses pips instead of numbers so that players don't get them confused for the other numerals elsewhere on the card. The card begins play upright, with the top left pip indicated by a teardrop shape and one pip pointing clockwise. After the first activation, the card is rotated 90° clockwise, so a new arrow shape and two pips are visible on the top left. The third activation shows another arrow with three pips. On the fourth and final activation, the card has been rotated 270° and now has an octagon "Stop" shape with four pips in it.

Work with the printer and their sheet size to maximize paper usage.
TODD SANDERS

CARD BACKS

To design the backs of cards, you'll follow similar principles as with frames or art placement. The added complication is that you have to be concerned about "marking" the cards so that they are recognizable when face-down. A reliably randomized card deck should have identical card backs. To that end, you'll want to follow some key rules.

Avoid Freckled Edges: Avoid key details like specks and dots being placed too close to the trimmed edge, since minute manufacturing errors may "mark" the cards by making those details more or less visible. Sharp-eyed competitive players will be able to recognize when a card's telltale freckle is visible or not.

Avoid Paralleling the Trim: You tempt fate if you place a line running parallel to the trim too close to the edge. With that printed line as a point of reference, it may make normal production errors more obvious and spur complaints from customers.

Avoid Unprinted Areas: Most professionally produced cards use a card stock with three layers. The two outer layers are what get actually printed on, but the middle layer is an opaque surface that prevents any light from passing through the card, thus making the front visible through the back. Nevertheless, you should avoid the risk by also designing your card backs to have a fully printed design that will guarantee the front is camouflaged. (This is why playing cards developed a tradition of intricate geometric and floral card back designs.)

For example, see the card backs in (Figure 4.21). I'm showing these card backs overlaid with the guidelines for the bleed, trim, and safe zone so you can see how the art has been designed to accommodate those specs.

A. The first card shows an envelope sealed by a string clasp. The texture is low contrast, so even if there is mis-registration, it's not going to be obvious. The seam of the envelope goes completely off the card to the edge of the bleed. When it touches the trim line, it's completely perpendicular to the angle of that trim line.

B. The second card shows a mottled texture flooding from edge to edge. The hexagonal border's flat edges run parallel to the trim, but it's within the safe zone so I'm not concerned about the cards being cut too close to that line. Because the texture is so low contrast, it won't be obvious if a tiny speck has been cut differently.

C. The third card has a high-tech motif of white lines at 90° and 45° angles. Note that these lines completely straighten out if they're going to bleed off the edge. Any sharp corners are resolved at the safe margin line. The outer border has a softly pixelated texture, but it's low contrast.

D. The fourth card has a fully illustrated back. It has many more organic lines and details, resembling a carved and weathered stone edifice. Even in this case, the artist has done his best to comply with the

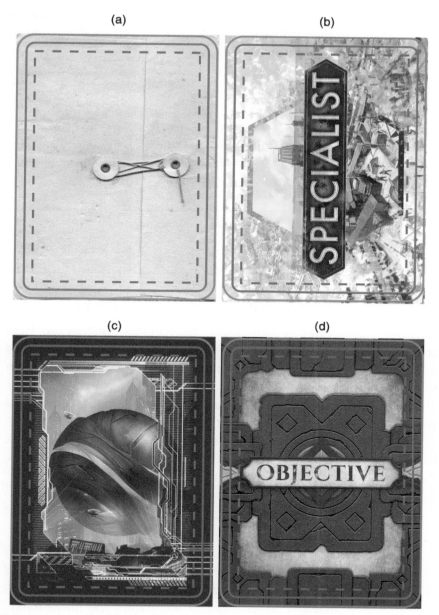

FIGURE 4.21 Card backs from (a) *Publish or Perish: Wiñay Kawsay* (2024), (b) *Seastead* (2020), (c) *Free Radicals* (2022), (d) *Clash of Cultures: Monumental Edition* (2021).

recommended safe margins and bleeds. Doing so has not harmed the aesthetics of the card back at all. Factory compliance doesn't mean you have to sacrifice subjective beauty.

BOX 4.10 ORIENTATION

If your card fronts are designed with a correct orientation, then it's helpful to also design your card backs with that same orientation. That makes it easier for players to draw from a deck and spare them the annoyance of rotating the card 180°. This can be easily done by placing the game's logo on the back.

Readability from across the table is very important and often overlooked!

ESTEFANIA RODRIGUEZ

ORGANIZING SPREADSHEETS FOR AUTOMATION

Developers and game designers use spreadsheets to organize large amounts of data, as you might find in a large card deck (Figure 4.22). These spreadsheets are also useful for graphic designers, since that same data can be used to automatically populate placeholders in a pre-designed template. This process is often called "Data Merge" in various layout programs, but your tool of choice might call it something different.

I find it's helpful for the whole project team to use a cloud-based service like Google Sheets so everyone has editing access to the same spreadsheets. Generally speaking, the spreadsheet is organized as follows:

• A column represents something that will change on each card. I tend to call this a "variable" as a broad term.

• The first row is what names each column, like the card's name, any artwork, its abilities, and any stats. Each column corresponds to a designated placeholder in your design program. For example, I work in Adobe InDesign, where I can set text frames and image frames linked via the Data Merge panel.

• Subsequent rows fill in the content of that variable. For example, if the first row of a column is called **Name**, then the next rows would have different names for each card. Row 1 would be **Adam**, Row 2 would be **Beth**, Row 3 would be **Carl**, and so on.

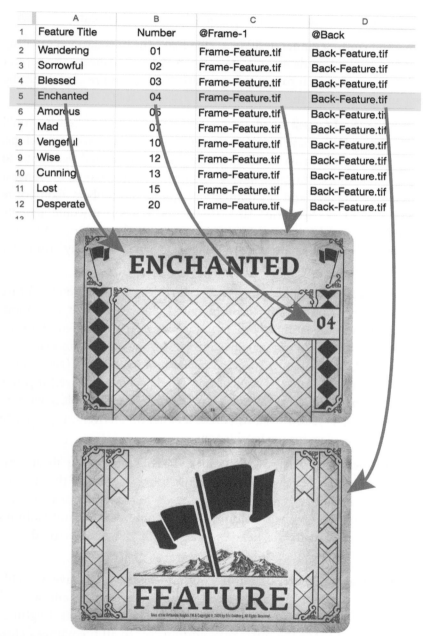

	A	B	C	D
1	Feature Title	Number	@Frame-1	@Back
2	Wandering	01	Frame-Feature.tif	Back-Feature.tif
3	Sorrowful	02	Frame-Feature.tif	Back-Feature.tif
4	Blessed	03	Frame-Feature.tif	Back-Feature.tif
5	Enchanted	04	Frame-Feature.tif	Back-Feature.tif
6	Amorous	05	Frame-Feature.tif	Back-Feature.tif
7	Mad	07	Frame-Feature.tif	Back-Feature.tif
8	Vengeful	10	Frame-Feature.tif	Back-Feature.tif
9	Wise	12	Frame-Feature.tif	Back-Feature.tif
10	Cunning	13	Frame-Feature.tif	Back-Feature.tif
11	Lost	15	Frame-Feature.tif	Back-Feature.tif
12	Desperate	20	Frame-Feature.tif	Back-Feature.tif

FIGURE 4.22   Example spreadsheet of a card deck. Note how the data in each cell corresponds to the images and text placed in the layout.

Here are some tips for how you manage your spreadsheet data.

Back and Front: Beginner designers often make the mistake of alternating front and back of cards as separate rows in the spreadsheet. The correct method is to treat each row of the spreadsheet as the *entire* card, both the front and the back on the same row.

Design for the Longest Card: As content begins getting filled in, you'll have some cards that have especially long passages. As the project develops, you'll find that it is easier to fill up empty space if you need to. It's not so easy to *create* that extra space later. Look for the longest name, the longest amount of effect text, and any double- or triple-digit numbers. Composite a fake "Worst Case Scenario" card. This is not a card that would actually ever really be produced, it just helps future-proof the design. Add some extra bonus space just in case the designer decides that they absolutely have to add another sentence.

Plan for Localization: Planning like this still doesn't protect you for future problems, since you've only accommodated one language at this point. Localizing and translating to other languages can triple the length of the text! Thankfully this is not usually something you have to concern your-self with if this is a brand new game in the prototype stage. (Needing to translate your game into 10 languages is a good problem to have.) If you're really thinking about localization, just make your text 100% black with no cyan, magenta, or yellow. That will make it easier for an overseas printer to replace one ink plate for the local language.

Header Row: Freeze this row so it's locked at the top of your sheet. This makes sure it doesn't get shuffled with the other content of the spread-sheet. As you add names for each column, do not skip any header cells. For example, if you named Column 1 then Column 3, but not Column 2. If there is a gap in the header cells, it will cause an error during automation.

Image Variable Headers: If this column is meant to have variable images, like different portraits, borders, or backgrounds, add an "@" before the column name. For example, **@Frame** or **@Art**. Note: Beginner designers often make the mistake of adding "@" to all file names below row 1. This is not necessary. You only need the "@" in the top cell, not the file names.

QR and UPC Code Variables: Some layout software allows you to automate the creation of QR codes directly in the layout without linking to a separate image. Rather than the @ symbol, this would use the # symbol in the header. For example, if you have a narrative game and you want to hide the outcome of each story choice behind a QR code, you can call your header cell **#spoiler**. Then this will encode your plain text content in this column into a scannable QR code. You can also use this function to activate texts, emails, or web links, but they each require unique formatting:

- Web Hyperlink: URL:`http://www.danielsolisgames.com`
- Text Message: SMSTO:phonenumber:Hello
- Email: MATMSG:\nTO:`usernamehere@emailaddress.com`\nSUB:Hello;\nBODY:;;

Image Folder: If this is your very first card design project, I suggest keeping all your files in one directory. Don't sort them into separate sub-folders yet. You have enough to manage on your first project.

Image Variable Names: In row 2 and beyond, each row should be the file name of the image you wish to place in the layout, like **Frame-Defense.tif**, **Frame-Instant.psd**, or **Portrait-SmilingFace.jpg**. Note that I like to name my image files by type first, since I tend to keep my source images in one big directory. Naming them by type keeps them roughly organized even if the local directory starts growing to hundreds of files.

Image Sub-Folders: As time goes on and you become more familiar with the card design process, you may instead prefer to group each image type into separate directories. For the spreadsheet to find those files, you must add a relative file path to the file name. For example, if you opted to keep all of your portraits in a separate "portraits" sub-directory, the proper relative file path might be **.portraits/SmilingFace.jpg**. However, the correct syntax of that file path may vary based on your design program, so see your program's help documentation for specifics.

	A	B	C	D	E	F	G	H
1	@SuitA	Color	@SuitB	@Hero	@Background	Name	Power	@Diagram
2	Suits_5.eps	Blue	Oval-Bard.tif	Hero_Bard.tif	Background_5.tif	Bard	Dance	Diagram_1.eps
3	Suits_5.eps	Blue	Oval-Druid.tif	Hero_Druid.tif	Background_5.tif	Druid	Grow	Diagram_2.eps
4	Suits_5.eps	Blue	Oval-Guard.tif	Hero_Guard.tif	Background_5.tif	Guard	Rescue	Diagram_3.eps
5	Suits_5.eps	Blue	Oval-Knight.tif	Hero_Knight.tif	Background_5.tif	Knight	Charge	Diagram_4.eps
6	Suits_5.eps	Blue	Oval-Mage.tif	Hero_Mage.tif	Background_5.tif	Mage	Vanish	Diagram_5.eps
7	Suits_5.eps	Blue	Oval-Summoner.tif	Hero_Necromancer.	Background_5.tif	Summoner	Summon	Diagram_6.eps
8	Suits_5.eps	Blue	Oval-Rogue.tif	Hero_Rogue.tif	Background_5.tif	Rogue	Sneak	Diagram_7.eps
9	Suits_4.eps	Green	Oval-Bard.tif	Hero_Bard.tif	Background_4.tif	Bard	Dance	Diagram_1.eps
10	Suits_4.eps	Green	Oval-Druid.tif	Hero_Druid.tif	Background_4.tif	Druid	Grow	Diagram_2.eps
11	Suits_4.eps	Green	Oval-Guard.tif	Hero_Guard.tif	Background_4.tif	Guard	Rescue	Diagram_3.eps
12	Suits_4.eps	Green	Oval-Knight.tif	Hero_Knight.tif	Background_4.tif	Knight	Charge	Diagram_4.eps
13	Suits_4.eps	Green	Oval-Mage.tif	Hero_Mage.tif	Background_4.tif	Mage	Vanish	Diagram_5.eps
14	Suits_4.eps	Green	Oval-Summoner.tif	Hero_Necromancer.	Background_4.tif	Summoner	Summon	Diagram_6.eps
15	Suits_4.eps	Green	Oval-Rogue.tif	Hero_Rogue.tif	Background_4.tif	Rogue	Sneak	Diagram_7.eps
16	Suits_6.eps	Indigo	Oval-Bard.tif	Hero_Bard.tif	Background_6.tif	Bard	Dance	Diagram_1.eps
17	Suits_6.eps	Indigo	Oval-Druid.tif	Hero_Druid.tif	Background_6.tif	Druid	Grow	Diagram_2.eps
18	Suits_6.eps	Indigo	Oval-Guard.tif	Hero_Guard.tif	Background_6.tif	Guard	Rescue	Diagram_3.eps
19	Suits_6.eps	Indigo	Oval-Knight.tif	Hero_Knight.tif	Background_6.tif	Knight	Charge	Diagram_4.eps

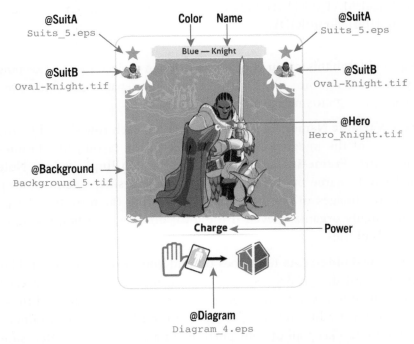

FIGURE 4.23 The actual spreadsheet used to automate the layout of *Trickster: Fantasy cards*. Note how both corner placeholders are duplicated, both being populated by the columns labeled @SuitA and @SuitB.

BOX 4.11 COMMON DEVELOPER MISTAKES

There are a few recurring errors you'll find that game developers will make in their spreadsheets. They won't notice these problems until the graphic designer has to start the layout automation process (Figure 4.23).

Case Sensitivity: Make sure your row names, file names, and file paths are all spelled and capitalized consistently. This is the most common source of errors when it comes time to automate the layout. A project member accidentally changing the column name **Title** to **title** can break the automation process. This error also occurs if file names in a spreadsheet have different capitalization than the intended file. If the spreadsheet content calls for a file named **portrait2.tif**, it would not find the file **Portrait2.tif**.

Unnamed Columns: If you have text in a cell whose column doesn't have a name, it will cause an error in your automation. This most often occurs when developers leave some stray notes far-off to one side or down below the spreadsheet. It's fine for them to use their own development spreadsheets in this manner, but the spreadsheet graphic designers use for automating layout should be kept very tidy.

Line Breaks: Developers are often working in word processor software where it's easier for them to read and write the text. Then they'll copy-paste that text into the spreadsheet, which may include one or more paragraph breaks within a cell. Unfortunately, those sneaky line breaks will be treated as a whole new card when the layout gets automated, which causes cascading glitches in the rest of that deck's layout. Let your developers know they should avoid putting line breaks within a cell. If they insist on paragraph breaks, I have two methods I use while working in Adobe InDesign. Both of these are just cosmetic line breaks. They don't actually break the paragraph. Instead, they make invisible words that are stretched so wide or have such extended letter spacing that the later text gets pushed to a new line.

- This method is what I once used most often. The advantage is that it allows you to control the vertical space between the two paragraphs. The disadvantage is that it's specific to the width of the text frame. Your developer also has to remember a special code word to activate this paragraph break. (YouTube: https://youtu.be/zaPnChlt0rE)
- The newer method just requires two spaces in a row, which InDesign will stretch out to force the next line of text down. The disadvantage is that you can't control the vertical spacing with this method. The advantage is that there is no special code to remember and it works with any text frame. (YouTube: https://youtu.be/iQmbAIUXaZE)

Special Characters: Writing software often automatically replaces plain punctuation with special characters, like replacing two hyphens with an em-dash or converting straight quotations and apostrophes into curved alternates. When copy-pasted into a spreadsheet, they're easy to miss to the naked eye. Unfortunately, these cause errors when automating layout, turning those special glyphs into ASCII gibberish. I recommend cleaning up the data at the source, removing all unusual characters if possible. If the developers insist on special characters, then make sure your spreadsheet is saved in a format that supports extended range of characters, like CSV UTF-16.

I am a huge fan of automating workflows where possible, so the data merging feature of Adobe InDesign and Affinity Publisher see *hefty* use from me. Especially for rapid card prototyping I find this an indispensable tool.

HEIKO GÜNTHER

Manufacturers work with files in CMYK. The RGB colorspace is intended for screens only. If you hand over final files in RGB, you may get surprised by how your game look when it gets printed.

LINDSAY DAVIAU

SUMMARY OF CARDS

As you design your cards, consider the context in which they will be played. Remember the different affordances required if the card is held in hand, kept face-up on a table, or flashed for a moment from the top of a deck. Your game may require cards to be played in particular orientations in a personal tableau, so plan your layout to accommodate vertical or horizontal arrangements. If cards serve multiple purposes, test the methods you can tuck, hide, and obscure parts of the card so only relevant information is visible. Above all, recognize the constraints of a small card and be realistic with your Dev team about how much they're asking one card to do.

You may notice this chapter focuses mainly on the design and production of paper cards. These range from pure card battlers (Hearthstone) to real-time speed running games using cards as an action selection interface (Neon White). Digital cards permit any length of text and on-the-fly customization. They can be modified to only show relevant data. They can expand to fill a whole screen or compress into a small icon on a virtual tabletop. With that freedom, it might seem irrelevant to consider the constraints discussed here. However, designing within paper's limitations also makes a digital card that much more accessible.

The more accessible your design, the greater chance it will be adopted by a broader audience. In designing your cards to have simpler text, clear icons, and consistent visual language, you may have only had a physical table in mind. However, the solutions for a physical environment *also* serve the digital environment.

Summary Questions

- How many different ways are cards used in your game?
- How long are they kept in hand, on a table, or elsewhere?
- Do you find testers squinting or tilting their heads to read a card?
- Is information readily available at the moment it must be referenced?
- When does a certain type of usage require a distinct layout?
- What usage takes priority over the others?
- How does the visual hierarchy correspond to that priority?
- In what ways can your card layout support fluency in the game's mechanics?
- Does the art style of your card layout match the game's fiction?
- Are any individual cards looking more cluttered than the rest?
- Can you discuss the problem cards with the Dev team to find a solution?
- How much unique art is needed for the whole card deck?
- What role does the artwork has in card play?
- Are card backs for different decks distinct enough to not be confused for each other?
- How does the card front resemble the card back?
- What plans have you made for localizing the cards into different languages?
- Are you automating the card deck layout or designing each card individually?

CHAPTER 5

Punchouts

INTRODUCTION TO PUNCH COMPONENTS

These components go by many names in the industry—Chipboard, Punchout, Punch Sheets, or Cardboard—but I typically just say "punch board" out of habit (Figure 5.1). They all refer to a variety of thick cardboard pressed between two glossy color laminate sheets on either side. A factory can create custom dies that perforate these sheets into different patterns and the resulting tokens can be punched out of the sheet. Delivering tokens still connected to a sheet protects them in transit until they're purchased.

Before getting too far along in your design process, consult with your factory representative to confirm they are able to achieve your requests. They'll offer solutions that best suit your needs at a budget you're able to sustain. They will also explain how they prefer to have their files delivered. The guidelines in this chapter are not universal standards, but they should get you most of the way toward how most factories prefer to receive their files.

Assume all punch board components require designated bleed, trim, and safe zones just like a card design. However, the thickness of the punch

DOI: 10.1201/9781003453772-6

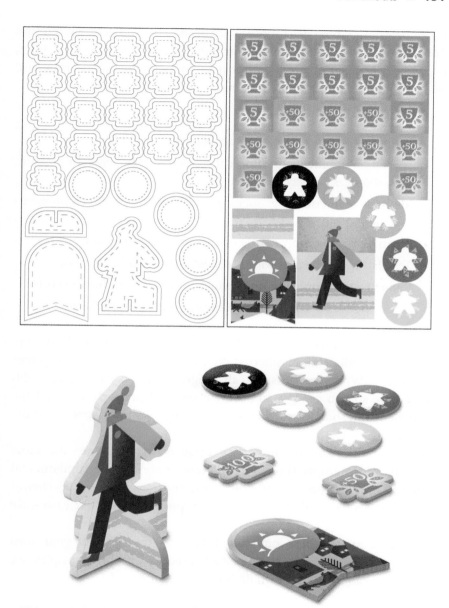

FIGURE 5.1   Example punch sheet from *Jokkmokk*. Top Left: The die pattern for this sheet: trim lines in pink, internal safe margins indicated by a green dashed line, and outer bleed lines in cyan. Top Right: The art layer for this sheet, with all artwork placed to align with the die pattern. Bottom: Example renders of the punched and assembled components.

board determines how strict those zones need to be. You need a minimum 3mm bleed and safe zone, but if your punch board is thicker than 3mm, expand the bleed and trim line to match. So if your punch is 5mm, also make your bleed and safe zones 5mm.

Issues to consider include:

- Planning how the art will interact with the trim line.
- Special requirements for different types of components, like tokens, tiles, standees, or player boards.
- Methods of interlocking, docking, and joining different components together.
- Planning the assembly of 3-D constructible components.
- Tesselating the die cuts within a sheet that can fit in your box.
- Reducing the number of unique die cuts to save production costs.
- Preparing files to clearly communicate your intent to the factory.

This chapter is formatted differently because it requires so much space to show you the full detail of different die cuts alone and arranged together on a sheet. Wherever possible, all diagrams are presented at 100% actual scale so you can get an accurate sense of proportion for all the components. In some cases, that means you'll see whole pages of just die cut patterns.

Many of the rules for designing these components are the same idea repeated multiple times for different contexts. The fundamental geometry and engineering of slots, cuts, and tabs don't really change that much. It's the application and execution that makes each use-case distinct.

Feel free to use these outlined designs as the basis of your own components. Once you've established a familiarity with the principles, see how far you can push your own designs to fit your game!

Always get a hard proof from the manufacturer, or better even, if possible, go there and oversee the production. [...] In the worst case, you need to tell the publisher to send back a *whole container* around half the world.

HEIKO GÜNTHER

PLANNING ART

Your job as the graphic designer or art director is to make sure your images fit the die cuts as intended. There are three main options for trimming the art for tokens.

Exact Trims: The shape of the token is the exact outline of the subject in the artwork. If the token shows a person, the trim line is that person's exact silhouette. If the token shows a tree, the token is exactly tree shaped. To achieve this effect, the artwork must be blended out to the bleed line. This method is best for depicting inanimate subjects, like coins, terrain, trees, or objects with indistinct textures that can tolerate being slightly offset. See Figure 5.2:

COIN—*Problem:* The coin's shiny details have stopped at the trim line, meaning that they will sometimes be cropped off-center. *Solution:* Either extend the shine all the way to the bleed line OR add an outer border so the shine stops within the safe margin (Figure 5.2a).

WATER TILE—*Problem:* This water tile has small landmasses that sit entirely between the trim line and bleed line, meaning they will appear inconsistently across various tiles. *Solution:* Either make the landmass more solid and contiguous so it can tolerate miscuts OR make the water texture more homogenous without high-contrast details (Figure 5.2b).

ROCKET—*Problem:* The rocket ship's artwork is entirely cropped to the intended trim line, meaning any miscuts will draw more attention. *Solution:* Extend the hull artwork all the way to the bleed line, removing any details that would be outside the safe margin. Use angles perpendicular to the trimmed edge where possible, so vertical and horizontal mis-registrations aren't as noticeable (Figure 5.2c).

CAR—*Problem:* The car has a similar problem as the rocket, however there is an alternate solution in this case. *Solution:* Rather than extend the artwork, you can expand the trim line so the safe zone margin roughly matches the car's silhouette. Outside the car, you can add simple landscape and sky textures to fill in the space (Figure 5.2d).

All of these bleed-extensions may look strange on the page, but they'll look fine when the component is punched out. Without these extensions, misalignments will be very obvious and look amateurish.

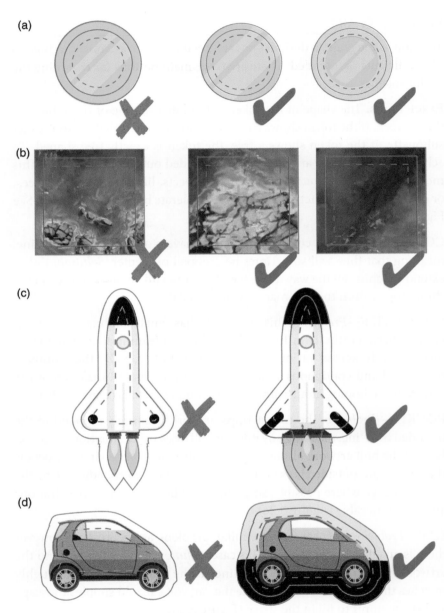

FIGURE 5.2   Examples of die cuts and the corresponding art.

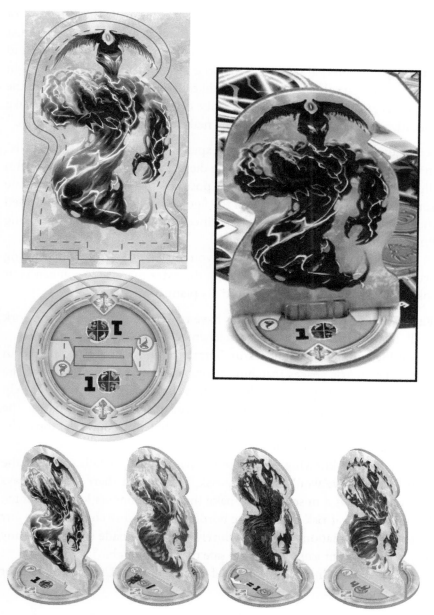

FIGURE 5.3   Elemental Lords from *Gates of Mara*.

Outer Trims: For artwork depicting people or animals, it's safer to not make the trim line hug the exact shape of the artwork. Instead, you must imagine the artwork's silhouette as your safe zone. It's also best to round out any sharp internal recesses, otherwise an especially deep notch might mar the art. You can put whatever you like behind the artwork to fill in the extra space. You may leave it blank white or add a background. Just make sure it's indistinct enough that it won't make misalignments too obvious.

See Figure 5.3: To save on production expenses, the four "Elemental Lords" in *Gates of Mara* all use the exact same die cut pattern. Artist Nastya Lehn illustrated each of the lords in similar poses that would fit within the safe zone of that die cut. On the base of the figure, you'll see that we duplicated the icons on both halves of the circle since the standee would be blocking line-of-sight for some players.

The advantage of this method is that you can have more freedom drawing artwork in any pose you wish. Adding the extra margin does mean your tokens might be larger than you initially planned.

Functional Trims: These trim lines have no correlation with the artwork at all. Instead, the shape itself has mechanical relevance in the gameplay.

See Figure 5.4: The standees in *Gates of Mara* may only be placed in certain geometric spaces matching their base. A square base can only be placed on a square space, a circle base on a circle space, and so on. To help recognition, the tops of the standees are cut to resemble their bases. The circle bases also have round tops. The square bases also have flat tops. The triangular bases have pointed tops.

Note that we knowingly put some beveled border details closer to the trim line than we would normally risk. That meant there would always be a chance that a miscut could make these components look off-center. We accepted that risk because the border bevels didn't communicate any gameplay information. They were purely decor. We made sure to keep any gameplay-relevant *icons* within the safe margin, though.

Your game can include any or all of these solutions. Use the best one for each component!

[Make] sure the design elements convey the theme of the game [and] Inform the players what the game is about.

KIRK W BUCKENDORF

FIGURE 5.4   Player Pawns from *Gates of Mara*.

TOKENS, COINS, AND CHITS

These components act as the basic currency of your game. For some games, they represent literal coins or resources that may be spent for certain actions (Figure 5.5).

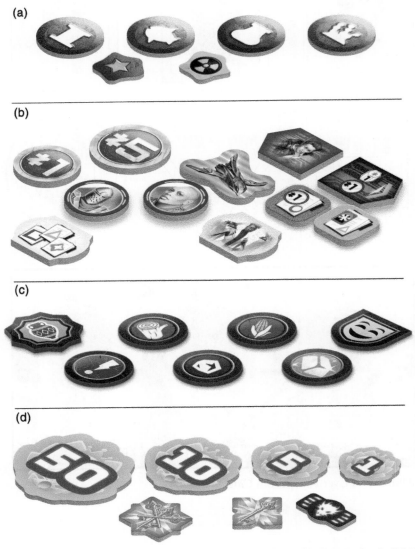

FIGURE 5.5   Assorted tokens from (a) *Seastead* (2022), (b) *Free Radicals* (2022), (c) *Clash of Cultures: Monumental Edition* (2021), (d) *Gates of Mara* (2022).

Sizing: The size of your tokens will eventually be restricted by the production constraints, like how big you can make your punch sheet and how detailed the die patterns need to be. Before worrying about those far-off concerns, it's best to focus on how the tokens feel on the table. Make your own mockups at home at various sizes and try manipulating them. Ask several questions:

- How often are the tokens handled during the course of play?
- Are they visible enough on the table or on the game board?
- Must they fit a certain slot or game space exactly?
- Can you pick up a flat token from a hard flat surface?
- Can they stack? If so, how high before it becomes unsteady?
- Can they be randomized in a bag without discerning their shape?

You can also reference the dimensions of real-world coins, such as US currency.

- Penny: 19.05mm
- Nickel: 21.21mm
- Dime: 17.91mm
- Quarter Dollar: 24.26mm
- Half Dollar: 30.61mm
- Dollar: 26.49mm

Then again, the bizarre idiosyncrasies of US currency may not be the best system to use as a basis.

Denominations: For a more rational structure, start at 20mm for your smallest token (a bit smaller than an inch), then increase sizes by 5mm increments for each denomination. So "1" would be 20mm diameter, "5" would be 25mm diameter, and "10" would be 30mm diameter. These size differences are enough to be noticeable, but won't result in a high-value coin that is too cumbersome to handle.

Quantities: When planning how many of each token denomination to include in your game, I recommend working in base-twelve, as in 12, 24, 36, and so on. For example, you might decide that for a two-player game, you need about 10 of your largest denomination, 20 of your middle, and 30 of your smallest. Those quantities are fine if you end up needing only two sheets, but they divide awkwardly if you need more sheets. Instead, increase those numbers to the nearest multiple of 12: 12 of your largest denomination, then 24 of your middle denomination, then 36 of your smallest denomination. Those quantities divide smoothly between two, three, or four sheets as needed.

BOX 5.1 EXTREMELY SMALL TOKENS

Some factories have difficulty producing punch out tokens at very small diameters. Tell your factory rep if any tokens are less than 20mm in size. The factory may have to use a different material to make such fine cuts, which will affect the token's durability and thickness. It may mean those small tokens need to be printed on a different stock, which adds to your costs.

Try to push for screen printed wood for important elements.

TORBEN RATZLAFF

TILES

Tiles are arranged to form the game's playable space. In a "tile placement" game, players strategically set the tiles according to certain objectives. The tiles interact with each other according to their icons and artwork. Tiles might also compose a randomized map that changes with each play session or is pre-set according to a campaign scenario.

Designing within the Safe Zone: Production variances are unavoidable and are more frequent with thicker stock. Keep any critical graphics within the safe zone of your tiles. That not only includes icons and text, but also any important artwork details.

Figure 5.6(a): The terrain tiles in *Clash of Cultures* are meant to be placed together and form a contiguous world map. They are illustrated with a green grassy border along every edge that encroaches 3mm into the trim line and expands 3mm out of the trim line.

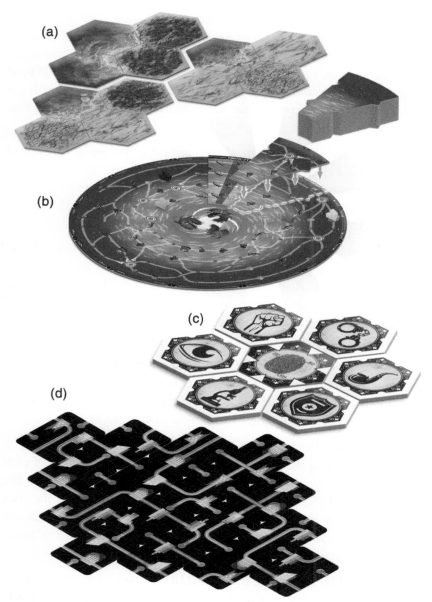

FIGURE 5.6 (a) Terrain tiles from *Clash of Cultures*, (b) water tiles from *Greece Lightning*, (c) hexagonal tiles from *Detective Rummy*, and (d) route tiles from *Light Rail*.

Global Tiles: If the tiles are in a shared central space, all players must be able to "read" the tile from any angle. It's best to avoid any text on a tile unless absolutely necessary. If the tile needs numerals, try to avoid numbers larger than 5 so you can use dots or pips instead of proper digits. If your numbers go up to 9, add a very clear underline or dot to distinguish a 6 from a 9. Make sure the terrain has distinctive high contrast features that players can recognize at a glance.

Figure 5.6(b): The water tiles in *Greece Lightning* are wedges arranged together to form a circular race track with branching paths through a whirlpool. A player must read the track clearly from any seating and regardless of the tile's orientation. All icons are designed to have distinct shapes and contrast sharply against the blue background.

Personal Tiles: If your game has players building their own personal play area, then you can approach their graphic design as if the tile were just a card with an unusual shape. The text may be oriented in one direction, accommodating the player who owns that tile rather than their opponents. Unlike cards, you don't usually have to make adjustments for the tiles being held in hand as a fan.

Figure 5.6(c): The tiles in *Detective Rummy* are placed onto a personal player board and owned by one player alone. All text and icons are kept well within the trim line. The background textures and borders are organic enough to allow for misalignments without exposing errors.

Designing Paths: Tiles may have paths that form a tangled network. The first step of designing these tiles is finding the exact middle point of each tile edge. This is where your paths will enter/exit the tile. Straighten the paths before reaching the trim, to be exactly perpendicular to the tile's edge. Paths should also be at least 3mm thick, so any two paths will still touch each other even if both tiles are printed slightly offset by 1 or 2mm. If possible, give your paths a soft or organic edge.

Figure 5.6(d): The route tiles in *Light Rail* have six terminals: two on the long edges and one at the short edges. Each path is 6mm thick. Each color of path also has an interior white detail to assist colorblind players.

Try to be bold with shapes. A player should be able to scan a board state and be able to identify pieces that are important to them.

RORY MULDOON

STANDEES

Standees are an economical option if you need freestanding pawns. There are two main methods of making a token stand upright: Intersection and Plastic Base (Figure 5.7).

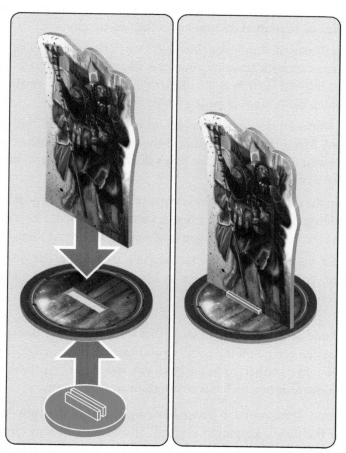

FIGURE 5.7 Example standees with intersection bases, plastic bases, and skirts.

Intersection: The standee is designed with a slot in the center-bottom. A separate "base" token has a corresponding slot along its top, so the two tokens interlock with each other, forming a stable X-shaped footprint at the bottom. Here are some basic specs for designing these slots.

A. Keep 6mm clearance between the slot and the rest of the trim line. More is better, since any narrow extensions of your standee are at risk of folding and fraying.

B. The slots should taper from a wide mouth to a narrow notch. Make the mouth slightly wider than the chipboard's thickness, so the pieces slide together. Make the notch slightly narrower than the chipboard's thickness, so mutual friction keeps the two tiles joined.

C. Both the standee and base must have wide, flat bottom edges. If your standee's artwork has a narrow base, like a superhero with tiny feet, or no implied bottom at all, like a flying superhero, then you'll need to widen the bottom of your standee quite a bit.

D. The standee's slot should be about 10mm minimum, but more is better. Make that the distance between the base's bottom and the narrowest end of its slot. The base's slot can be any length, but 10mm is also a reasonable goal.

E. Align the slots to the standee's center of mass to avoid any imbalanced wobbling. If the standee's shape is unusually biased, like a dinosaur with a long extended head, you might need more bases to stay upright.

F. As for visuals, consider what imagery will go on the intersecting token. You can use this space to identify player colors, terrains, or factional associations.

The downside of intersection bases is that assembling and disassembling the standee can scrape off the printing and cause a frayed edge. If you opt to keep the token connected to the base, you risk damaging the standee in storage unless your box includes customized storage inserts.

Plastic Base: These molded bases have short clasps that grip onto the bottom of the token, keeping it vertical. The base shape can vary quite a bit, but stock shapes are usually circles or squares about 1 inch in diameter.

G. If your bases are opaque, you may want to raise your artwork up a few millimeters so none of it is obscured by the base's clasp.

H. Make sure that your game boards have been designed with the base's footprint in mind. It's even better if your board spaces are 2 or 3mm larger than that footprint, since some injection molding leaves an extra flange along the seam.

Skirts: If your game needs uniquely shaped plastic bases, try making skirts instead. This is a punch board token with a slot in the center designed to fit the clasp of a plastic base. You nestle the skirt around the clasp of a standard plastic base. Then you clasp the base to the standee. Because the skirt is full-color, it can also convey additional information with icons or text.

I. In *Gates of Mara*, standees have different levels of access to spaces on the board. To keep MSRP down, I used custom shaped skirts that matched the shape of the board spaces. This let me add factional icons and gameplay reminder graphics to the bases.

Make sure you have enough components for everyone!
ESTEFANIA RODRIGUEZ

CUSTOM PLAYER BOARDS

The simplest personal player boards are flat rectangles of thick paper stock with tracks and special spaces printed on them. Effectively, these are over-sized reference cards. Without accommodations like slots and holes, any cubes, pawns, or tokens placed on these boards are prone to jostling out of place. Even so much as a stiff breeze or a stray shirt sleeve could ruin your game night. It's more common for personal player boards to be made from layers of custom die cut punch board (Figure 5.8).

Top Layer: This is the most visible part of the player board. It has holes sized to fit wood or plastic components like cubes or meeples. These slot safely into the board to resist jostling. For example, the square spaces of the Clash of Culture are about 10mm to fit 8mm cubes.

Bottom Layer: The bottom layer has any extra information that may depend on whether the hole is filled. For example, in *Seastead*, buildings move from your player board into the central play area, thus revealing icons on the player board. Make sure any icons or text on this layer are small

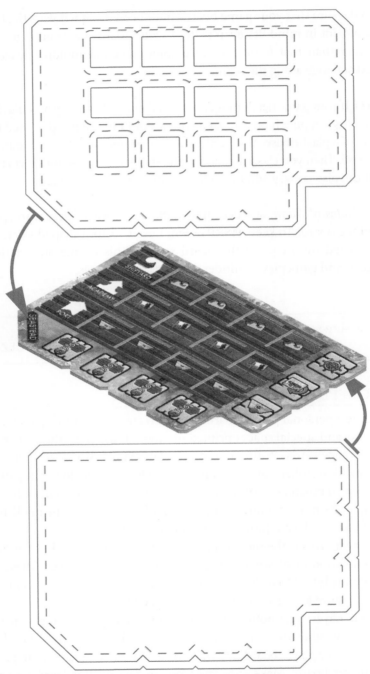

FIGURE 5.8 Die cut and artwork of both layers of the *Seastead* personal board.

enough to be about 3mm away from the top layer's edges. Also consider what will be visible on the underside of this layer, since it will also be visible.

Spacing Bleeds and Die Cuts: Include a bleed for the interior cuts of your top layer. Keep at least 6mm between any two trim lines. If you need any text between two tracks, those trim lines will need to be even further apart to make room for that text.

Arranging Track Spaces: Here are several options for arranging the holes in a die cut track (Figure 5.9):

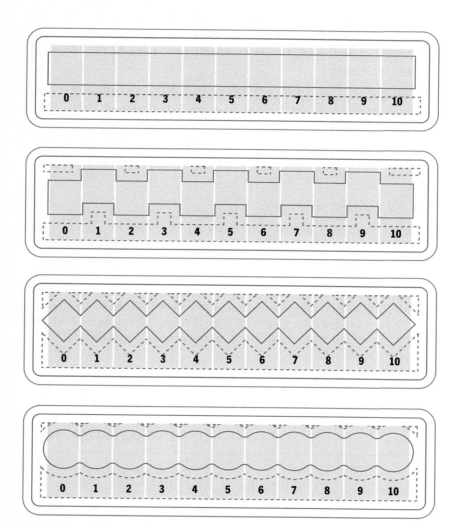

FIGURE 5.9   Die cut tracks.

- **Straight Strip**: This track is designed for a cube to slide smoothly along the track without interruption. This is useful if your track's increments are tightly spaced, but the cube might be nudged out of position by accident.
- **Offset Squares**: This track has overlapping squares offset up and down by about 3mm. This makes clear increments for your track, but the small tabs between each increment may become frayed over time.
- **45° Diamonds**: This track is composed of squares tilted 45°. This lets you keep the track clearly horizontal or vertical, but it does need some extra space for its unusually wide bleed and safe zone. To avoid frayed notches, I recommend rounding the nubs in that demarcate each increment.
- **Caterpillar**: This is just my term for this shape. I'm not sure it has an industry standard yet. This style of track is designed for a cylinder rather than a cube. The track is composed of overlapping circles with rounded nubs between each increment. This has the advantages of the diamond track without the extra space required for its die cut.

BOX 5.2 FACTORY ASSEMBLY

If you're planning for a multi-layer player board, it usually won't be part of your punch board sheet. It will be a separate file so the factory workers can print and glue it in-house. You can of course make single-layer player boards which are just the top layer, without any bottom. The functionality remains, but without the added assembly costs. More recently, some games have shipped with double-sided tape so players assemble their own boards. Consult your options with your publisher and your factory rep to find the best compromise between customer expectations and your budget.

Make sure to look at your color choices with colorblind filters to at least make sure the colors look different for different kinds of colorblindness.

LINDSAY DAVIAU

INTERLOCKING COMPONENTS AND PUZZLE JOINTS

Many games have punch board components that must interlock with each other flat on the table. Often this is done to create a larger play space than

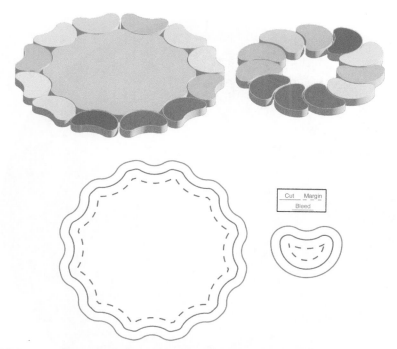

FIGURE 5.10   Prototype concept for *Sea Glass* game.

a single punch board component could create on its own. Sometimes the join doesn't have to be completely secure, only good enough to keep the play area tidy. In either case, the design considerations are the same. Let's begin with a loose join first.

In Figure 5.10, I have a prototype game called *Sea Glass*. The central board represents a large circular island with rounded concave indentations around its perimeter. The game also has "sea glass" tokens that have the same rounded indentation, making them look like fat crescents. Each round, players draw the same number of tokens from the bag and place them around the island. The tokens slot gently into the island, but also into each other, forming chains. When players land on a spot of the island, they collect the chain of tokens at that location. The tokens' crescent shape allows players to make "necklace" arrangements with their collected sea glass tokens by rotating each token a few degrees, until the outermost tokens touch each other as shown in the example.

In Figure 5.11, the circular race track is composed of 12 modular wedges that lock into each other with very shallow tabs and slots. We didn't want

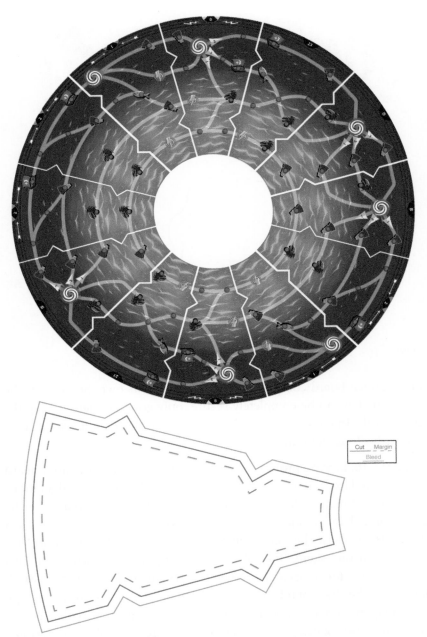

FIGURE 5.11 Circular board assembled from individual wedges in *Greece Lightning*.

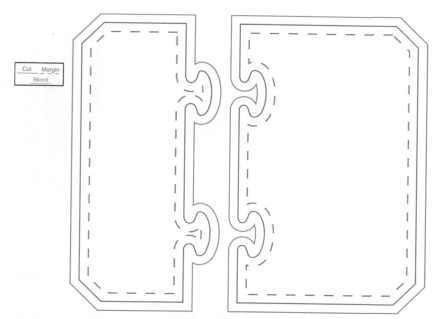

FIGURE 5.12   Die cut pattern for interlocking boards.

to use proper jigsaw puzzle joins because the tiles needed to be easily disassembled. However, they still needed to be held securely in place when a complete circle was put together. We settled on the die cut shape shown in the example, with each wedge having a tab and a slot that would securely bond with its neighbor. When the full circle was assembled, the interlacing tabs and slots were enough to hold the whole ring in place.

In Figure 5.12, in *Marvel: Age of Heroes*, the player's long-term objectives were represented by a pair of interlocking boards. On the left was a narrow "Mission" board that had worker placement spaces, each with unique prerequisites. On the right was a "Villain" board that had special game-play conditions and different point values for using the matching on the worker placement spaces. By randomly pairing the Mission and Villain tiles together, it made each objective unique in each play session. These tiles had to stay locked together throughout the game, so we used a proper jigsaw puzzle joint, with a tab that had wide flanges that prevented the tiles from being pulled apart.

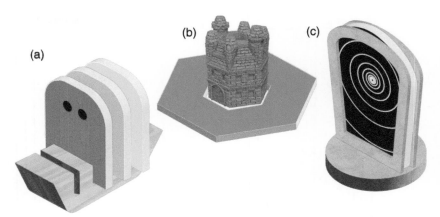

(a) (b) (c)

FIGURE 5.13   Punched components custom die cut to interact with 3-D components.

A. These small wooden boats come with one or more carved grooves for flat cardboard to stand upright. This bakes in key game mechanics, like a ship's crew capacity (Figure 5.13).

B. Plastic city buildings are designed with footprints that match the holes of certain terrain tiles, making it clear where that building may be placed.

C. These plastic magical portals have room for circular punched discs to be inserted. The discs may be swapped out to show how a portal's destination has changed.

BOX 5.3 BLENDING PUNCH WITH WOOD OR PLASTIC

Recent games are experimenting with using the best attributes of punch board alongside molded plastic or carved wood components. Plastic and wood have the satisfying heft of a real object, but lack the customizability of printed matter. Meanwhile, punched components require some complicated geometry to approximate the volume and density of plastic or wood. By making both materials interlock with each other, a designer can maximize each material's utility.

[Manufacturers] usually have great solutions to problems you did not yet know you would have, and can save you a lot of trouble later on. Mostly.

HEIKO GÜNTHER

3-D CONSTRUCTIBLE COMPONENTS

For added table presence and "toy factor," it's becoming more common for games to include fully constructed objects that customers assemble from flat-packed punch board elements. How complex you make these items is up to you and your customer's tolerance for some at-home assembly work and whether your game box can store the fully constructed object (Figure 5.14).

Hinged Corners: Some factories can slice shallow cuts into punch boards without cutting all the way through. This makes a natural hinged corner to ease construction and saves you a little bit of space on your sheet. Discuss this option with your factory rep to see if they can do it and what technical considerations will need to be taken into account. In my experience, it's a good option if you do not plan for your object to be disassembled. The hinges can become quite weak with overuse and may tear apart.

FIGURE 5.14   The dice tower from *Wingspan* is designed to be disassembled into two pieces so it can be easily stowed inside the box base.

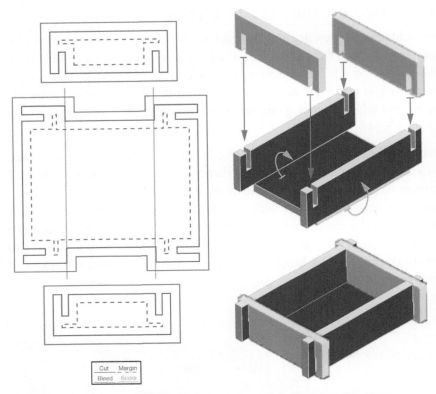

FIGURE 5.15   Die pattern and assembly instructions for a punch out tray.

Sizing: Plan for the height, width, and depth of your object to be at least 10mm less than the internal volume of your box. If any other components span that volume, like the rulebook or main game board, then you must make the depth that much shorter to accommodate their extra bulk. If you cannot fit your objects in the box, then it must be disassembled after each game, causing wear and tear. Make it easy for your players to disassemble the object so it doesn't get damaged.

Tray: A tray is usually a rectangular structure with four walls and no top. The diagram shown in Figure 5.15 shows the die pattern for a tray with an inner base about 30mm × 40mm. When assembled, the walls rise up to 15mm, but the inner height is slightly less since the base may take 2–3mm, depending on the thickness of your punch stock. The whole assembly is composed of just three pieces. The largest piece includes the bottom of the tray and the longest side walls. The walls and base are attached by a scored hinge, shown by the yellow line. The smaller walls slot into the notches of the longer walls, locking them upright. Note that if a player grabs the tray from the narrow wall, they might pop out of place. However, most players will grab the tray from the longest walls where they have a more ergonomic grip, so there is less chance for the tray walls to come apart from each other.

Four-Walled Alcoves: To make a privacy alcove, you're making a box with only three walls, but with a "roof" panel at the top. In this case, the two side walls and long outer panel are assembled together first. The back wall panel has a thin slot near its top and the roof panel has a protruding tab matching that slot's width. The final step of assembly is to insert the roof panel so it interlocks with the side walls and keep pushing it until its tab inserts into the back wall's slot (Figure 5.16).

Privacy Screen: A privacy screen takes fewer panels than the alcove, shaped more like a theatrical stage. The side panels each have diagonal scores. The middle panel has extra height and a customized die cut along the top that loosely traces around the silhouette of the portrait (Figure 5.17).

Dice Tower: This is a component in some dice-based games to ensure the dice are fairly randomized. Players drop dice into the open top of the tower. A series of internal baffles force the dice to randomly tumble, eventually sliding down into a short-walled tray to keep the dice from scattering across the table. Dice towers can take many forms and are not even restricted to rolling dice. If the bits that fall in the tower are small enough to navigate the baffles, anything can be dropped into the tower. In the example on Figure 5.18, *Age of Dirt* uses a tower to randomize wooden figures representing cavemen adventuring through a deadly mountain passage. The survivors that fall out from the bottom are available for players to use as workers.

Dials: Dials are rotating displays used to track resources or numerical values. Players can easily adjust the dial to reflect changes in their status (Figure 5.19). Dials allow players to conceal information, such as an intended action for a round. At their simplest, dials consist of a top layer with a window or a pointer to indicate a current value, a bottom layer with all possible statuses or numerical values, and some kind of fastener that locks these two layers together. The fastening is secure enough to keep

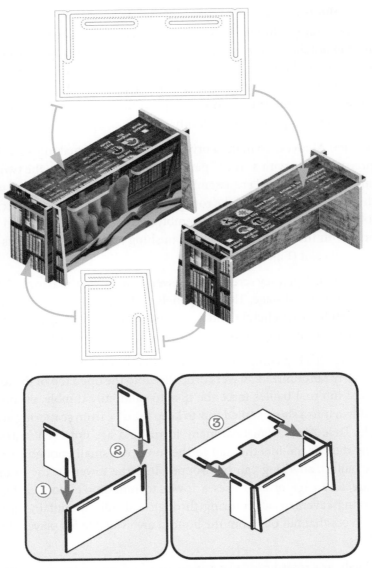

FIGURE 5.16   A privacy alcove from *Publish or Perish: Wiñay Kawsay.*

the layers pressed together, but gentle enough to allow the layers to rotate independently. When you design your dial information, remember that the ridge around any window or pointer may obstruct the view if seen at an angle, so keep some extra space around your numbers and icons.

FIGURE 5.17   A privacy screen from *Sidereal Confluence: Remastered Edition*.

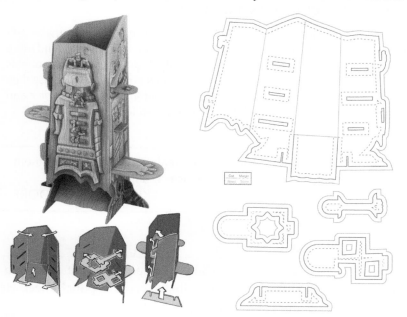

FIGURE 5.18   A tower with interior baffles from *Age of Dirt*.

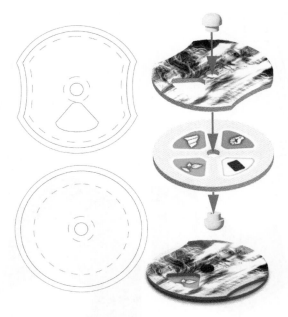

FIGURE 5.19   Dial from *Kardashev Scale*.

BOX 5.4 PAPERCRAFT CONSTRUCTIBLES

Papercraft is the art of using thick paper or thin cardstock to make 3-D objects. Unlike punch boards, card stock allows for multiple folds and more complex shapes, at the cost of less durability. Usually these components have to be stored or disassembled carefully when not in use, otherwise they will get crushed or dented. The advantage is that they're much lighter and can be shipped in a fraction of the space required for punch boards.

Construct all your components in the real world and playtest them live to get a feeling of scale, ease of use, and fiddly-ness.

KIRK W BUCKENDORF

DESIGNING PUNCH SHEETS

Once you have designed the individual components, the next step is planning how those shapes will be distributed across a punch sheet. Here are some basic guidelines to follow (Figure 5.20).

FRONT

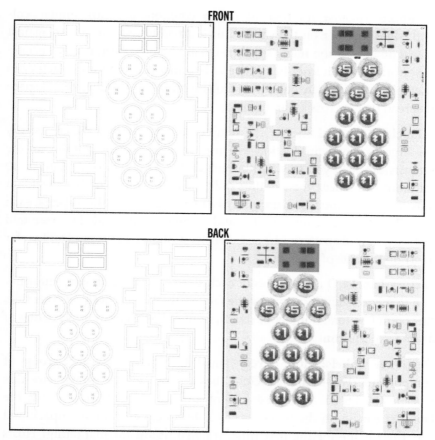

BACK

FIGURE 5.20   Example punch sheet's die cut pattern and artwork, front and back, from *Free Radicals*.

Sizing Sheets: The maximum height and width of the sheet is about 20mm less than the size of your box. This gives enough clearance for the factory's workers to quickly pack sheets into the box. (This also makes it easier for your customer to take the sheet out.) Talk to your factory rep if you need to add a few more mm to stay within your budget. It may be possible, but at the cost of slower production and assembly.

Spacing Tokens: Keep at least 6mm of clearance between any two trim lines, including the outer edge of the sheet itself. Thankfully the standard 3mm rule for bleeds keeps 6mm between any two components anyway.

Grouping Tokens: It's best to group components with similar colored edges together on the sheet. This is an additional insurance against misalignments. If too many small pieces are on one sheet, it may become so perforated that it loses integrity and becomes difficult for the factory to assemble with adequate quality control. Be careful to give them extra space or spread them across separate sheets.

Balancing Dies and Sheets: The setup costs for making a die are usually the largest part of production expense, so reducing the number of die patterns can help you stay within budget. For example, you might fit 50 coins onto one sheet, then 20 tiles and 10 standees onto another sheet, but those are two unique die patterns. Instead, make two identical sheets, each with die cuts for 25 coins, 10 tiles, and 5 standees. (Recently I've been told that each new die pattern isn't as expensive as it used to be, but I still prefer to err on the side of efficiency.)

Factory Labels: On both sides of each sheet, add the following information in a consistent location for the factory workers to notice: Game title, sheet number, total number of sheets, front or back. For example: *Gates of Mara* **(3 of 5) Front**.

Customer Labels: Add a very small text label for each group of components. For example, "Gold" beside gold tokens. Make sure this label is OUTSIDE the bleed line of any component. (Don't risk the label appearing on the token itself.) Labels help customers unpack and sort their game for the first time. It's also useful for marketing! Hosts of unboxing videos know what to call each component as they take the sheets out of the box.

Back Sides: The back of your sheet should be horizontally mirrored from the front. Anything on the left of the front will be on the right of the back, and vice versa. A good factory will warn you if there is a discrepancy between your front and back files, but it's always best to catch this detail early before file delivery. Arrange your die cuts to be as symmetrical as possible so you don't have to worry so much about accurate mirroring.

Background Fill: Fill background art or texture in the spaces between all the tokens. Every element of a game's first impression should be considered, including this small detail. Even though the leftover punch board may be thrown away, the "ooh" and "aah" of that first look make the customer more excited to play.

Assembly Instructions: In any free space you have between components, add instructional diagrams for assembling constructible components like dice towers or privacy screens. Often these components only need to be assembled once and you may not want to take up space in your rulebook for this one-time setup.

Extra Lift: Your game might have a component tray that is a bit shallower than the inner box. If this is the case for your game, add some instructions on the sheet warning customers to save the leftover punch sheets and stack them *underneath* the component tray. This will give the tray enough lift that the tray remains flush with the upper lid. Of course, if you *do* want your customer to throw away the leftovers, you might add that note somewhere on the sheet as well.

Remember to account for time at the end of a project if you will be putting together all of the printer specifications and mockups to show component shapes, sizes, colors, and breakdown of each number of tokens. It's easy to only think about the creation part, and not the logistics!

BRIGETTE INDELICATO

FILE PREP

Most graphic design programs will allow you to set your own bleed depth on any document. Make sure this bleed is set to a minimum of 3mm. When you export the document as a PDF, look for an option labeled "Include Document Bleed Settings" or words to that effect. Turning on this option ensures that your document's bleeds will be included in the resulting PDF.

Factories will have their own preferences for how they want to see the artwork interact with the die cut. I've seen this file preference from some manufacturers:

- One PDF with the die cut layer visible overlaid on the art. One page per sheet. The top layer is the die cut. The bottom layer is the printed artwork.

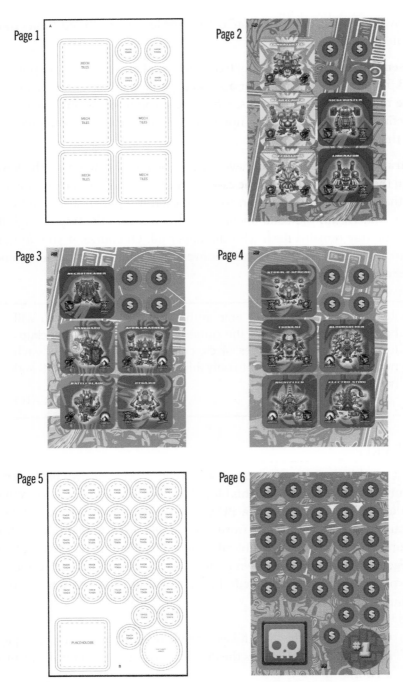

FIGURE 5.21 Page order of a punch sheet PDF, front and back, from *Atlantic Robot League*.

Page 1

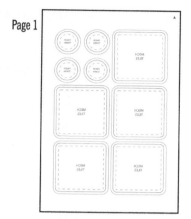

Page 2

Page 3

Page 4

Page 5

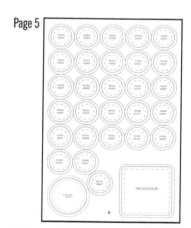

Page 6

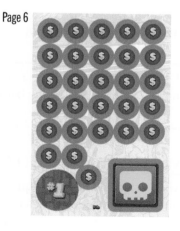

FIGURE 5.21 (Continued)

- One PDF without the die cut layer visible, only the printed art. One page per sheet. Only one layer, the artwork alone.

However, I've seen even veteran designers accidentally export PDFs with the die lines flattened against the artwork, making the layers inseparable from each other. A good factory rep will notice this error before processing the submission, but mistakes happen. It's entirely possible that they'll go to print without confirming that this was an error on the designer's part. To be safer, I prefer the format shown in Figure 5.21:

- One PDF for the front and one PDF for the back.
- The first page shows the die pattern alone. For an extra degree of safety, you can add disclaimers to the die pattern pages like "GUIDELINE FOR DIE CUTS—DO NOT PRINT."
- The subsequent pages show all of the artwork using that pattern, with only the artwork visible, not the die pattern. Make sure your page orders on the front file and back file are identical, so the factory knows which sheets are meant to be paired together (i.e., page 2 of the front file goes with page 2 of the back file).
- If there is a second die pattern, show that alone in the next page.
- That will be followed by any sheets using that pattern.
- This order continues, alternating one die pattern page and any number of artwork sheets.

Before submitting your files to print, make sure your linked images are all effectively 300dpi, CMYK, and your fonts are functioning properly.

Design with production in mind so you don't have to clean it up or make compromises on the back end.

JACOBY O'CONNOR

SUMMARY OF PUNCHED COMPONENTS

Punched components are unique in their capacity to be the most utilitarian commodities or eye-popping centerpieces. How you use them is up to the demands of the game, the practical budgets of manufacturing, and the creativity you can bring to bear. Designing punched components requires balancing superficial appearance with functional precision. Absent any wooden or plastic components, those punched components may be the most tactile element of the game's user experience.

The pragmatic considerations may seem endless: Thickness of cardboard, minimum bleeds and safe zones, easy assembly and durability of constructible components, ease of storage, shipping and packing, and so on. It may seem daunting, but habit and repetition make these concerns second nature to an experienced designer. Then you can get excited about making the best-looking components that wow players!

- *Potion Explosion* includes a large dispenser of glass marbles that randomly sorts them into several troughs.
- *Camel Up*'s original edition has a punch board pyramid dice-shaker, with a rubber band keeping a trap door shut at the pyramid's apex.
- *Celestia* centers around a big airship with generous space for each player's pawn to stand upright.
- *Age of Dirt* has a "cube tower" where players drop in their wooden cubes. The cubes may rest in hidden platforms or knock down cubes that had been dropped in previous turns.

Over time, designers will innovate new uses for punched cardboard components. As necessity demands, you might discover some new feature of punched components that no one else had considered!

Summary Questions

- How will your punched components be used in play?
- Will they intersect or interact with other components?
- Have you afforded enough space on the punched component for that interaction?
- For multi-layered boards, have you checked that the bottom layers correctly align with the windows of higher layers?
- How big is each punch board sheet?
- Have you made efficient use of that sheet's space to minimize the number of unique die patterns required?

- Do you have at least 6mm between any two trim lines?
- Does your artwork have at least 3mm of bleed going beyond the trim line?
- Have you given the artwork at least 3mm of internal margin to be safe for possible misaligned cuts?
- Does your trim shape have thin, pointy elements that might be prone to damage over time?
- If designing constructible components, have you made enough room for the slots to interlock?
- Have you confirmed the thickness of cardboard so your slots are tight enough to keep interlocked pieces held together by friction?

CHAPTER 6

Game Boards

INTRODUCTION TO GAME BOARDS

Game boards are among the oldest surviving artifacts of gameplay from the ancient world. Fragments and depictions of the game *Senet* survive from as early as 5000 years ago. However, that's all that remains. No complete, intact, contemporaneous written rules for *Senet* exist today. We can only infer rules from the pieces and what depictions we can find (Figure 6.1).

Nevertheless, the board and components give scholars enough clues to make an educated guess at how the game is meant to be played. The board is a 10 × 3 grid of square spaces, with visual indications of a serpentine path from one corner of the board to the opposing corner. Accompanying player pawns have doglike heads, implying a directionality in their intended movement—they have a "forward" and "backward." The final five spaces have special decoration, which suggests that they behave differently than the proper 25 spaces. From these scant pieces, we now have a rough approximation of the game that humans enjoyed when in the neolithic era.

Today's boards are packed with information and it can be overwhelming for a new player. Your task is to guide attention to where and when it is most relevant. A well-crafted board conveys critical reminders, offers specific in-game actions, and allows quick assessment of the current

DOI: 10.1201/9781003453772-7

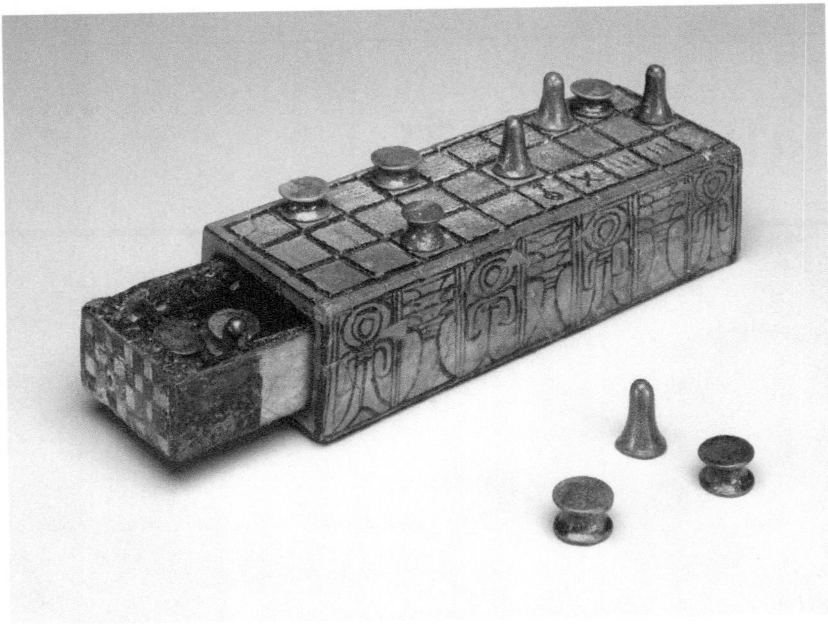

FIGURE 6.1 Senet gaming board inscribed for Amenhotep III with separate sliding drawer, ca. 1390–1353 BCE. Faience, glazed, 23⁄16 × 31⁄16 × 81⁄4 in. (5.5 × 7.7 × 21 cm). Brooklyn Museum, Charles Edwin Wilbour Fund, 49.56a–b.

game-state—somehow doing all that without looking like a distracting tangle of visual gibberish.

Pay close attention to the *subjective* responses from testers. Note their first impressions when they first see the initial setup. If you hear something like "wow, this is complicated." Now you must ask, *is* the game complicated or does it just *look* complicated because it's not clear where their focus should be? Solutions might come down to ergonomics, like pawns accidentally bumping into each other or resources being difficult to reach.

This chapter will give you tools to approach this process with a degree of clinicality, but it's never a true science. It's science-ish. Graphic designers have rules of thumb that result in good design MOST of the time, but we can't always get it right every time. We just aim to make the game as playable as possible and the interface is the means by which we achieve that.

While you incrementally hone your board design, try not to evaluate it as "good" or "bad" without context. Consider your goals and whether this board achieves those goals. That's a more achievable metric by which to judge your progress and invests less ego in the process. Try not to take it personally when you get negative feedback. It's not about you, it's just the board and how well it's working at the job it is meant to do.

In the end, you want all the beginner players to achieve enough fluency that they can easily scan and evaluate the game-state at a glance. That elevates all players to a roughly equivalent skill parity so the game is a test of strategy and tactics, rather than the ability to literally see the board.

[Boards are] where you can really let your theme and art shine. Transport the player.

JACOBY O'CONNOR

NOISE VS. QUIET

Designing pages and cards at least offers you the convenient assumption that players will read those objects from a predictable orientation. Not so with boards, which have to be parsable regardless of the player's seated position.

Invariably, someone will be in the "worst" seat, having to read labels upside-down or recognizing geography from an awkward angle. Consider your design from that player's perspective and you'll do a good service to the entire group.

You must first distinguish "quiet" areas against "noise" areas and adjust relative visual clutter to naturally draw the eye to where it's most salient at any moment. Imagine your board as a noisy room full of people. It can be hard to distinguish one speaker amongst the din or identify one person in the crowd. An amateur designer will try to make important areas bigger or add effects to make them stand out, but this can be a costly use of limited space. In addition, it just means that the overall effect is to make the board even noisier.

Instead, you want an aura of quiet around the most important spaces of the board, like one guest at the party clearing a gap in the crowd to showcase their dance moves. For example, your game board may include some reminder text about the flow of rounds, phases, and steps. This is not an interactable area of the board and could be distracting. So don't give it a

FIGURE 6.2   Main game board for *Atlantic Robot League*.

special background, make the text at most half the size of other board text, and tuck it into a far corner where it won't be in the way.

In Figure 6.2, see the main board for *Atlantic Robot League*. This game is set in an exciting future of competitive giant robot battles. It called for lots of color and flair fitting a pro sports environment, but must still serve the practical concerns of actual people around a table.

On the top edge, small slots are outlined in white for players to place a display of cards. Just below that, reminder text is set in sharp white against a greatly darkened background. The charts are formatted with borderless cells, using fills for each row and generous space between each column. The arena floor is illustrated with lots of scratches, saturated colors, and elaborate hazard stripes, yet the central grid is clearly defined by white squares. The bottom slots show well-defined spaces where each team's tiles will be stacked when not in play. Taken as a whole, this is not a "quiet" board, it's full of color and detail, but distinct zones are easily discerned from the non-functional artwork.

When talking about interfaces, which games are, at a most fundamental level, one should never underestimate the destructive power of poor UX design.

HEIKO GÜNTHER

BOARD SIZE

Game boards are constructed from thick chipboard material sliced into equally sized panels. The panels are hinged with strong fabric tape so they can fold down to a size that fits into the game box (Figure 6.3).

The actual art of the game board is printed on a separate paper sheet adhered to the chipboard. That paper usually has about 20mm of extra bleed so it can grip around the edges.

If the board is single-sided, the back side is covered with plain black matte paper that prevents the wraparound paper from peeling up. Often this paper also has a textured finish that keeps the board from jostling on top of a smooth table surface.

If the board is double-sided, then the black paper is replaced with "Board B's" graphics. Board B is often either a variant map for extra replay value or a slightly different board layout for a smaller or larger player count. Board B's art typically doesn't have the enormous wraparound bleed and is actually a few millimeters smaller than the total board size. This is to avoid Board B's paper edge from sticking out and becoming peeled or frayed over time.

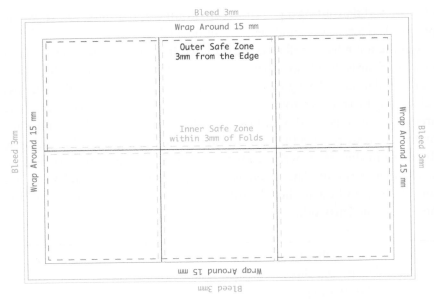

FIGURE 6.3   A Die-line for a 6-fold game board, 300mm wide and 200mm tall.

Whatever your board size, imagine double that size for the necessary table. That affords your players with enough room for their arms, personal components, and other items they may want to keep on-hand. Even if you want to make a luxury, table-hogging board, you'll face obstacles purely from a logistical limitation. For many factories, the maximum board size is 700mm × 1000mm (about 27 inches tall and 39 inches wide). If your board must be bigger than that, you'll have to make separate boards that players position adjacent to each other.

If your board is small and doesn't have to be folded, then at most it should be about 30mm smaller than either axis of your inner box lid. This gives it enough room to be secure in a component tray. Your product might not have such a tray, in which case you can push those limits. Consult with your factory rep just to be sure.

Most often, your board will be bigger than the box and must be folded to be safely stored. Let's assume "N" is any inner square box lid size, minus 30mm on each axis. That is the size of one panel of your folded board. Here is how that translates to your overall board dimensions:

- 1/2 (Two Panels): Your board opens like a book, for a maximum size double *N* along the largest axis and *N* on the smallest axis.

- Panorama (Multiple Panels in a Row): The board folds like an accordion, expanding to a wide horizontal panorama. A maximum size N on the smallest axis and N multiplied by the number of panels necessary to reach your desired board length. Note that most factories will still cap this length at around 1000mm total.

- 1/4 (Four Panels): This is by far the most common board type since it offers the best balance between playable space and safe storage. The maximum dimensions are $2N \times 2N$.

- 1/6 (Six Panels): This is typically the maximum number of folds offered by the factory as a standard option. The maximum dimensions would be triple N at the longest axis and double N at the shortest axis.

A folded board is usually the heaviest single component, so you don't really want that to move a lot in the box.

HEIKO GÜNTHER

BOARD TEXT

While it's usually best to make a board as language-neutral as possible, sometimes you just have to add text to make sure the game is easy to play. Here are some tips for handling text on your game board (Figure 6.4).

Selecting Alignment: Decide whether the board has a universal "up" and "down" direction for the board. If it does, one player is going to have the "good seat" because they can read everything easily. This might actually be a good feature for newer players to take the better position while the experienced vets can adapt elsewhere. If there is not a universal alignment, set predictable rules for how you align your text labels. For example, if you have card slots around the perimeter of your board, then those text baselines can run along the edge to match. Otherwise, the other text defaults to an established universal orientation.

Folds and Creases: If your board is folded, there are areas where the board must be creased or cut so that it can fold cleanly. These areas are often the first to become damaged over time. Even a faint crack might erase a letter or punctuation in your text. Keep text at least 3 mm away from any cuts or folds.

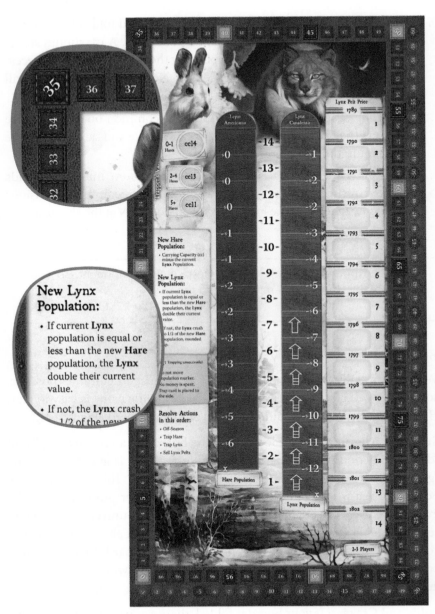

FIGURE 6.4   Game board for *LYNX*.

Bilateral Boards: Under normal circumstances for a multi-player game, there would be no way to arrange text labels so they're perfectly oriented for all players. However if you're designing a strictly two-player game, then you do have the privilege of mirroring labels so both players can easily read them.

Font Choices: As noted earlier in Chapter 1 (Typography), you'll want to use fonts that are easy to read but still have a touch of the game's flavor so the player can be better immersed. A sans serif font would look out of place in a pirate themed game just as hand-drawn calligraphy might be odd in a cyberpunk game. In all cases, the priority is readability though. If you're using an ornate font, give it plenty of visual quiet around the letters so their florid details don't get tangled into the background.

Avoid All-Caps: Words aren't just read by their individual letters, but by their overall silhouette of the entire word. The distinctive ascenders and descenders are what make the text easier to scan. When you make a word all-caps, it flattens the top and bottom, making the silhouette a solid indistinct rectangle.

Set a Consistent Style: Determine the general purpose for the different texts on your board. For each purpose, set a consistent style. That way, it's predictable and clear when text is labeling a gameplay zone that players should pay special attention to. Coordinate the text styles with other components that may interact with the board as well, like card titles, tile effects, or resource tokens. You'll want all of these components to feel unified and consistent, yet still distinguishable as play requires.

Which elements are the most central to gameplay, and which ones are more secondary?

BRIGETTE INDELICATO

ADAPTING REAL MAPS

If your board includes a map, you have a unique design challenge on your hands. The scale may represent anything from a skirmish among rival ants to vast interstellar civilizations (Figure 6.5).

Whereas a real-world map's goal is to represent reality as closely as possible, your map is part of a game and will have to be compromised to facilitate gameplay. Any labels must coexist with physical components

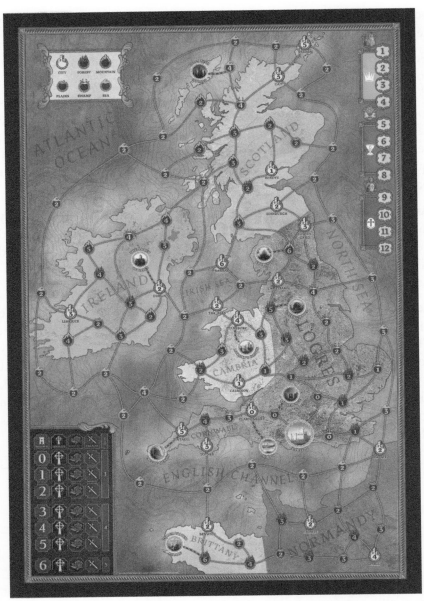

FIGURE 6.5   Game board for *Tales of the Arthurian Knights*, based on real-world landmasses.

and seated positions surrounding the table. Cities and landmarks might be depicted far away from their actual location, raising a few eyebrows from anyone who knows the area well. Note that this is only a problem for maps based on the real world. If you're making a fantasy world for your game, that map can look however you deem fit for the benefit of a better play experience. For everyone else, here are some examples of how you can keep the authentic flavor of your map while still keeping your game ergonomically practical.

Several board games are set in the contiguous US, so let's use that as a case study. The US map has wildly different scales for its states. Somehow the game developers have to make tiny Rhode Island, vast Texas, square Wyoming, spindly Florida all equally convenient play spaces. A single pawn might spill over Delaware yet be dwarfed by California.

Here are a few solutions to this problem.

Abstract Zones: Rather than an accurate map of each state's borders, you can abstract the map into 50 zones of roughly equal geometric area. You can keep the relative adjacencies of each state as well. See the map in *Rolling America* (2015) from GameWright.

Node Maps: Instead of concerning yourself with borders, identify key strategic locations on your map and link them together with paths of your own design. This allows you to space apart nodes as much as you need, even if they drift quite far from their actual location. See the maps of *Ticket to Ride* (2004) from Days of Wonder and *Pandemic* (2008) from Z-Man Games.

Floating Zones: You can keep your realistic map artwork in the background board, but overlay it with standardized zones in roughly the right place to represent their territory. This still has the disadvantage of some areas being more crowded, but at least makes the competitive areas clearer. See the map in *1960: The Making of the President* (2007) from GMT Games.

Grids: If your game theme only loosely connects to the real territorial borders of your map, you might instead overlay it with a plain grid of squares, hexes, or even just regularly spaced dots. This still allows you to implement special geographic rules for certain cells of the grid with a more tenuous connection to real geography. See the maps of *Empire Builder* (1982) from Mayfair Games and *TransAmerica* (2001) from Winning Moves.

Abstract Regions: Finally, you can simply group your smallest real-world regions into areas that roughly match the area of your largest regions. In the example here, the Eastern US has been merged and divided into a North East, Mid-Atlantic, and South East zone. A handful of neighboring states west of the Mississippi are merged as well, resulting in about half the number of actual states but a more feasible play space for a functioning game.

I try to incorporate the theme into the design as much as possible, but I might compromise on the thematic accuracy to prioritize user experience.

STEPHANIE GUSTAFSSON

Never use the horrible Mercator projection for a world map.

MIKE MARKOWITZ

TERRAIN ART

Many games use different types of topographical terrain (Figures 6.6 and 6.7). The challenge is that so many of them use the same set of colors. How can you tell a "field" from a "plain" or a "forest" from a "jungle?"

Pick an iconic geographic feature to exaggerate in your chosen terrain and exclusively use that on that terrain. For example, a real-world prairie may have the occasional tree, but for the sake of clarity, restrict trees exclusively to forests. The real world has nuance, but game interfaces do not.

Here are some recommendations for common terrains that may be in the same color family and thus need more distinctive details for ease of reference.

Fields, Hills, and Forests are commonly coded green:

- For fields, use irregular tufts of three lines, an icon for short grasses. If your fields are meant to be inhabited by farmers, you can add slight accent shades indicating long tracts of arable land.
- For hills, use a sparse cluster of semi-circular bumps. Your main goal is to differentiate this terrain from mountains, which are more likely to use sharp triangular shapes.
- For forests, I suggest using a much darker shade of green from either hills or fields, tightly clustered with bushy trees. As an extra accent, you can add some autumnal accents of red and orange leaves.

FIGURE 6.6   Map tiles from *Clash of Cultures: Monumental Edition*.

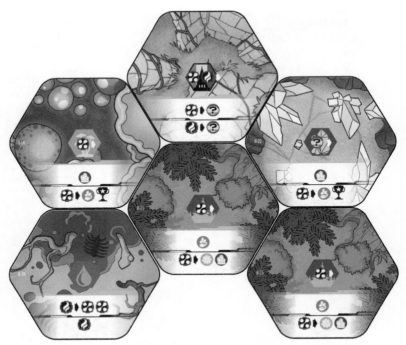

FIGURE 6.7   Map tiles from *Shapers of Gaia*.

Ponds, Lakes, Rivers, and Oceans are commonly coded blue:

- For shallow waters, use a lighter shade of cyan with minimal details and accents. This terrain looks calm and inviting, as a contrast to the more turbulent deep waters.
- For deep water, use a darker shade of cerulean accented by tall white-capped waves. Add shadowy forms of deep-sea megafauna, like sharks, whales, and squids.

Plains and deserts are commonly coded yellow:

- For deserts, stamp sand dunes repeatedly across the entire terrain. If your desert is meant to be more flat and baked like the American southwest, instead use saguaro cacti or tumbleweeds as your icons.
- For grassy plains, show tall waving stalks of wheat or colorful sprinkles of wild flowers. Signs of human cultivation are also useful,

like regularly spaced rows of crops or the occasional hay-stuffed scarecrow.

Arctic terrain and alpine mountains are commonly coded gray:

- For arctic conditions, exaggerate the smooth shiny flatness of the ice sheet covering the ground. Include subtle shine-lines where light refracts from its glassy surface.
- For mountains, exaggerate the dryness of the conditions by showing more bare rock, large boulders, and the occasional faint swirling wisp of high-altitude wind.

Avoid large areas of dark saturated colors. ABOVE ALL, do not assume it will look good on the table top if it looks good on the screen.

MIKE MARKOWITZ

PLACING INTERACTION POINTS

As your game board is being developed, try to find where players will interact most often with each other. Talk to the game's development team and ask which worker placement spaces get used most often, how tall figurines will be, and generally where most of the attention will be focused.

Cool Down Hot Spots: Your primary goal is to identify where there might be "hot spots" of too much activity concentrated on too small of an area. Hot spots can make the game feel cramped and fiddly, regardless of the actual game mechanics. Make sure those areas of the board have plenty of extra room for player pieces and resource tokens. Consider if the hot spot can be divided and spread apart into multiple locations so players don't converge so much on one exact area.

Warm Up Cold Spots: As a secondary concern, you and the developers may identify some areas of the board that do not get used as often. These areas can usually be shrunk to fit fewer figurines and components, with tighter margins between placement spaces. As a secondary benefit, this difference in size also implicitly communicates the relative importance of different board areas, which is helpful for orienting new players.

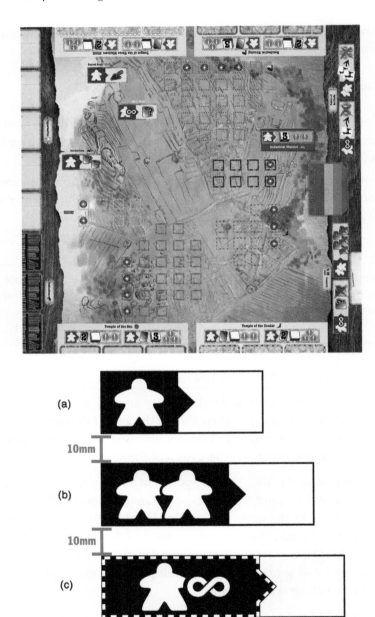

FIGURE 6.8 Top: Game board from *Publish or Perish: Wiñay Kawsay*. Bottom: Samples of different types of worker placement locations and how they may be sized or spaced for different amounts of interaction.

Worker Placement Spaces: If only one worker is allowed in a space, it should be sized to fit that worker's footprint or silhouette. If multiple are allowed, it should be large with an indefinite border. In the examples of Figure 6.8, there are several types of worker placement spaces with distinct rules:

A. This space may be visited by one player using one pawn.

B. This space may be visited by one player using two pawns. It may only be visited once.

C. This space may be visited by any number of players, each using one researcher. Players may also re-visit this space.

Break Apart Sandwiches: Imagine players around the board for a worker placement game. As a cost-saving measure, you might initially arrange those placement spaces in an efficient grid so the board can be smaller. Visualize a player selecting a space in the center of the board or at the opposite side. How many other spaces does their arm cross over along the way? Each of those is a risk for a shirt sleeve knocking over figurines or stray elbow scattering various tokens, all irrevocably scrambling the game. The easiest way to avoid this situation is finding any three spaces that are directly adjacent to each other, like a sandwich. Move the middle space away from the other two somehow, like off-setting its alignment. You'll find that the most convenient arrangement is usually a loose ring or a checkerboard pattern.

Keep things simple, and accessible. Trying to say more with less is hard but it can really pay off in so many ways. […] You can say a lot with a shape, color, pattern and/or a number.

ESTEFANIA RODRIGUEZ (*POPCATS FIGHTER*)

CARD DISPLAYS

Card displays are special spaces on a board that are filled with cards randomly drawn from a deck. There are a few best practices to consider as you design these displays, the first of which is whether the cards must be placed entirely on the board at all (Figure 6.9).

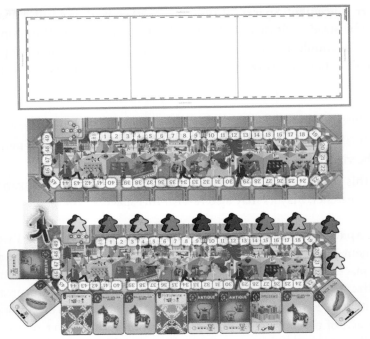

FIGURE 6.9   Game board from *Jokkmokk: The Winter Market*. Top: The die cut for the trifold board. Middle: The final board design, trimmed to size. Bottom: The game set up at the start of play, with cards and other components positioned at the indicated card slots around the perimeter of the board.

Extra Margin: A flat card on a flat rigid board can be rather difficult to pick up, so if your game requires frequent drawing and replacement, I caution against putting a card slot entirely on the game board. If you do put it on the board, make sure there is about 25mm of open margin surrounding the card space so players can slide and grab the card with their fingertips without bumping other components. This also creates a more forgiving surface in case the table gets bumped.

Working with Sleeves: Game fans often sleeve their cards to make them last longer. An added benefit of this is that they're easier to pick up from a flat surface since the sleeve has just enough extra flexible tactility. If you expect your players to sleeve their cards, then add between 5mm and 10mm of extra height and width to your card slot's dimensions. Even if players don't sleeve their cards, the extra room will still be helpful.

Pickup Grooves: If your production budget allows, consider carving a narrow slot or deep embossed groove along the top of the card space, about 70mm wide and 15mm tall. (Of course keeping the usual 6mm minimum safe zone between any two die cuts as well.) This allows players to gently press the top edge of the card down, which levers the rest of the card up and makes it much easier to grab. Note that this introduces some small risks of the cards being bent in the process, so some players may not like this feature since they want to preserve their cards as long as possible. (Sleeves would make that a moot point.)

External Card Slots: As an alternative to placing the card entirely on the board, you can indicate card positions with a tab shape that bleeds off the edge of the board. This still defines the number of spaces in the card display, but allows players to put the cards outside the board where they may be more convenient to grab. (Dedicated board game fans often have special neoprene mats that are just pliable enough to serve this purpose.)

Aesthetics: While cards may cover up most of the board during play, you should always consider the first impression of the bare board. The "ooh" and "aah" of a pretty board is valuable to make new players excited to get started. Consider the case of a path-building game like Tsuro, in which players will gradually cover the entire board with square tiles. There's no objective reason for that board to be so lavishly illustrated, yet it always draws admiring comments. Players will be staring at this object for up to 30 minutes so it's just nice to add an extra touch of luxury.

Consider the overall table footprint when boards and cards are placed on the table.

STEPHANIE GUSTAFSSON

DESIGNING ACTION SPACES

Your board may need key spaces where players place their figurines or other components. Sometimes these are single spaces signifying a special effect, like a worker placement space. In all cases, the number of players and the size of their components is the primary factor you must consider (Figure 6.10).

If you know the dimensions of the player components, you can use that as a basic unit of measurement for the board spaces.

FIGURE 6.10   Example of visually designating different types of action spaces.

A. **One player may place one worker:** Make the action space just large enough for one figurine and include one exact 1:1 scale silhouette for that footprint.

B. **One player must place multiple workers:** Make the action space large enough for however many figurines are required, but consult with your game developers to know what a typical maximum investment might be. Represent this indefinite cap by dashing the outline around the silhouette.

C. **Multiple players may place here once, using one worker each:** Divide the action spaces into color-coded areas matching each player color and give each space enough room for one figurine. Each player has one footprint available.

D. **Multiple players may place here once, using two workers each:** As above, but just double the amount of space for each player and dash the outline of their respective silhouettes.

E. **Unlimited placement:** Same overall dimensions as noted above, but don't color code the action spaces. Instead show a dashed silhouette with an infinity symbol. Offer enough space for each player to place one figurine. (Players can stack their figurines if they run out of room.)

F. **Spending resources:** Most worker placement games also demand an expenditure of resources in order to activate a certain space. In this example, we have a variant of space A, where only one player may place one worker here. However, that player must also spend the two resources indicated by the circular icons.

G. **Prerequisites:** Some worker placement games have "unlockable" spaces that are only accessible given certain game-states or other individual conditions. It's important to make such prerequisites very visible so players understand they can't count on accessing that space until the noted conditions are met. You don't want players facing the disappointment of a critical action being unavailable when they had expected it to be. In this case, the space is only available on round 3, visualized by an hourglass and the Roman numeral III. The entire action space is surrounded by an extra border, indicating that entry is barred until the indicated time.

As you arrange your board spaces, I suggest giving them an amount of clearance matching their height. So if the figurine is 15mm tall, then no other space should come within 15mm of it. This helps keep them visible even if fully occupied and prevents the pieces' height blocking certain lines of sight. It's not a panacea, but it definitely helps.

Remember that the space's shape also helps convey game rules. Let's say you have pawns with square, circle, and triangle bases. You can design the board spaces to have corresponding shapes, reminding players that certain pawns are meant to go in certain places. This helps internalize a core game rule without having to read a rulebook.

It's ok if your board is busy with lots of crazy themes, but the parts of the board that you actually interact with need to be very easy to identify and read.

BILL BRICKER

DESIGNING TRACKS

Tracks signify victory points (VPs), skill tree advancement, or some other progression. Tracks present a difficult challenge, since a significant area of the board could be reserved for spaces that are typically only used once and rarely occupied by multiple players at a time.

Numbering Tracks: Some game boards opt to only show the numbers of every fifth or tenth space on a track, which I never really understood. I assume my players have a limited resource of mental bandwidth and I don't want them wasting it on a willfully obtuse track. So, this is me giving you permission to number all of your track spaces. You can still signify every fifth and tenth space with larger, bolder, higher contrast numbers, but please number all of them.

Sizing Spaces: If the tracks are relatively short, then you can afford to make the spaces big enough for each player to have one figurine with a little extra room. As the tracks lengthen, you'll have to compromise by gradually shrinking the outermost spaces where it's less likely that players will share a space. (Of course, if your game forbids players from sharing spaces in the first place, you can just make the spaces big enough for only one component.)

VP Track Length: Your longest tracks will usually be for VPs, typically between 50 and 100 spaces. You want each player's current standing to be easily read at a glance, but there are undoubtedly more important and interactable parts of the board that should take visual precedence. For the most part, it's best to make the spaces just big enough for one player piece. If you can, make the first 20ish spaces double or triple that, since players will typically share these spaces earlier in the game.

Arranging Tracks: There are three methods of arranging tracks:

- **Perimeter:** The track is a simple border running clockwise around the outer edge of the board. This is easy to read and avoids any important areas of the board. Best for your highest-value game information, like VPs. The example in Figure 6.11 shows the VPs along the outside edge of the display board from *Princes of Florence*.

- **Linear:** This track follows a single line, but may be arranged as clean lanes (such as the Knowledge track from *Free Radicals*). If your linear tracks must be compared to each other, it's best to arrange them as clearly as possible so as to ease that comparison. Otherwise, you can make more serpentine arrangements that thread haphazardly around the board. The paths of a racing game or the randomized tracks of Robo Rally would fit this category.

- **Graph:** The VP track is arranged in a grid, with rows from 00 to 09 left-to-right, then dropping to another row from 10 to 19, then another row from 20 to 29, and so on. This arrangement is favored among engineers and mathematicians. It's best for games that have double-digit scoring jumps, especially for endgame scoring.

Always be willing to revise and modify drafts. Game development is an iterative process that cycles between two phases:
(1) proliferation of complexity
(2) ruthless simplification
Most design teams are good at (1) and then neglect (2).

MIKE MARKOWITZ

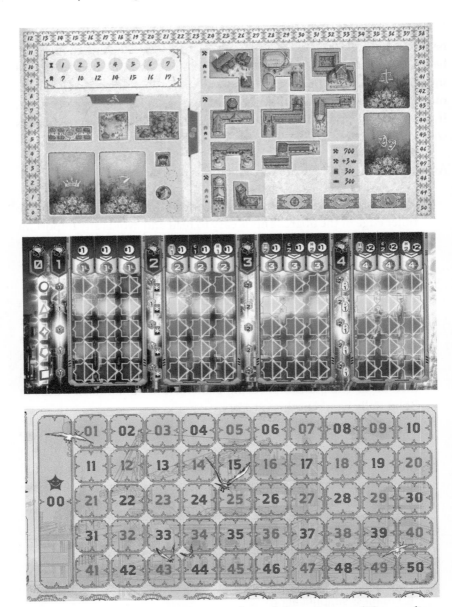

FIGURE 6.11   Example of a perimeter-style track from *Princes of Florence*, linear-style tracks from *Free Radicals*, and a graph-style track from *Rebuilding Seattle*.

SUMMARY OF GAME BOARDS

Creating an engaging and functional game board requires all the skills discussed in this book so far: You must have clear typography, helpful language-neutral iconography, fundamental understanding of contrast, and creating an intuitive visual hierarchy.

The paramount challenge is information density. Having the full breadth of a large game board can lull you into thinking you can pack tons of information. It takes careful management of emptiness as well as content to avoid your game board from overwhelming a new player. Above all, you must ensure that key information is easily discernible ... And oh yeah, it all has to look pretty, too.

Graphic design for game boards requires a creative approach to problem-solving. You'll provide helpful visual cues that make the game so intuitive that players could guess the answer to a rules question.

- If a track has one direction, there should be some arrows in that direction. (And any illustrations should also help suggest that linearity.)
- If there are worker placement-style conversion spaces, those transactions should be depicted in a consistent visual language. (Such as illustrating frames and backgrounds to reliably correspond to the same game mechanics.)
- If certain locations are only unlocked by certain conditions, they should be hidden or set apart from the main accessible areas. (Perhaps even being separate sub-boards that only get added after being triggered.)

These and other techniques will help your game board be as intuitive as possible.

Summary Questions

- How does your board's color scheme reflect the game's theme and help guide player's attention?
- How is your board's typography enhancing the player's understanding of the rules?
- Have you tested your iconography to make sure it's visible under different lighting conditions and comprehensible to most players?

- How does the game board interact with other components, like player pawns, cards, and tiles?
- Have you given adequate space on the game board for multiple pieces, if allowed?
- In places where certain actions like movement or placement are not permitted, what indications have you provided to remind players of that prohibition?
- Are you using "empty" space to make physical interaction with the board easier, like making enough room for fingers to manipulate cubes and tokens?
- Are there any thematic elements of the game that should be included on the board's visuals, like textures, motifs, and borders?
- How does the board change over the course of the game?
- Will certain elements be obscured once components are placed on top?
- How are you taking advantage of hiding and revealing to focus attention where it's most pertinent?
- How have you made the board accessible to players with colorblindness or other visual impairment?
- How many of the game's rules can be inferred just by looking at the board?

CHAPTER 7

Rulebooks

INTRODUCTION

We ask too much of rulebooks. With so many styles of learning out there, somehow we expect rulebooks to satisfy them all.

- **Readers** are happy to learn an entire game by studying the book alone, though they're a rare group. Whether they like it or not, they are the teachers of the group and the book is their handy script.

- **Watchers** prefer to learn from a video or at the table from a friend. They'll closely observe the movement of components and cards, only referring to the rulebook if there is a specific question to answer.

- **Doers** are the "let's just play" people, preferring to learn on-the-go. They came to play, not read. For them, the book better be as quick and easy to navigate as possible, lest the game night be ruined by a dry recitation of opaque language.

Those three modes are a lot to ask of one slim stapled pamphlet, and yet we expect that from rulebooks in every board game.

This chapter won't teach how to *write* the rules, at least not much. The entire discipline of technical writing is its own field that could fill its own volume. Instead, I'll focus on how you can present your rules as clearly as

DOI: 10.1201/9781003453772-8

possible, in a roughly logical order, and avoid common visual pitfalls that can make rules difficult to parse for most learners.

THE FLOW OF THE BOOK

While laying out a rulebook, imagine teaching the game at the table. The worst case scenario is when the whole table is learning the game straight from the book. Reading aloud a poorly organized manual tests the patience of even the most generous guest. A clear structure can avoid spoiling game night. Here is a useful template to follow for each "chapter" of the book (Figure 7.1). This is not a cure-all, just a simple framework in the absence of any other organizational guide.

1. **Front Cover:** Often just the box art, logo, and a paragraph explaining the theme of the game. **Goal:** Let the player know who they represent, their goal, and the "mood" of the game.

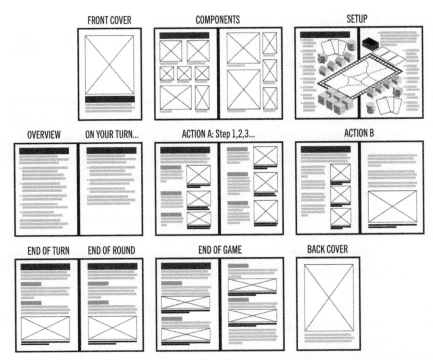

FIGURE 7.1 An example of how a rulebook is organized during the layout process.

2. **Components:** Outline all the pieces used in the game. Don't explain the purpose of each piece, just label them. **Goal:** The player should know the name of each piece in the game, though not necessarily its function in the game.

3. **Setup:** How to prepare the central play area, each player's personal area, and any tertiary areas necessary for play. **Goal:** After following these steps, players should be ready for their first turn.

4. **(Optional) Setup Guidelines:** If as a part of setup, players must decide certain roles to play or certain modules to include, use this section to very loosely describe the play experience for each option. **Goal:** Players can make somewhat informed decisions in their first game. Even if they don't know the mechanics, they should know if an option is "complex" or "aggressive" or "strategic."

5. **Overview of a Game:** This is a brief overview of the game's time structure, such as definitions of a "turn," "phase," or "round" in your particular game. This can also mention some critical events that recur throughout the game, like scoring phases, combat, or a random event deck. **Goal:** Players should know loosely how long the game will last, how it will end, and the general rhythm of play.

6. **"On Your Turn …":** Outline what actually occurs within a player's turn. Describe any mandatory upkeep before or after a turn as well. **Goal:** Players should know their basic options when it's their turn.

7. **Action Steps 1, 2, 3 …:** The most granular explanation of the steps or options of a player's turn, including diagrams and examples. The bulk of the book will be devoted to these sections. **Goal:** Players should have a general understanding of the consequences of each choice they can make on their turn.

8. **(Optional) "Housekeeping" End of Turn/End of Round:** If there are any extra mandatory actions that must occur at the end of a player's turn or after each player has taken a turn, describe them here. **Goal:** Help players remember to do any necessary steps before the next segment of play begins.

9. **End of Game:** What triggers the end of the game and any final scoring? **Goal:** Players should understand some paths to victory; how their cumulative choices build to a certain strategy.

10. **Back Cover:** A refresher overview for readers who have already read the rulebook. **Goal:** Jog a player's memory for how a game plays so they don't have to open the book more often than necessary.

BOX 7.1 INCREMENTS OF 4 OR 8 PAGES

A book's page count must be measured in certain strict increments. Usually this is 4 pages, 8 pages, 16 pages, or 32 pages, but the printer has final authority. Keep to increments of 8 pages for most rulebooks. The front and back cover count as pages, so bear those in your calculations as well!

Graphic design works alongside illustration in a game to make it a pleasing and attractive product that is enjoyable to interact with.

BRIGETTE INDELICATO

Communicate the intent of the game.

TODD SANDERS

PAGE SIZE VS. BOOK LENGTH

When you set up your pages, leave at least 10mm margin from the edge of the sheet along the top and outside edges. Leave about 20mm margin from the inner "gutter" and the bottom edge (Figure 7.2).

Your rulebook's page dimensions should be about 15mm smaller than the box's dimensions. Therefore, if your box is 300 × 300mm, the rulebook should be no larger than 285mm × 285mm. Please note that just because you *can* make the rulebook this large, doesn't mean you *should* do so.

Most of the time, rulebooks become this large because industry designers have been trained that customers are discouraged by very thick rulebooks. If a game has a reputation for being difficult to learn, it can deflate sales and hurt revenues. With those risks in mind, you may be tempted to simply enlarge the pages so that there are fewer of them. A bigger, thinner rulebook should be more approachable, right?

The problem is that there is an equally vocal contingent of customers who dislike the enormous footprint of the largest rulebooks. Even if it allows for larger text, clearer examples, and more diagrams, those more entrenched board game customers would happily tolerate a rulebook with twice as many pages and half the footprint.

Neither of these two demands will be equally satisfied. They're both valid. This is why I generally default to an A4 size rulebook, even if the box

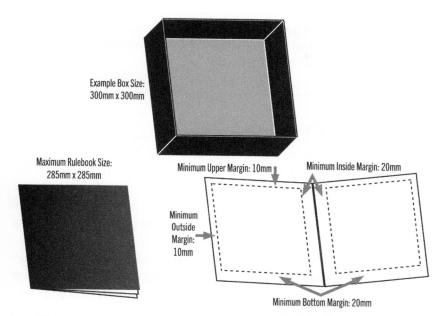

FIGURE 7.2 For a sample box size of 300mm × 300mm, the maximum size of the rulebook should be 285mm × 285mm. The margins on these pages should be 10mm on the top and outside, 20mm on the inside and bottom.

is large enough to allow a bigger book. A4 may still result in a book that is too thick for some, or a page that is too large for others, but at least it's a familiar size that will get the fewest complaints. As an added advantage, it can be printed at home, which makes it great for online support and errata.

BOX 7.2 VAST COSMIC FORCES OF PASSIVE VOICE

Game designers have a habit of using passive voice, third-party tense because it sounds more official. "The player will do this, the player will do that." It makes rules sound more opaque and indirect. Here's my tip for catching passive voice in text: If you can add "… by vast cosmic forces!" to the end of a sentence, it's probably too passive. For example: The cards are shuffled at the beginning of the Economy Phase … **by vast cosmic forces!**" Instead, try a present-tense, second-person, declarative voice. For example: "Shuffle the deck at the beginning of the Economy Phase." Note that the active voice isn't *necessarily* shorter than passive voice, but the goal is to make the text clearer. Being succinct isn't the goal in itself. If brevity makes the text clearer, good. If elaboration makes the text clearer, that's good, too.

Actually playing the game helps me understand it a lot better. I know what's important on the cards and in the rulebook and I can adjust my design accordingly.

TONY MASTRANGELI

ONE TOPIC PER SPREAD

Treat each double-page spread of your rulebook as a full "unit" of the rules explanation. Don't let a major topic traverse the page-flip, so the reader comes to expect the end of a topic is within their field of view at all times. The first spread in Figure 7.3 shows that structure. The entire set of components is displayed as one spread, with no spillover to the next page.

Most manuscripts aren't written with this structure in mind, since there's no way for the game designer to accurately predict how their word count would paginate in the final layout. If necessary, you can divide a page into half for tinier divisions of information. You can split vertically as seen on the left page of the second spread in Figure 7.3, dividing the content into two columns. This can also be done horizontally, as seen on the right page of the third spread in Figure 7.3, with a header appearing halfway down the page.

Avoid placing a top-level header lower than the middle of the page, since a hurried reader can easily miss it as they scan the book. Fill any "gaps" with relevant information and images. For example, in the vertically split page, a large image of the Round Track fills the extra space, since that component is most relevant to the topic of Game Structure. That allowed the subsequent content to end naturally closer to the bottom of the page.

If there is not enough practical content to fill in a topic's designated space, I'll check in with the game designer to see if there's anything else they'd like to add, like an example or sidebar. For example, on the right page of the second spread, "City Size" doesn't quite have enough text to fill in that column. The original rules text didn't call for any examples or visual references here, but a visual example of the five sizes of city doesn't hurt and only helps.

If there is truly no other content to fill in any gaps, then add non-instructional images, like illustrations, decorative motifs, or loose textures.

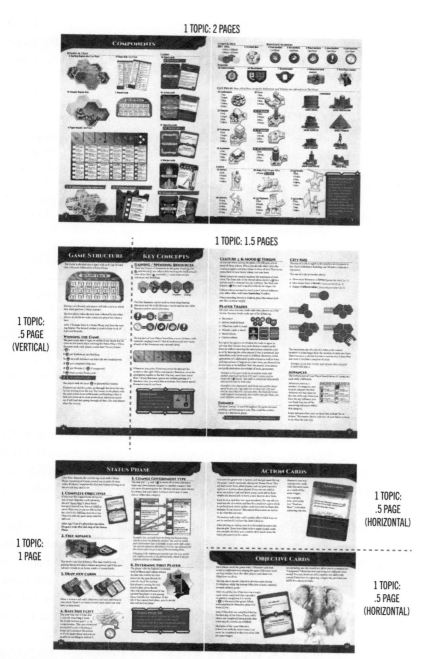

1 TOPIC: 2 PAGES

1 TOPIC: 1.5 PAGES

1 TOPIC: .5 PAGE (VERTICAL)

1 TOPIC: .5 PAGE (HORIZONTAL)

1 TOPIC: 1 PAGE

1 TOPIC: .5 PAGE (HORIZONTAL)

FIGURE 7.3   *Clash of Cultures: Monumental Edition* (2021).

For example, in the right page of the third spread, "Objective Cards" didn't quite have enough text or component content to fill in that half of the page, so the empty space is filled with an illustration of a soldier facing a war elephant.

> **BOX 7.3 "KEEP" OPTIONS**
>
> Never split a paragraph between columns and definitely not between pages. If a paragraph traverses a break, just start that paragraph on the next column instead. Your layout program should have a function to do this automatically. Look for a function called "Keep Together" or "Keep with Next." These give you more granular control to force paragraphs to remain intact if they would traverse a column break or a page break. That's much more convenient than manually adding line-returns or adjusting the margins of a text frame.

Hierarchy is the biggest thing I pay attention to. The visual language of a game should have a clear path of understanding and that's often achieved by the hierarchy of typography, symbology, color and shape.

RORY MULDOON

ADDING EXAMPLES

Now that we have the spacing established, we should make more room for visual examples, diagrams, and other supplementary information. In ideal circumstances, insert a visual example after every paragraph of a rulebook, on the assumption that each paragraph has introduced a completely new rules concept.

Explain one rule at a time, without diverging into a tangent or edge-case. Then demonstrate that simpler rule with a clear visual example. Then introduce more nuances or exceptions, each time offering further examples. This creates a recurring rhythm: Introduce, then demonstrate, then elaborate, then demonstrate again. Repeat as often as the rules require until that entire game rule is completely explained, then proceed to the next rule.

At the top of Figure 7.4, you'll see a page from *Colosseum: Emperor's Edition*. This is a good example of a very typical rules presentation. The big header at the top of the page sets the subject of this section, "Phase

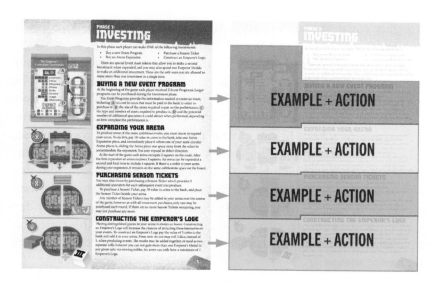

FIGURE 7.4   *Colosseum: Emperor's Edition* (2017).

1: Investing." The rules of this phase are entirely contained within this one page. The first paragraph is a brief introduction of the phase and overview of the four options you have during this phase. The sub-headers are more granular explanations of each of those options. Thankfully, each option had roughly equal amounts of rules text, so a diagram fits beside each sub-header.

At the bottom of Figure 7.4, you'll see the next double-page spread from *Colosseum: Emperor's Edition*, "Phase 2: Acquiring Event Asset Tokens." In this phase, players will participate in an auction until each player has won a set of tokens. This involves several rounds of bidding, winning tokens, and refreshing of tokens in the central market. Unlike the prior phase, this phase's rules text did include a fully written "For Example" section. In fact, that section was long enough to fill almost half a page. I did not attempt to design one giant diagram that shows all of these micro-actions at once. Instead, I broke the text into individual paragraphs, added divider lines, and inserted a smaller example beside each paragraph. This treats the example as a series of smaller moments, with easily discernible differences between each moment.

It's important to highlight the differences in expressing the flow time here. Whereas Phase 1's examples show mutually exclusive forks in the road that can be taken, Phase 2's examples are meant to show a consecutive sequence of events. Now that I look back on this layout with several years of hindsight, I could've made this distinction clearer. I could have given the examples of "Investing" different colored backgrounds so they are clearly different actions, then keep one color background for Phase 2's example. I also could have used different styles of dividing lines for the two different example diagrams, perhaps downward pointed chevrons for Phase 2, showing that you're meant to read it from top-to-bottom as one whole process.

BOX 7.4 SHOWING PLAYERS IN EXAMPLES

It's usually not necessary to depict the actual human players in a gameplay example. If you must, show them as simply as possible and clearly labeled, either "you" and "opponent" or by unique names mentioned in the example text. Try using very short names beginning with A, B, C, and D without rhyming or alliteration.

Walls of text suck. Let the rulebook breathe. Don't crowd the pages with tons of text. It's better to add an extra 4 pages and create some space.

BILL BRICKER

COMPONENTS SECTION

Imagine your reader has just opened their new box and they see your list of components. This acts as a manifest, confirming that the reader has indeed received a complete product. Toward that end, components sections should be a full page or a spread. (In especially small card and dice games, they may fit in half a page on the front cover.)

The components should be neatly organized into a clear structure, with enough space between each component, so that there is no confusion about which pieces belong to which category. They should be individually labeled for ease of reference. In ideal circumstances, a player will be able to take out each piece from the box and immediately know what it's called, how many there should be, and what other related components they should find (Figure 7.5).

Group components by type as follows:

Boards: Show the central game board and any tertiary displays shared by all players. I recommend *not* showing a player board though, since there will be a separate section for components owned by individual players.

Cards: Show an example of one front and one back from each deck. To save space, you can show the back tucked halfway behind the front. Remember to round the corners of your card images so they look professional. If a deck has many slight variants of what the front looks like, don't show them all. Just show one and save granular "anatomy" for a later part of the book.

Tokens: Show one of each type of resource or currency here. I recommend displaying it flat so players know the distinct silhouette of each token along with its art. If you have multiple values of the same resource, like 1VP, 5VP, and 10VP, they can all be grouped tightly together to show their association.

Markers: These are unique components showing general progress along a track, like showing the current round of the game. Some games might keep these under the definition of "token," but I find it useful to have a separate term for them.

FIGURE 7.5   *Seastead* (2020).

Player Components: This is where you show one instance of each of the components that a player will keep in their personal area. This is any component in their player color, such as personal boards, track markers, privacy screens, unique role cards, starting decks, or miniatures.

Within each section, keep the scale of components consistent. So if you're showing a card at 35% actual scale, show ALL cards at 35%. This makes it easier to recognize the difference between a mini card, a poker size card, and a tarot size card. However, you don't need to keep the same magnification between *different* sections. You may show tokens shown at 200% of actual size and game boards shown at 10%. What's important is that players recognize a component on sight.

BOX 7.5 AVOID FORWARD-REFERENCING

Give your book's content enough room to explain enough of a concept when it is most pertinent, and not before. Ideally, you won't need any "forward-referencing" parenthetical notes like "see page XX, then come back here to page YY to continue." That forces the reader to jump around the book unnecessarily. Just explain everything as best you can when it is most relevant, in order. Note that there is an exception to this guideline if the referenced section is immediately visible, like "see next page" or "see next section." In those cases, you can be more lenient about forward-referencing since it doesn't force the reader to jump around the book too much.

If there's any text that can be replaced with images, do it!

LINDSAY DAVIAU

SETUP SECTION

On the next page (or the next spread), you'll see the full game setup with all components at their correct scale to each other, arranged as if they were on a table.

Most often, the graphic designer won't have much editorial authority over how the text is structured. The traditional Setup page keeps text separate from the diagram. One area of the page will be a sequenced list of instructions. Another area will be the corresponding diagram, with small numbered tags around the diagram, each corresponding to each step of the instructions. This traditional Setup is so common that many players and publishers take it for granted. However, it is not always the best way of presenting this type of information.

Instead, borrow some lessons from comic page design. In comics, when a character is speaking, they have a bubble of dialogue near the speaker. Similarly, you can break up the text into small boxes and place each box as close to the corresponding area of the game as possible.

This doesn't mean you have to abandon a specific order to your game setup either. You can still number the text blurbs as you like, ideally arranging them in a clockwise pattern starting from the top left, proceeding around the game area. In any case, it's very helpful to have a visual connection between text and component. It's closer to the natural act of teaching a game and pointing to an area of the table or a particular piece.

If your game has different setup instructions for different player counts, give the most attention to the *ideal* player count. (Most games have such an ideal count, whether publishers care to admit it publicly or not.) Usually any differences can just be noted in the text. If it is necessary to visually show the differences, those alternate setup diagrams can be shown at a much smaller scale. The components can also be simplified into plain silhouettes rather than show the actual art.

Figure 7.6 shows both the traditional and comic styles of Setup diagrams in *Free Radicals*. This game has extremely asymmetric player roles, with each player effectively using their own unique mini-game to interact with a central board. There was one main rulebook that covered the rules for that central area and separate double-sided sheets for each player's individual mini-game rules.

The top spread is the Setup diagram from the main rulebook. The left page shows the Setup instruction text as a numbered list. The diagram below it has circular numbered tags pointing to the corresponding areas of the finished central setup. Step 4 of the Setup asks players to pick which faction they will play, consulting a separate section that describes the general gameplay for each faction's mini-game. Integrating this content into the flow of the Setup text, made it too cluttered. Instead, those overviews are their own facing page on the right side of the spread.

The bottom image shows the Setup diagram from one faction's player aid. In this case, there wasn't enough space to decouple the text from the diagram. Originally the text was formatted as a numbered list, but the setup didn't require a particular order. So I removed that numbering and instead placed each paragraph around the diagram as a small "bubble."

BOX 7.6 HYBRID TRADITIONAL/COMIC SETUP

If you really must keep your text flowing in a standard column, you can still take a half-step toward the "comics" layout. Try using this system of vertical lines and arrows leading from the text to the indicated area of the game diagram. That way you have the clean flow of a pure text document but the visual ease of the "comics" style.

Be a part of the cold playtests, where new players are recruited to read the rules and play the game with no outside help.

KIRK W BUCKENDORF

SETUP TEXT DECOUPLED FROM THE SETUP DIAGRAM

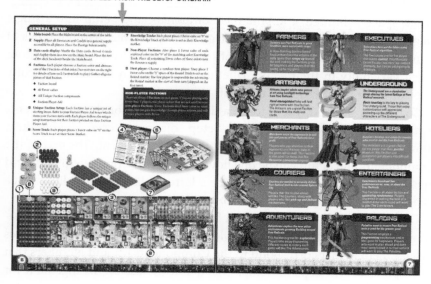

SETUP TEXT BLENDED INTO THE SETUP DIAGRAM

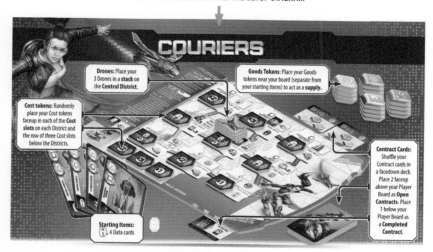

FIGURE 7.6   *Atlantic Robot League* (2022).

MERGING COMPONENTS WITH SETUP

When space is limited, combine the Component and Setup into a single diagram. This usually only works for games with fewer than ten types of components and about 10–15 steps of setup. It's also best for games without much variability in their setup, whether it be for player count, difficulty level, or some other modular element.

To do this method, you'll forgo a dedicated page for the Components section. Instead you'll have the Setup diagram serve double-duty, showing both the game area and each type of component. The text of the Components and Setup will be one flow of text, with Components first and the Setup second. Components will be a **lettered** list taking as little space as possible. The setup will be a **numbered** list.

On the diagram, you'll use small flags or tags floating around the diagram, just like a Traditional Setup style. However, you'll have two categories of flags. Letters that correspond to the Components list and Numbers that correspond to the steps of Setup. This is not the easiest arrangement for players to read, but does save you a lot of space, cutting up to two or three pages, depending on the size of the game.

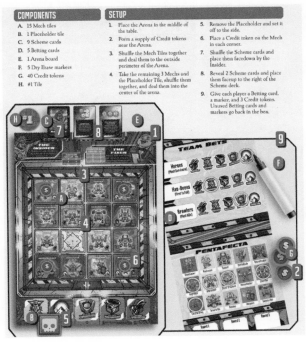

FIGURE 7.7   *Free Radicals* (2022).

Figure 7.7 shows the hybrid layout from *Atlantic Robot League*. This rulebook had to be limited to four pages and they were relatively small pages at that. So to conserve space, Components and Setup are on the same page. The Components list is lettered and the Setup instructions are numbered. In the diagram, letters are in round circles and the numbers in blue squares.

BOX 7.7 PERSONAL SETUP

If your game requires each player to have their own personal area, with their own board, tokens, cards, and so on, do *not* include the player areas in your general setup diagram. Instead, make a separate diagram zoomed in close enough to clearly demonstrate one player's area. This works best if the text is written with a clean division between setting up the central area and a player's personal area.

Highlight important keywords. Add clear and easily understandable sections and headlines. Show components, icons and game situations.

TORBEN RATZLAFF

RULEBOOKS AS GAME BOARDS

There's a small subgenre of board games that use a book as a "board." For some games, a large portion of the rulebook is devoted to a tutorial scenario played directly on its pages.

Krosmaster Arena's tutorial has you play through simple scenarios with short goals on each page spread, literally putting your miniatures and terrain markers on the pre-printed maps. The scenarios increase in complexity until you're ready to graduate to the proper game board.

Gloomhaven: Jaws of the Lion, *Stuffed Fables*, *Sleeping Gods*, and *ISS Vanguard* present new scenarios with every page. Typically new rules are presented in a block of explanatory text beside the map, along with a summary of any special components used for this scenario.

Sagrada Artisans forgoes the conceit of a map, instead just presents different stained glass patterns for you to color in. Each double-page spread offers a different set of tools at your disposal, along with constraints to stay within.

Using a rulebook as a game board is an unconventional approach with some unique considerations.

Binding: Consider how to leave a book open, flat, and stable on a game table. Comb-binding or spiral-binding allows the book to lay completely flat, though some discerning aesthetes may find it unsightly to have a large gap in between the two pages. Traditional staple-binding (also called "saddle-stitched") will require some firm weights to force the pages to lay flat.

Compact Space: By integrating the rulebook and game board into one component, you get space-saving design. This can be beneficial for players with limited table space. However, the size also restricts the complexity of the game board and the scenario. The more complex the scenario, the more text you'll probably need, which in turn competes with the space available to actually play out that same scenario.

Accessibility: You should have all necessary rules visible alongside the playable surface, so players don't have to flip to a previous page for a reminder of basic rules. Scenarios should have few distinct variations on a consistent baseline game system.

Fragility: Rulebooks are typically not designed to withstand the wear and tear of being used as a game board. Over time, frequent folding and unfolding may lead to damage. This may be less of a concern if the game is intended to be "one-time use," but it's hard to shake a board game customer's impulse to protect their games from damage.

Customization: A book-as-board offers changing terrain and a guided experience over time. If you find one book's maps too small, you can add a second book with its own map pages that pair up against the main book's maps. For example, *Bargain Basement Bathysphere* has three maps, each on its own large folded folio (Figure 7.8). The first few scenarios are only played on one of these maps, but as the campaign continues, pairs of maps are put together.

FIGURE 7.8   An early concept for *Bargain Basement Bathysphere*. Each episode of the campaign would be played directly on a comb-bound rulebook. Development would eventually lead us to go in a different direction, but I still liked the concept.

> **BOX 7.8: TIGHTLY BOUND GAMES**
>
> Some games' rules resist being formatted in a linear structure. For example, when the first step of play requires you bid on an auction, but you don't yet know the relative values of each item in the lot. You require additional context to make an informed decision, but if the rulebook keeps trying to dump all that information too soon, it front-loads the rules piecemeal. As the rulebook designer, you must give *just enough* information that is most pertinent to *this* moment in play. Not the whole game all at once, but enough to get the reader/player to the next page of the book, then the next, and the next, trusting that each topic will be fully elaborated in its own due time.

Poor usability can ruin otherwise flawless games, jarring design decisions leave the most sour taste after an otherwise delicious game.

HEIKO GÜNTHER

SUMMARY OF RULEBOOKS

Rulebooks are the voice of the game designer made real. It is the primary conduit between the game designer's head and the game player's table. Yet, it's too often the last thing a game designer wants to deal with. They're occupied as it is just making the game good enough, but then communicating every nuance of strategy in writing feels daunting.

The challenge is only compounded once we accept that people learn in different ways. Linear players would rather use the rulebook as a step-by-step guide through the first couple of games. Referential players hate such hand-holding and would prefer to use the rulebook as an official writ, emerging only to answer any rules questions, then being put away. Visual players would prefer the pages be filled with visual examples unpacked into granular beats. (The list of psychographics could go on.)

One book (or two, or three) won't satisfy every possible learning style that comes to your game. Try to manage your expectations and don't take it too hard if players still struggle with your rulebook even after many rounds of revisions. The best you can do is approach this multi-faceted challenge with good faith, clear intent, and well-practiced skills.

Summary Questions

- What is the visual hierarchy you're showing on each page and every double-page spread?

- How are you using color coding to help players find their most pertinent information when it's needed?

- How have you balanced creating a comprehensive reference with a thematic artifact? How does it inform AND excite?

- Are you sufficiently spotlighting urgent and important rules that ensure the game functions as intended?

- How have you incorporated the techniques of visual storytelling in the layout of play examples and infographics?

- For players who want to learn the game out of the book step-by-step, how much are you forcing them to jump back and forth between different sections?

- Is information presented when it is most pertinent?

- Do you have some pages that are overly dense while others are overly sparse? Have you discussed these problem areas with your Dev team to find ways to parse this information more evenly?

- For players who prefer to use the book as an on-the-fly authoritative rules reference, what visual cues have you included to make reference easy as possible?

- What typographic or visual differences are you using to delineate between types of content, like instruction, flavor, example, appendix, and designer notes?

- Have you discussed with the game designer if there are some interactions and strategies left unstated, so players can discover them on their own?

CHAPTER 8

Boxes and Packaging

A COVER IS A PROMISE

Books were my first entry into professional graphic design. In that business, with razor-thin profits and expensive production, I learned "you shouldn't judge a book by its cover" was the exact opposite of a graphic designer's goal. If a customer can't discern the game's theme, mood, play style, and other key selling points from the cover, then that is a lost sale and a bit less job security for the whole team.

I learned this even before online sales and tiny stamp-size product images became the predominant shopping experience, so now it's even more important for a package to make a good first-glance impression. So no, the true axiom to follow is this: A cover is a promise.

Customers will judge the book (or game) by its cover whether they acknowledge it or not. So the graphic designer's job is to make that judgment as accurate and enticing as possible. You're setting a bread crumb trail from a first impression to a final sale. Every step in between should be carefully considered and discussed among all decision-makers. Personal taste and subjective whim will definitely play a factor in this process, but it's important that all team members at least accept that they share a few common goals:

DOI: 10.1201/9781003453772-9

- Honestly convey this game's qualities.
- Target the audience who will enjoy this game.
- Sell this game to that audience.

Board game packaging is not just a shipping container. It's an introduction to the customer, so they know "this game is for me." You should already be familiar with the game's key themes, components, and nuances. You'll ensure its outward appearance meets or exceeds the expectations of the intended players. With luck, you'll even find unexpected appeal *beyond* your target audience, growing your customer base beyond what you had initially anticipated.

All the prior lessons in color, iconography, and typography will come into play as you design your game box. In addition, this chapter will discuss:

- Selecting a box type to suit the components, market pricing, and customer expectations.
- Identifying visual trends so your game stands out in its category.
- Designing a graphic brand that reflects the game's personality.
- Formatting the back of the box to present a good snapshot of the game's selling points.
- Properly accounting for wraps, folds, and other production constraints.

In Figure 8.1, we see three very different box covers. *Clash of Cultures: Monumental Edition* promises epic conflict between historical civilizations. In particular, the publisher wanted to have a war elephant on the cover as a promise to customers that this edition of the game included elephant miniatures, which had been missing in the original base game. The cover of *Jokkmokk: The Winter Market* shows an idyllic Swedish village fair illustrated in a much simpler folk style. This promises a calm, friendly play experience. The cover of *Bequest* depicts two supervillains seemingly coming to an agreement, but are secretly holding weapons behind their backs. This promises a more vicious and sneaky time.

Always give your illustrators a template […] so they understand how the box will be laid out.

KIRK W BUCKENDORF

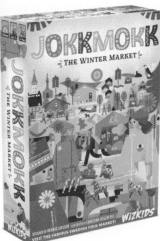

FIGURE 8.1   Box design for *Clash of Cultures: Monumental Edition*; *Jokkmokk: The Winter Market, and Bequest*.

WHO USES THE BOX, AND HOW?

The box design's success should be measured by how well it serves as a tool for each user.

Publishers spend a LOT of money up front due to tooling costs, art expenses, and overseas shipping. The easiest way to recoup that cost is to sell to a distributor, who orders units by the thousands. Publishers will present their upcoming catalog at distributor events where representatives can take a close look at the box, inspect the components, and of course play the game.

Meanwhile, the **Distributors** who order bulk quantities of games don't want those boxes gathering dust on their warehouse shelves. They offer a degree of curation to help the retailer sort through each month's new releases. Some larger publishers bypass distribution by directly contacting larger retailers, but most publishers and stores are too small and numerous for them all to talk to each other directly. The distributor acts as the inter-mediary between both parties, but in that role they're also a gatekeeper between the publisher and retailer.

Next, **Retailers** have a store to run and bills to pay. Once this meant only operating an actual brick-and-mortar store, but now they compete against online-only retailers also serving the games market. In response, the physical stores have branched out to offer their own online ordering with competitive discounts. Their aim is to present their inventory to the customer looking to buy for themselves or as a gift for someone else. The retailers decide how the product is displayed.

Even then the sales cycle isn't over yet! The game's **Owner** just bought this hot new game they're excited to play, but they have to convince their friends to spend their limited leisure time learning an entirely new game's rules. Just imagine that owner, holding the box out hoping someone will be interested in playing. It definitely helps if the box looks exciting, fun, and intriguing enough to be worth that investment of time and energy.

This is why you'll sometimes see dodgy decisions in box design. What appeals to a distributor may not look great on a home shelf. What makes a tasteful, elegant addition to a home collection may be drab to a retailer's eye. Thankfully, there are some compromises that help:

- **Stickers on Shrinkwrap:** Imagine you're shopping for a game as a gift. You don't know games, so it would certainly help to see shiny

FIGURE 8.2   Boxes for *Seastead, Dice Conquest*, and two editions of *Kodama: The Tree Spirits*.

gold seals guaranteeing that the game is a hit. Adhering those seals to the outside of the shrink wrap won't mar the box itself.

- **Box Sleeves:** Though it adds some extra cost, higher-end games have retail-friendly outer sleeves wrapping like a dust jacket around the entire box. Then the box itself has a much more minimal design that isn't quite so loud.

- **Targeted Panels:** You can design just one- or two-side panels with all the loud, poppy retailer graphics to draw attention, like awards blurbs and high-contrast colors. The remaining sides can appeal to the collector, with practical information and clear legible text.

In Figure 8.2, you'll see the *Seastead* box I designed for WizKids. The WizKids trade dress typically doesn't call for player count to be displayed on the front cover, but this is strictly a two-player game so the publisher felt it was important to emphasize that. To further support this, the cover art features two characters serving distinct roles in the operation of a seafaring colony. Any other characters are depicted very small, barely noticeable among the other textures.

The box for *Dice Conquest* also broke the usual WizKids trade dress for entirely different reasons. The publisher wanted to showcase the custom set of dice that comes included in the game. The box itself was relatively small already, so that forced the game title to be somewhat squished along the left. We improvised a composition with the large blue dragon along the top, since that's the final boss in the game. It made sense to give him top billing.

The original box for *Kodama: the Tree Spirits* was packaged in a horizontally oriented box to emphasize the natural landscape themes. Unfortunately, retailers reported those boxes would sometimes be hidden behind taller boxes on the shelf. When the game was picked up by a new publisher, they kept the same art but rotated the composition vertically so the title could be larger and higher.

BOX 8.1 A NOTE ON LANGUAGE

If you're aiming for a worldwide audience, your game's title and key information may need to be presented in multiple languages. Consider how your design will appeal to and inform customers in different regions. Whether due to legal mandates or simple practical budgeting, your box may need to include space for 2–5 different translations of the game's back text, legal disclaimers, and title.

> Keep the box as small as possible without making your publisher wince. [Publishers] think that a bigger box will sell better. They will not believe you that this does not matter a lot when selling online.
>
> HEIKO GÜNTHER

IDENTIFYING VISUAL TRENDS

Markets have a love–hate relationship with originality. To some extent, you need to be familiar with what a customer expects a game of a certain type to look like, yet you also need it to stand out from that category somehow. Identifying visual trends helps you navigate a very narrow path between satisfying expectations and spotlighting novelty. Try to be clear-eyed about your game's best attributes and avoid assuming your game is utterly original. Analyze your game's key features, then find as many other games are out there with those same attributes.

In Figure 8.3, you'll see cover designs for two editions of *Ascending Empires*. The 2011 edition foregrounded a lone soldier overseeing a planetary attack, which sold the game as primarily a combat-driven experience. That implicitly grouped it with crunchier space campaign games which all depicted similar scenes of space war, usually set against a black starry background. About 15 years later, I inverted the color scheme to be mainly white, as a literal contrast against the other games in this category. I was targeting the shopper who wanted a big space game, but with a more streamlined and elegant game system. This is one simple example of identifying a visual trend, i.e. "space games have black space backgrounds," and take a calculated risk to stand out from that trend, i.e. "use a white background to stand apart, but still showcase spaceships and starfighters." Calculated or not, it is still a risk, so do your research on your game's category and assess how much you can safely stray from those existing trends.

On BoardGameGeek, run a quick search and filter your results by mechanisms, genre, and themes. Then rank those results by various user ratings, ownership, and release dates. You're looking for a few trends in these searches.

Color: Look for an average color scheme across the game covers. Squint your eyes and blur your vision, removing all the fine details. See what color seems to dominate your particular type of game. You'll probably find that nature-themed games trend toward greens and yellows. Western themed games use more muted leathery earthtones. Austere

FIGURE 8.3   Top: The original cover of *Ascending Empires* had a dark logo against a dark background in an irregular font, which impeded legibility. The scene of planetary bombardment emphasized combat, but the game is as much about city-building and space exploration. Bottom: WizKids' proposed cover for a new "Zenith Edition." The new edition is mostly white, which is unusual for a space-themed game that usually has a space-black cover. The circular framing element represents the disc-based dexterity mechanics of the game's combat, a unique feature of this game compared to others in the genre. A large mothership and fighter escort pop out of the frame, but are not in direct combat, since this game is not only about direct action. (Note: This game has since been published by Play to Z Games, not WizKids.)

games lean toward stark minimalism OR hard-pivot to bold colors exaggerate the theme.

Subject: Generally, whoever is featured on your cover is taken as a proxy for the player, demonstrating the central "verb" of the game. Direct-confrontation games tend to show grim combatants in high-stakes struggle amidst fire and destruction. Cooperative games tend to show groups of competent professionals huddled together on a problem or looking outward toward a greater unseen threat. Family games show zany antics. What are the subjects doing on the covers you see?

Art Style: Where does the cover illustration fall in a range between realism and abstraction? Realism would be a 100% accurate rendering of a person or scene, like a photograph from a historical archive. Abstraction would not be representational at all, like geometric shapes or floods of colors and textures. Most cover art is somewhere in between, with cinematic flourishes, painterly details, cartoonish proportions, and selective editing to express a certain perspective.

Shapes, Borders, and Motifs: In the chapter on card design (Chapter 4), we discussed how certain border shapes are often associated with different genres. If you're researching a futuristic sci-fi game, you might find a lot of rigid straight lines randomly interrupted by 45° angles. If it's an optimistic future, those borders would be filled with clean brushed steel or just plain white. If it's a dystopian future, the metal texture would be corroded and some of the straight edges would be nicked and weathered. What visual commonalities do you see in your search?

Unusual Packaging: While the majority of strategy and hobby games stick to reliable rectilinear boxes, occasionally a game will come out with an unusual form factor. Party games might come in cloth pouches. Dice games can be sold as cardboard tubes. Small card games can be sold in blister packs that include a velvet drawstring pouch for storage. In all cases, these eye-catching packages sacrifice easy display and risk annoying local store owners.

To be honest, your customer won't be conscious of *why* a certain game looks like an epic fantasy, historical simulation, or wacky party. They just get a vibe. It's up to you to know what creates that vibe at a granular level.

People might only look at the cover for 3 seconds, and you want them to come away with one strong impression. Prioritize your message.
LINDSAY DAVIAU

BASIC SPECS OF A BOX

For now we'll assume you're designing a traditional two-part box with lid and base. Here are some basic guidelines to follow for your design (Figure 8.4(a, b)).

Height and Width: Make sure your box is at least 15mm taller and wider than your largest component. Usually that largest component will be your

FIGURE 8.4 (a) Top lid for WizKids box trade dress template established in 2021. This provided a consistent starting point for designing each game box, rather than starting from scratch with every new game. (b) The bottom lid of the WizKids trade dress. This established cross-promotion spaces on the four side panels of the inner lid. The three "hooks" along the side gave the marketing and events team the basis for pitching a game to various channels. The placeholder text also gave the writing team a simple template for how to describe each game.

FIGURE 8.4 (Continued)

folded game board, but it may also be your unpunched sheets or even just the rulebook. For example, if your largest component is the game board that folds to a 150mm square, then the box should be at least 165mm tall and wide.

Depth: It may be difficult to estimate how deeply your components will stack up inside the box, so consult with your manufacturer for how they recommend to efficiently pack your contents. The base will be 2–5mm narrower, shorter, and shallower than the lid, so account for that in your estimates. Generally, you can assume the following depths for the following components:

- 1 Sheet of Punchboard: 3mm, but may need more space to prevent damage.
- 50 Cards: 25–35mm, depending on stock thickness and coating.
- 16 Page rulebook: 3–10mm, depending on the paper weight.

3mm Corner Edges: Maintain a minimum of 3mm clearance wherever the artwork folds between the visible faces. (In total this is actually 6mm of clearance, with the fold at the center of that margin.) For example, while our cover artwork may flood across the entire box lid, the game title, publisher identity, and tagline never get closer than 3mm to the edges.

18mm Outer Bleeds: The artwork for a base and lid is printed on adhesive paper that is pressed against a blank cardboard shell. To maintain that adhesion, the artwork needs an additional 18mm of bleed so the paper can fold into the inner surface of the shell.

Resolution and Color: As always, make sure your artwork is all at least 300dpi and CMYK color mode. Some printers may also request that your black text be plain black, with no cyan, magenta, or yellow in the mix.

File Format: When I deliver my box files, page 1 is the box lid die line alone, centered on the page. Page 2 is the full lid artwork without the die line, but aligned to match the die line's position exactly. Page 3 is the box base die line alone, centered on the page. Page 4 is the full base artwork, again without the die line but aligned to match the die line's position. Separating the die line from the artwork lets the factory create their molds to cut the paper properly.

Ask for a template from the manufacturers if you haven't been supplied one.

RORY MULDOON

ANATOMY OF A BOX COVER

Maintaining a clear visual hierarchy is important for an impactful cover that serves its function (Figure 8.5). The following is the most common content you'll include on a cover, in order of most important to least important.

The game title should be big and legible even if the cover is shrunk to a thumbnail.

Art should accurately depict the vibe of the game.

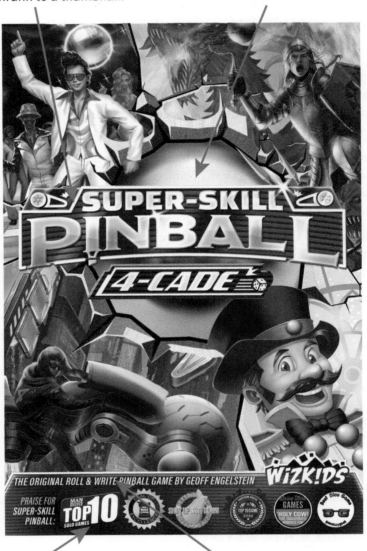

Awards lend credibility but can clutter the design.

Summarize the premise of the game in one brief sentence.

FIGURE 8.5   Cover of *Super-Skill Pinball* (2020).

Title: Maintain at least 5mm of lower contrast around the title, so it really pops. This is especially important for unusual words like "Terraforming," "Anno," or "Imperium." You don't want any busy artwork coming too close to the title, obstructing the letterforms. You may even want to widen that margin to a full centimeter in the case of vertical orientations where the logo is shrunken to a fraction of its usual size. (Needless to say, you should be using a font that is easy to read as well.)

Art: The basics of art direction are worth a whole book of their own, so this is only a cursory overview. Your box art will be the public face of your game and it's important that it accurately represents your game's intended experience. If this is your first time art directing for a box cover, here are some very safe choices for a reliable cover. First, depict the main activity of your game, like building, fighting, or co-operating. (For example, in a two-player competitive game, it makes sense to have a bisected composition with opposing factions or armies facing each other in hostility.) Second, if players represent individual actors in the game's world, depict those characters engaging in the game's main activity. (For example, if certain characters have unique powers, then show those characters using those powers.) Following those two basic guidelines will result in a clear and simple cover, though not exactly groundbreaking.

Credits: Crediting the designer on the front cover is standard practice for all modern board games. Account for the extra room for multiple designers. If your game has a lead artist, include their credits on the front cover as well, near or below the game designer. Finally, make sure you're correctly using any non-English characters that the designers may have in their name, like é, ç, or ø.

(Optional) Tagline: This is a one-line description of your game, like "The Game of Global Domination" or "The Action-Packed Roll & Write Pinball Game." This is a great opportunity to coin your own category. For example, *Sushi Go* uses the tagline "The Pick-and-Pass Card Game" to introduce the concept of a drafting game to a broader audience.

Publisher Identity: For most publishers, you should keep the company logo and branding relatively modest. At WizKids, the current board game trade dress keeps our logo on the bottom-right corner, embedded in a footer that spans the bottom of the cover.

(Optional) Game Stats: Some publishers prefer to show the player count, age range, and play time directly on the front cover. This is generally for games aimed at very young players, so be careful that you're not unintentionally giving that impression for your more complex game.

Complement the illustration and don't compete with it.

JACOBY O'CONNOR

ANATOMY OF A SIDE PANEL

The side panels are kind of like four miniature covers. Since your game is likely to be stored with one side panel facing out, it's important to treat each side as a chance to sell the game (Figure 8.6).

Title: Follow the same principles as the title design on the front cover.

Game Stats: Unlike the cover, I consider it mandatory to include the player/age/time on every side panel. This is especially the case if you don't include the stats on the front cover.

Publisher Identity: While I prefer to keep the publisher brand modest, it should still be consistent. If a loyal customer buys several games from your catalog, it's courteous to put all the game stats and publisher logos in the same position across those boxes. This is especially important for multiple games within the same franchise.

Orientation: Rotate each panel's layout to accommodate vertical or horizontal storage. Ideally, one long panel and one short panel are horizontal while one long panel and one short panel are vertical.

Vertical storage means the game is shelved like a book. Most games have fairly long titles that don't lend themselves well to vertical orientations. You

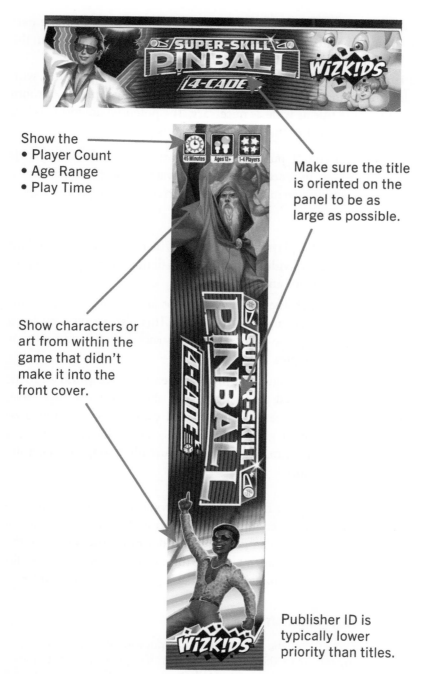

Show the
• Player Count
• Age Range
• Play Time

Make sure the title is oriented on the panel to be as large as possible.

Show characters or art from within the game that didn't make it into the front cover.

Publisher ID is typically lower priority than titles.

FIGURE 8.6   Side panels of *Super-Skill Pinball* (2020).

may need to design a tall "stacked" version of the title logo for these particular use-cases. Still, the art will likely be much more prominent than the title, which means it should be especially recognizable at a glance.

Horizontal storage means the game is stacked among other games, with the side panel being short and wide. Thankfully this gives plenty of room to make the game title as wide as necessary. The potential downside is less room for any artwork, but that's an acceptable risk.

Art: As a general rule, I put the following artwork on the side panels flanking the title logo. In order of priorities—Avatars, Locations, Creatures. In all instances, emphasize the variety of experience the player can expect when they play.

a. AVATARS tell the players who they are in the game. These might represent literal individuals in the game's fiction, or simply be representative mascots for an in-game faction.

b. LOCATIONS pitch the game as more of an adventure tale, promising unusual vistas and exotic locales. This also works well for a civilization-level game where you construct major landmarks or advanced technologies.

c. CREATURES can range from mythical beasts to real-world animals. For a combat-focused game, it's best to show the most aggressive, predatory looking creatures. (Teeth and claws!) For a subdued or ecologically oriented game, it's better to show the creatures in a sedate and calm posture. (More like a nature photograph or scientific journal illustration.)

If your game's only art is the front cover, then you can simply treat the side panel as a narrow or wider version of the front cover. In Photoshop or some other editing program, you can crop layers and arrange them to fit in the available space on the side panel. I reserve this as a last resort since I prefer to show MORE with a side panel rather than just repeat the front cover.

BOX 8.3 TITLE PLACEMENT

The narrower your panel, the higher you should put your title. For example, on a tall skinny rectangle, the title should be in the upper third so it's the first thing the customer reads from top to bottom.

The left and right side will need to have art that will stand on its own, vertically on the shelf. Then the top and bottom half should have artwork that displays horizontally.

KIRK W BUCKENDORF

ANATOMY OF A BOX BASE

Imagine you are working at a convention booth. An interested customer picks up a box and asks you, "Hey, what's this game like?" It's such a broad question. Do you focus on the mechanics? The victory condition? Aaaack! So you look at the back of the box, desperate for some lifeline. Oh no, it's just a display of components with a dense paragraph about the game's fictional setting. Not even a tagline to summarize the core idea of game-play! While you're skimming the text for some key points, the customer has walked away. Oh dear.

This is a dramatic example, but it happens all the time. If you're lucky enough that a potential customer has been enticed enough to look at the back of the box, this is your chance to close the deal or lose the sale. The back of the box should present a good snapshot of the game's selling points. Here's the order of priority I recommend for all the back content (Figure 8.7).

Summary: This is the block of text explaining the key points of the game. Lower your expectations of how much reading a customer is willing to do. You have to be a ruthless editor. Keep it under 100 words, or about 3–5 sentences. Answer the main questions of the game's premise. Write in a direct, second-person declarative voice: Who are you? How do you win? What's in your way?

Overview Diagram: Put together a diagram of your board, cards, and other components that show a typical game in action. Try to make the game state match what would be permitted by the rules. Aside from that basic accuracy, make the game look as exciting as possible. Add special effects like arrows to indicate movement or starbursts to show physical impact between components.

Stat Block: As with the side panels, it's important that a potential customer easily find the player count, age range, and game length.

Summarize the pitch for the game.

Form a three-part hook describing the main actions or premise of the game.

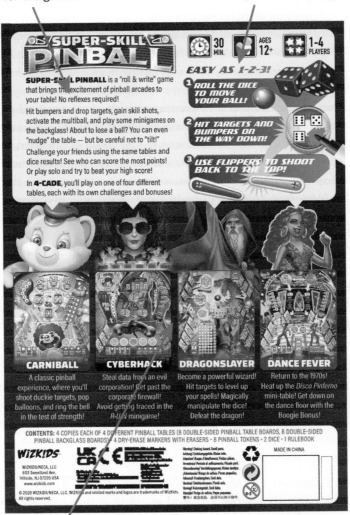

Showcase the components in their best light.

Reserve space for any necessary legal markings.

FIGURE 8.7   Box base of *Super-Skill Pinball* (2020).

3 Hooks: I always include a sidebar of three panels that outline the basic ideas of the game. If the game is designed for a mass market audience and the rules are simple enough, we will try to summarize the core gameplay in three steps. (See Super-Skill Pinball.) If the game is too big and complex to summarize the literal in-game actions in three steps, then we'll go more broad and highlight three interesting hooks of the game. (See Sidereal Confluence.)

Contents: List all the components included in the box, such as boards, cards, pawns, etc. Make the quantities as accurate as possible, especially for cards and three-dimensional components. In the case of small tokens whose quantities might shift up and down over the course of the graphic design process, you can list the minimum guaranteed quantity and a plus sign, like "100+ Health Tokens, 20+ Gold Coins."

Credits: If you have not credited the game designer or lead artist on the front cover, you should at least do so on the back cover.

Legal Stuff: Your mandatory box markings will vary greatly depending on your regional market.

- **Location:** Disclose where your game was manufactured, like "Made in Mexico."

- **Contact Info:** You may need to include your publisher's mailing contact information, website, and/or phone number. You may also need to include similar info for any localization partners, shipping affiliates, or licensors.

- **Minimum Age:** You may need to repeat the game's intended minimum age in plain text. Make sure it matches what's in your stat block! It's easy to forget to keep them synchronized.

- **Safety:** Your box may need to include safety and testing indicia for the UK, Europe, or other territories. Each has its own mandatory disclosures, so make sure you're obeying them all.

- **IP Marks:** Include trademark, registration, and copyright disclaimers required for the game. Your publisher's contracts and licensing partners will dictate the terms that must be used in these disclaimers.

- **Barcode:** The entire distribution retail system relies on barcodes and "Stock-Keeping Unit" or "SKU" numbers to accurately track inventory. Place your barcode somewhere easily findable, but where it won't interfere with the general sales pitch for the game. Your publisher should provide you with the game's UPC/EAN13 barcode. A barcode should be around 30mm wide, but may be cropped to as thin as 15mm tall. DO NOT stretch the barcode.

- **Lot Space**: Keep at least 5mm of clear white space beside your barcode so the factory can print a lot number. This lot number is how all parties can identify the source of mishandled or misprinted units in case they have to be recalled.

We've begun adding a 3-step how-to-play on the back of the box. I think that's a great selling point and is even more important than showing all the components.

BILL BRICKER

THREE TIPS FOR WRITING A SUMMARY

If you'll excuse the brief digression into editorial guidelines, I have some basic tips for writing a punchy summary of your game.

Summarize in the First Sentence. Tell the player in one sentence who they are in the game's fiction, what they do, and perhaps what's in their way. Phrase this in the direct language in second-person tense. For some examples, look at the summaries currently on BoardGameGeek for the most popular games in their rankings.

- *Twilight Struggle*: Relive the Cold War and rewrite history in an epic clash between the USA and USSR.
- *Wingspan*: Attract a beautiful and diverse collection of birds to your wildlife preserve.
- *Great Western Trail*: Wrangle your herd of cows across the Midwest prairie and deliver it to Kansas City.

Focus on Verbs. Focus on what the player will do in the game. Note how the three summaries above each begin with an action phrase. "Relive" sells

Twilight Struggle to history buffs. "Attract" emphasizes the beautiful art-work in Wingspan. "Wrangle" distinctly evokes the old west. Here are a few more examples that lean even harder into verbs.

- *Puerto Rico 1897*: Compete against other newly independent farmers to hire workers, sell crops, and build island infrastructure.
- *Race for the Galaxy*: Colonize, develop, and conquer alien worlds while taking advantage of your opponent's actions.
- *Clank!*: Claim your treasures without attracting the dragon in this deck-building dungeon race.

Limit the Use of Proper Nouns. Many games are set in original fantasy and sci-fi settings with all sorts of unique concepts, each of them with Capitalized Names To Emphasize Their Significance. However, that's all gibberish without some basic grounding. Here are some examples from games with rich lore that doesn't clutter the basic pitch.

- *Netrunner*: Control a megacorporation or become a cyberpunk hacker in an asymmetric cat-and-mouse game.
- *Aeon's End*: Reach your full magical potential to defend the last remnants of humanity from terrible monsters.
- *Twilight Imperium*: Trade and struggle to expand a starfaring empire across the galaxy.

Keep Text Short. This is not the space to go into extensive details about deep interactions. Notice how in the Pandemic box, the text never says "spend 5 cards of a kind and visit the CDC to cure a disease." That is simply shown in a diagram. The text itself just says "discover the cure for the disease." Also, try to avoid any gamer jargon. Even something as seem-ingly ubiquitous as "build your engine," will be very esoteric to the casual customer.

Close with Goals. This is the first question most casual customers want to know. In Fingerguns at High Noon, the goal is to just survive by not being targeted by your opponents. In Diamonds, you want to have the most crystals. Among Thieves was the slight variation on this format since it doesn't focus on the victory condition. Instead, we decided to close with the prisoners' dilemma inherent in the game as that was the more interesting hook for sales.

The back of the box needs to help sell the game. […] I hate when I just get one piece of art and some thematic text. I want to see the components, know what the gameplay is like, and see the game in action.

TONY MASTRANGELI

COMMON PACKAGES

Unless you're doing something really unique for your game's shelf presence, your package will typically fall into one of four types:

Two-Part Boxes are the most common board game package, engineered for durability and efficient storage. This style of box consists of a lid and a slightly smaller base inserted within the lid. The base box offers you some extra room to add secondary trade dress that will only be visible when the box is opened. This might be an opportunity for a bio about the game's designer, some guidelines for storing the components, or just general lore about the game's setting. The inside of the lid or base can also be printed upon, though this is less common in modern games and likely to be limited to one color of ink (Figure 8.8).

Tuckboxes are excellent for small card games, though much less durable than a two-part box. They consist of a single sheet of cardstock folded and glued to create a rectangle that tightly holds the card deck and other incidental components. The primary opening is a large flap along one edge that tucks into the box, using friction to keep it in place. There is a perception that a tuckbox commands a smaller price, so it's been underutilized in today's market. However, as customers become more conscious of their personal budgets and a publisher's ecologically sustainable business practices, perhaps tuckboxes will make a return (Figure 8.9).

Blister Packs are a transparent plastic shell adhered to a rigid sheet of cardstock, like you might find for a child's toy. On a spectrum between customer satisfaction and retailer convenience, blisters lean heavily in favor of the retailer. They can be shelved with other games or hung on a space-efficient rack. Blisters don't leave behind any reusable packaging for the customer to keep on their home shelf, unless they include some kind of

FIGURE 8.8   Two-part box template from *WizKids*.

FIGURE 8.9 Tuckbox design template from *WizKids*.

flat-packed tuckbox, cardboard tube, or cloth bag. Otherwise, these packages are best for expansion content, where it's assumed the customer already has a larger box with room for these extra components. When you're designing

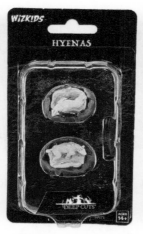

FIGURE 8.10   Blister pack design from *WizKids* Deep Cuts line of miniatures.

a blister pack, remember that the blister shell and its contents will obscure a large portion of the backing card. Keep any critical logos or indicia very far from the blister area (Figure 8.10).

Tins are solid metal boxes with a short lid nested onto a larger base. The advantage of tins is that they can be easily embossed or debossed to add a slight 3-D element to the cover art. They're also very good at protecting their contents. However, any dents or dings can create permanent damage and that may cause a retailer to discount those units, resulting in less profit for the publisher. It's fair to expect up to 10% of your print run to experience some degree of damage, so you may need to produce that many extra units to compensate (Figure 8.11).

Tubes are a very special case where the packaging is part of the game's pitch. *Martian Dice* and *Zombie Dice* are packaged in hard cardboard shipping tubes, emphasizing their portability. *Tenzi* packs dozens of dice into a skinny plastic tube that can be hung on a retailer's peg board. The abstract two-player game Pente was once sold as a long thin tube, but that required the board to be made of a thin pliant material like cloth or vinyl. This does create a very convenient and economical form factor, but isn't practical for most board games. For example, the original edition of Junk Orbit became quite a hefty barrel when it was all assembled. In almost all cases, even if a game was once sold in a tube, it eventually gets repackaged in a more traditional box for a more economical printing (Figure 8.12).

FIGURE 8.11   Tin box packaging of the original edition of *Timeline* (2013).

FIGURE 8.12   Tube packaging for the original edition of *Junk Orbit* (2018).

Cloth Bags are a lovely item when they're made from good material and embroidered with a tasteful design. However, they're very delicate, so they're usually sold within another package listed above. For example, the game *Wonderland* uses very few cards and no other components. For some added value, Renegade added a velvet bag where the cards could be safely stored. The cards and bag were all packaged in a standard two-part box (Figure 8.13).

Button Shy Games's signature is producing small card games in plastic wallets that can fit up to about 36 cards. The games are usually only 18 cards, so the extra capacity is filled by an accordion-folded rules leaflet. In order to keep the production as economical as possible, they hand-assemble every copy of every game on their own. This indie spirit has earned Button Shy a well-deserved reputation for customer service, high quality, and innovative experimentation (Figure 8.14).

FIGURE 8.13   Cloth bag in *Wonderland* (2018).

FIGURE 8.14   Wallet package for *Anthelion: Conclave of Power* (2019).

The right package aligns the publisher's sales goals, the audience's expectations, and the retailer's necessities. Consult with all your stakeholders to find the right balance between all these interests.

Create mock-boxes of your games so you can hold them and see how they sit on shelves.
JACOBY O'CONNOR (RACCOON TYCOON, MOSAIC)

Keep an open mind when taking feedback and making revisions. [...] At work, we give feedback to make something better, not to break each other down.
ESTEFANIA RODRIGUEZ

COMPONENT TRAYS

For larger boxes with lots of components, it's standard practice to provide some kind of structured internal storage to contain all the bits. Because they must fit the components exactly, there is little wiggle room for your technical tolerances. Consult closely with your manufacturer and publisher to ensure all component counts and sizes have been correctly tallied. Any errors could result in an unusable tray and a waste of resources.

A typical component tray has a set of "wells," or deep depressions that can contain all components of a certain size. In some cases, particularly delicate pieces demand their own individual wells. Usually cards get stacked up and stored into a deck, though some games will subdivide that space with extra thick divider cards that have a labeled tab. Dice and tokens are most often commingled into a single bowl. Game boards are usually held stable by slightly shallower impressions along the top edge of the component tray, letting the boards seal in the loose bits in their respective spaces.

While you want to ensure that the trays are designed to securely hold each component in its designated place, you must also make it easy for players to remove and return components. For cards, this means making the wells about 5mm taller and wider than the actual card dimensions, or adding an extra-large thumbhole, or slightly angling the bottom of the well.

Your tray will most likely either be made from a "vacuform" plastic sheet or a folded cardboard sheet.

"Vacuform" is short for vacuum forming (Figure 8.15). It involves heating a plastic sheet until it becomes pliable, then pressing it against a hard mold with a vacuum where it solidifies into its intended shape. Each indentation

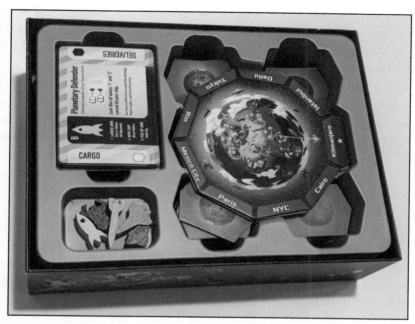

FIGURE 8.15 Vacuum formed tray from *Junk Orbit*. Folded cardboard divider from *Sundae Split*.

can weaken the overall integrity of the sheet, so you usually need some space between each well to reduce stress. This helps make sure no cracks appear where the tension is greatest. This is a popular option since it allows so much fine contour control to accommodate custom shapes. It's also resistant to moisture and mold problems.

Cardboard trays are very large sheets of cardstock that are cut and folded along a pattern to create walls within the box base. Unlike vacuum forming, cardboard can be printed with full CMYK color so you can add some thematic details to make your unboxing experience feel more special. Since the walls can be as thin as folded cardstock, this option is great for small box games. However, your compartments will be limited to rigid straight lines and sharp angles, not curves or bowls.

Pressed or molded pulp is composed of paper fiber shaped into bowls and wells, similar to a vacuum formed tray. The material is usually sourced from recycled paper or cardboard waste. They can also be recycled to form new materials, which makes it a very sustainable option. While cheaper and more ecologically friendly than plastics, it can be quite vulnerable to moisture and mold. You may need to take extra measures to control the humidity during transit. For example, molded trays can be dipped or sprayed with wax to seal them. This is a good option when you need extremely thick walls for your trays to protect very heavy parts.

Note that whichever option you choose, some especially dedicated customers will inevitably replace the tray with their own homemade or artisan-created version that suits their needs better. With that possibility in mind, I favor the cardboard tray option as a way to avoid creating plastic waste.

Everything should fit neatly.

MIKE MARKOWITZ

STAT BLOCKS

A board game box should show the number of players the game requires, the recommended age range for those players, and how long the game takes to play. Those three attributes are what the average customer wants to see right away (Figure 8.16). It's easiest to use generic icons for these concepts,

FIGURE 8.16   Time, age, and player pictograms of different games. Left to right, top to bottom: *Atlantic Robot League, Bequest, Blob Party, Fantasy Realms, Greece Lightning, Jokkmokk, Publish or Perish: Wiñay Kawsay, Rebuilding Seattle, Sidereal Confluence, Tragedy Looper, Trail Story: America, Unboxed, Yosemite,* and a generic universal set of pictograms. Far Bottom: Pictograms from *Bargain Basement Bathysphere* including an additional "Scenarios" section.

but I like to give them some personality that fits the game's theme. Here are some tips!

Time: Use a circular icon to evoke a clock face or a sun. If you can't figure out a circular icon that fits the game theme, it's safest to default to an hourglass.

Age Range: Show two differently sized subjects from the game. The larger one represents an older player and the small one a younger player. I sometimes take character art from the game and make them blank silhouettes. If your game doesn't have characters per se, you can use inanimate objects or animals to represent age.

Number of Players: Normally you'll see this represented by players at a table, sometimes in thematic costumes. However, I prefer to get more figurative by just showing around four subjects of any kind. The actual number of subjects I show is what the publisher and designer feel are the optimal player count.

Placement: Those icons should be clearly visible as the box is displayed on a shelf or on its side. Some publishers refrain from putting these icons on the front of the box so as not to tarnish their expensive cover art, but at the very least it should be on the side panels. At WizKids, we put the icons on two opposite side panels and on the back of the box. This leaves two cleaner side panels and a front cover if the retailer wishes to display the box in a different orientation.

Additional Info: Besides these three pieces of information, your game may have additional details of interest to a potential customer.

- In *Bargain Basement Bathysphere*, we wanted to highlight that it was a full 20-scenario campaign for a single player, so we added a small book icon to the other three standard pictograms. This might be useful for story-driven or "legacy" games as well.
- In an "escape" or "puzzle" style game, you might want to show the relative difficulty level. A brain can represent "mental challenge" or a skull representing "deadliness," but I prefer "signal" bars like you would see on your phone screen.

BOX 8.4 AGE TESTING

When a minimum age is very low, the game may require more stringent safety testing to be deemed legally appropriate for young players. That regulatory testing is at the publisher's expense, so sometimes it's easier to just cut off the minimum age at 13 or 14, even if a smart 10-year-old could play it just as well.

The box is a 3 dimensional shape, use that to your benefit. Understand FLGS display games in different ways and key information should always be prominently displayed.

TODD SANDERS

Publishers sometimes fear that a strict player count or inconvenient time span will lose them a potential sale. As a result, there is some "vanity sizing" in this info. Player counts inflate. Estimated durations shrink. All regardless of how the game is best experienced. So if I could offer a few requests to the industry as a whole, I'd like to put forward the following.

Be Accurate (as possible): You may have a great game for up to 3 players, but only so-so for up to 6. Most of the time, this will be listed as a 2–6-player game with no further details. I request that player counts be narrowed to their optimum or that the expanded player counts actually scale well. If neither is possible, then just be straightforward about which player counts are "Recommended."

Be Accessible: Use icons and pictures in addition to plain text. The back of a box can especially be intimidating if it's a wall of text. Thankfully the industry as a whole typically does a good job of communicating the core concepts visually as well as textually. In many cases, the information is presented in a language-neutral format as well.

Be Findable: This is probably the easiest request to fulfill. Please make game info as readily available as possible. No matter where I turn the box, I'd like to see the game info immediately readable. I understand wanting to maintain the artistic integrity of the front of the box, so you can keep that clear if you like.

Be More Informative: Here are some things I'd find useful to know. How long is the first time you play? How does the game change based on player count? How much strategy, luck, interaction is involved? How much will the downtime between turns test my child's patience? At a certain point, these are just judgment calls based on customers' subjective experience, but I would still like to know what the publisher thinks first.

- PLAYERS: 2–6 • Best for 4 • Extra downtime at 6 players • Uses an AI deck for 2 players.
- TIME: 30 Minutes • +15 for the First Game • +10 for fifth and sixth players.
- AGE: 12+ • Requires Reading & Math • ~5 minutes of downtime between turns.
- Intricate cardplay • Nuanced language • Minimal luck • Endgame calculations.

You can see this information formatted as a kind of standardized nutrition label. That's obviously too lengthy to put on every side of the box, but there's usually room on the back or a discreet bottom panel. And perhaps a nutrition label is too dreary for something that's supposed to be fun, so another format would be more appropriate. In any case, I do think we need to keep pushing for clearer information communication so customers can make an informed purchase.

It's easy to get comfortable with how something looks on the screen, but seeing things full size and in three dimensions can really help you see how the final product will look and feel.

BRIGETTE INDELICATO

DESIGNING THE GAME TITLE

The key to designing a game title logo is intent. Do not get hung up on "good" or "bad" as a binary. The only thing you can control is whether your design is intentional. "Good" and "bad" will always be subjective to the viewer. If there is an error or flaw in your design, at least be able to say it was a conscious choice rather than an accidental oversight. Here are a few ways to spot intention in your logo, using my process for designing the *Kokoro* logo as a case study (Figure 8.17).

Intentional Legibility: When I was designing the logo for *Kokoro: Avenue of the Kodama*, I knew this game would be aimed at a broad range of players, including families. "Kokoro" is an unusual word in English, so I wanted the

DEFAULT FONT: SUPER HAPPY FUN BALL

Kokoro

VARIED BASELINE HEIGHT / ROTATED O's / ADDED IMPERFECTIONS

Kokoro

ENCLOSURE ENSURES LEGIBILITY / OFFSET MAKES IT DYNAMIC

ALTERNATING STROKES GIVES THE LOGO SOME DIMENSION

FIGURE 8.17   Process of designing the logo for *Kokoro: Avenue of the Kodama*.

text to be as easy to vocalize on sight as possible. There should be consistent widths in the letterforms and no ostentatious accents that would harm legibility. Still, this shouldn't be something as boring as Helvetica. I began with the font Super Happy Fun Ball, which had a nice big O and a sharply pointed K in uppercase and lowercase.

Intentional Imperfections: Repeated letters tend to look too perfect and mechanical, so I had to keep an eye on differences between the multiple O's and K's in "Kokoro." I adjusted the bar lengths on the initial K to make it more distinct from the lowercase k. Then I adjusted the baselines of all the letters to balance out the negative spaces. I enlarged the last O to make room for a little Kodama peeking out of the tree in the illustration. This also helped balance out the visual weight of the very large initial K.

Intentional Background: A retail product logo should be legible against either light and dark backgrounds. Make an "enclosure" around the letters logos to fill in any spaces in letters like R and O. In this way, the logo provides its own background so it stays legible regardless of its context. In the case of *Kokoro*, I expanded the stroke around the letterforms, making it much darker than the base letters. This made sure it would be legible even if it were placed on a light background. I slightly offset that enclosure to the lower left. This added a little bit of dynamic energy, again making the product feel more fun and light-hearted without impeding legibility.

Alternate Stroke Weights—Thin-Thick-Thin-Thick …: When you add strokes around the letters, they should alternate thicknesses. This is a common last bit of polish in retail logos. For example, my finishing touches to the *Kokoro* logo are a very thin dark stroke behind the white letterforms and behind the entire enclosure. In effect, this made a concentric series of strokes: White letters, surrounded by a thin black stroke, then a thick red stroke, then thin black stroke.

Make a Lock-Up with a Subtitle: If your game includes a secondary subtitle, as in this case with *"Avenue of the Kodama"* then consider how you can unite the main title with that subtitle while maintaining their visual hierarchy. You always want the main logo to be read first, but they should be a unit.

BOX 8.5 WHICH FONT?

For new designers making a logo for their game, the most common question is "which font should I use?" That's a fair first step, of course. Most of us have a long list of options, so it seems like any one of them could be the magic solution on its own. Just remember that it's only a first step, not the last.

Make good contrast for the title, so you can read it in low light. [The] title must be visible on ALL sides if the product is for retail.

JEPPE NORSKER

For an extra touch, you can add subtle details to your box that reward in-person viewing. Note that these techniques really do work better in real life where they can be appreciated up close. Video and static thumbnails don't really do them justice (Figure 8.18).

UV Coating is a clear coating applied to the box art, either across the entire box or in selected areas to create extra glossy areas to sections of your cover art. This effect works especially well when your box art is printed on a slightly matte surface, so the difference in luster is more apparent. It's best for logo titles and foreground characters, making them appear closer to the viewer. If possible, make your intended UV coat a vector illustration so the edges are crisp and sharp.

Metallic Stamps are a thin sheet of pigmented foil adhered to the box art to create especially reflective surfaces. Discuss your options with your printer to see what foil standards they have available. This technique is best reserved for premium upgrades, anniversary editions, showcasing awards and acclaim. While they look great when they're in mint condition, they can be prone to scuffing and peeling over time.

Holo Foil stock is a special kind of paper with an iridescent surface, sometimes showing waves, swirls, or other patterns. Depending on how much ink is printed on this paper stock, you'll see more or less of this effect through the artwork. You can partly control this effect by instructing the factory to print a flat opaque layer on certain sections where you don't want the stock to be seen.

FIGURE 8.18   Various game title logos.

Debossing sinks small depressions into the surface. **Embossing** raises elevated areas from the surface. Either technique may be more difficult to achieve depending on the thickness of your packaging cardboard stock. If the stock is thin enough to allow debossing or embossing, it may be too delicate to adequately protect your game! This is why you normally only see this used in tin boxes.

A note of caution again: Because most games are shipped with completely sealed shrinkwrap, that shiny plastic surface will greatly diminish the impact of any of these techniques. They'll really only be appreciated *after* the game has been purchased, when it's already part of someone's collection. That's why it's more often used as a stretch goal for crowdfunded games that bypass any storefront retailer concerns.

Don't forget to work with bleed, and to print and mockup your boxes! You'd be surprised to know how often you can overlock direction when you design a flat box.

ESTEFANIA RODRIGUEZ

Always check if the publisher has decided on a printer, and if so, find out the file preparation requirements they prefer.

STEPHANIE GUSTAFSSON

SUMMARY OF BOXES AND PACKAGING

This chapter serves as a starting point for designing boxes and packaging. There's a bunch more we could discuss but I think this serves as a pretty solid base for the most common packaging you'll encounter in your career. No doubt you'll find a few rare projects with outlandish packages made from unusual materials in irregular shapes, but those are so unique that they'll require in-depth planning with the whole team. This chapter should give you the tools to begin that discussion so you can more quickly address the special circumstances of a more idiosyncratic package.

Just remember that the box serves multiple purposes and satisfying one purpose may sometimes compromise another. A package has to be durable enough to protect the game's contents during the rigors of overseas shipping, but must also not be so cushioned that customers complain about "boxes of air." The box must jump out to potential customers browsing a store rack or a digital catalog, but also be modest enough that it's suitable for home display on a collector's shelf. You'll have to find your own path between all of these demands.

Above all, the package is the game's first impression. Consider how you will initially present the game's themes and mechanisms to the uninitiated. Present the game's most positive attributes as clearly as possible. Even if someone doesn't buy the game, they should at least know what the game is about.

Summary Questions

- How would you characterize the mood of the game? Serious or humorous? Casual or competitive? Militaristic or Peaceful?
- How are similar games packaged and presented?
- In what ways can your package stand out from its category, while still clearly signaling that it is part of that category?
- How well does the packaging reflect that intended experience?
- What is the unboxing experience like for the customer? What is the first thing they see, then the second, then the third, and so on?
- What considerations have you made for the box's structural integrity?
- Is the package future-proof? Should it accommodate expansions or additional components?
- Do you need to consult with any regulatory or advisory committees before finalizing the package design?
- How have you accommodated international localizers?
- How can tactile elements in packaging enhance the overall gaming experience?
- Are there any unusual materials, like magnets or textiles, that may need additional oversight for international shipping?
- Is the game title legible on all sides of the package?
- Have you taken any measures to make the packaging more ecologically sustainable, such as minimizing the use of plastic?
- If so, what additional measures have you taken to ensure the package will not be subject to damaging elements during transit?
- Does the game require additional components not included in the game? If so, is that clearly communicated on the package?
- Have you had uninitiated people look at the package and give their first impressions?

CHAPTER 9

Conclusion

INTRODUCTION

My goal with this book was to share as much of my experience and knowledge as possible so that you'd be more prepared for your role as a graphic designer than I was when I started. Even if I succeeded in that goal, I realize that's only one person's perspective. No one designer could be a representative sample of the entire profession.

In order to get a more comprehensive view, I sent out a survey on several design topics, including card design, typography, rulebook layout, and more. We had 14 total respondents as of this writing. You've seen some individual curated responses throughout this book already. This final chapter collects a few more questions and replies that felt more appropriate to present all at once.

First, I'll give an overview of my own response and then follow with some curated responses from the survey participants. My hope is that showing these answers together makes it more evident how much common ground is shared by many designers, but also the many unique paths that can lead to being a graphic designer for board games.

DOI: 10.1201/9781003453772-10

GETTING STARTED AS A GRAPHIC DESIGNER

Over the years, I've met many graphic designers who work for board games. They've come from all walks of life with varying degrees of experience before being put into this role.

My own career began in the art program at a state university. The university actually had several schools offering their own versions of a graphic design curriculum. The journalism, architecture, and fine arts programs each graduated a cohort of designers into the field every year. Naturally, each school thought they were training the "real" designers while the rest were dubious at best. This was my first exposure to the myriad paths one might take to becoming a professional designer. It also taught me to not take academic pedigree very seriously. A desire to learn is more important than *where* you learned.

It was during this time I was first exposed to the world of board games. I bought a copy of *Pente* and *Carcassonne*, which hooked me immediately. In my off-time, I designed a string of abstract board games and released the rules for free on my personal blog "Luchacabra." None of these games are very good, but that wasn't really the goal. I was giving myself opportunities to use the Adobe suite of tools to make boards, cards, diagrams, and other graphics.

After graduating, I was hired as an intern at an advertising agency specializing in rebranding credit unions across the United States. I was promoted over time into more of a leadership role, managing other designers and leading strategy direction. I dabbled in script-writing, video-editing, and lots of meetings. So many meetings. Throughout it all, I continued my interest in board games and pursued freelance gigs where I had time. After about eight years in the ad business, I decided to make a change to working full-time as a freelancer. I had built up enough contacts that I could string together some paying gigs over about two years. Eventually I got hired by one of my freelance clients to work as a full-time in-house graphic designer. Around 2019, I took the chance for a promotion at WizKids Games and I'm still there as of this writing.

I asked survey participants "How did you get started in graphic design for tabletop games?" and they fell into a few loose categories:

Gamers-Turned-Designers

These are the respondents who began their career as fans and hobbyists within the board game community, eventually finding their niche as graphic designers.

I first started by working on my own games, and then after a couple of years I started working at Funko Games. I began by doing instruction layouts, component designs, and factory ready files.

ESTEFANIA RODRIGUEZ

Making speculative [...] redesigns of games I was enjoying, and posting them on Facebook groups and BoardGameGeek.com. Eventually a couple of publishers took notice.

RORY MULDOON

I enjoyed board gaming and my husband suggested I try freelancing in the game industry.

STEPHANIE GUSTAFSSON

I began by redesigning components in games I did not like. The board for Manhattan was first.

TODD SANDERS

Designers-Turned-Specialists

These are the professional graphic designers who narrowed their focus to the niche of board game development and production.

Through the connections I made by testing our game at local groups and events like Unpub, I was able to take on more and more game-related freelance jobs.

BRIGETTE INDELICATO

I hold a Masters degree in Design from 2000.

JEPPE NORSKER

Pros-Turned-Designers

These are folks who were already working in the tabletop games industry and found a role as graphic designers.

I'm a graphic designer by profession with a 10 years background in video games. I started out designing and doing art for board games about two years ago.

TORBEN RATZLAFF

I was working as an illustrator for Stronghold Games and we needed some graphic design work done.

BILL BRICKER

A job just kind of fell in my lap. I had a game design published by Petersen Games […] After some discussions, they signed me on.

TONY MASTRANGELI

Out of college, I got a part-time job at Hasbro Toys hand-assembling box prototypes. That got my foot in the door to apply for a graphic design position in Hasbro's games department.

LINDSAY DAVIAU

It looked like fun, so I went there. It actually is fun, so I stayed. In spite of the pay.

HEIKO GÜNTHER

WHAT I WISH I KNEW

I asked survey participants what they wish they had known when they were a novice designer entering the tabletop industry. In my case, I wish I had known more about automation features that would've spared me some long-term physical injuries like carpal tunnel syndrome and ulnar nerve impaction. If you work in Photoshop or Illustrator and find yourself doing repetitive tasks, record them into a batch action so they can be done with one click. If you do repetitive tasks in InDesign, search for any scripts that can do that work for you.

Here is how survey participants responded:

It is important to prepare your files correctly for print. Imagery should be supplied as RGB for best color fidelity and you as the designer should handle the color conversion to CMYK for print.

STEPHANIE GUSTAFSSON

I wish I had some real training in Indesign. Youtube has been a fantastic resource, but it took a hot minute to get my feet under me.

BILL BRICKER

Spend a little time up front in setting up your files with naming, linking, and a structure that will save you and other artists a LOT of time later.

KIRK W BUCKENDORF

The best relationships I've had are those where there's a good up front discussion about what the client needs and what services I can offer.

RORY MULDOON

It's a small, small industry with very tight margins. For the most part, you will be working for less money and benefits than an equivalent job in other industries.

TONY MASTRANGELI

Always assume things will take longer than you think they will.

BRIGETTE INDELICATO

TAKING FEEDBACK

While I don't think it's necessary to go to a full university program to learn graphic design, I did find the experience valuable for my own work habits. Our professors warned us that clients would want to see Option A, B, and C, regardless of how strongly you tried to recommend one path forward. Clients ask for multiple options because they want a sense of ownership process. They want to know that every course has been considered. So while I was a freelancer, I did my best to check in with the client regularly, first giving them a collage of images as a standard reference document. If they approved that reference, we could always compare our current status to that document and see if we were drifting from that goal.

Here is how survey participants responded regarding how they handle feedback and revisions.

I'm always happy to revise based on feedback. This is a collaborative effort and while some voices might carry more weight than others, all of the opinions should be explored.

BILL BRICKER

Mostly take notes, and separate them in categories like rules, gameplay, graphic design, etc. and refer to those notes when setting up the final files and rulebook.

KIRK W BUCKENDORF

If the feedback is subjective then I would rather have discussion so I can understand where those changes are coming from.

RORY MULDOON

I try to never present anything until I think it will solicit feedback on what is important. [...] Be clear of what the scope of the project is and what scope creep looks like. Get the contract signed.

JACOBY O'CONNOR

I try to minimize revisions due to how I structure the initial design presentations and working slowly with sign-off as the project moves along.

TODD SANDERS

Suggestions [from] other people can be valid while still having a suboptimal solution in mind.

TORBEN RATZLAFF

COLLABORATING ON A TEAM

Whether I'm a freelancer temporarily joining a project or an in-house designer overseeing multiple ongoing production schedules, I have to work with all sorts of specialists and keep everyone aware of our current status. My workflow has changed a lot over the years, but it's roughly settled on this basic process:

Orientation

Meet with the project's decision-makers to discuss goals, audiences, budgets, scope, and constraints. I ask if there are any manufacturing boundaries that have been determined before we had this meeting, such as using certain materials or a fixed size for some components that can't be exceeded. Aside from constraints, I also ask about their ambitions. What would they want to see in the game if they got their biggest wish?

Vision

I search for some prior examples of products that achieved the client's goals, such as miniatures, custom screen printed wood, or an unusual box. I also gather some examples of games and other media that share a theme with the project. I submit some reference images to the team for them to review and approve before we proceed to actual original work. This helps save some early "sketching" stages so I don't have to start from a purely blank page.

Assets

While I do this searching, I request any text documents, original art, and other assets the client wants to use in the project. I want the text to be as finished as possible, but it's inevitable that text changes will continue far into the layout process. There's something about seeing text in a real layout that makes errors more obvious than a text document. I just caution the team that it can be much slower and more costly to make simple text edits outside of the writing/editorial stage.

Ideation

I typically work on a game logo and box lid first, since these are among the earliest assets a publisher needs for the marketing campaign. It's common that art is still being illustrated while I work concurrently on the graphic design. I try to include the artist(s) in my layout updates, soliciting their early sketches so I know how my layout can best complement and support their work. The artist wants to know how the publisher's trade dress will overlap their illustration. I check in with the team once I have a rough draft design of a box cover, so the team has an early look at where we're headed. Get their approval in this direction before proceeding.

Updates

I continue sending regular and frequent updates to the team, making sure they're all signed off at each update. The last thing I want to do is backtrack on weeks of progress because a client is not happy with the current direction. The client will want some time to discuss and review each milestone, so I try to stagger my work across multiple components so that I can keep momentum on one item while another is being evaluated. This is partly why I send such frequent updates, because I don't want to waste time on one direction if it might be backtracked. I always save my review PDFs with the creation date in the file name so we maintain version control across the project.

Comments

I mostly use dropbox to share my periodic updates with clients so they can highlight sections of the page and comment on them directly. I know some clients prefer using Google Drive to serve a similar function, which is also fine. Mainly what I like is the ability to highlight specific areas when writing a comment, so I know when a client is looking at a particular paragraph or sentence rather than an entire page. This is also why I save each new draft as a new file, so that the client can still see the comment history from the prior draft and compare it to the new draft's updates so they may verify everything's been resolved.

Delivery

Eventually, after several rounds of comments and updates, the files will be approved. Most of the time I do not have direct contact with the factory, since the client or project manager has been coordinating with them separately. All I need from the factory is confirmation that all my files have been saved with the proper sizes, bleeds, margins, color mode, resolution, and so on. Once the file is sent to the factory, they'll send back a digital proof so the client can give it one final check and sign-off. Then it goes to production and my part of the project is done!

Here is how survey participants responded about collaborating with game designers, illustrators, and other team members:

I love Slack for communicating, Google for sharing spreadsheets and word documents, and Dropbox for sharing files. (The files on the hard drive automatically sync on Dropbox so that (a) I have an instant back-up, and (b) other folks on my team can access them as soon as I save them.)

LINDSAY DAVIAU

Graphic designers are often brought in later in the equation but I think we have a lot to offer in how a game might develop.

RORY MULDOON

I typically get involved in game design as early in the play testing as possible. [...] I tend to prefer using slack because it lets me share proofs with the team in a more trackable way.

JACOBY O'CONNOR

I try to minimize contact with the game designers, preferring to work through the publishing project manager.

TODD SANDERS

Get a common job understanding with the illustrator about what you try to achieve and how to keep design and illustrations consistent.

TORBEN RATZLAFF

Index

Note: Page numbers in *italics* refer to figures.

A

abstract-icon-color-pattern pairings 59 (box), *61*
abstraction 44–47, *45, 46*
action cards 111
action spaces on game board 205–208, *206*
Adobe Fonts 12 (box)
Aeon's End: Legacy 125
aesthetics 205
Age of Dirt 175, *177*, 185
age testing 267 (box)
alphanumeric characters in diagrams 78–80, *80*
Among Thieves 95, *96*, 255–256
Android: Netrunner 112 (box)
Anthelion: Conclave of Power 261
art
    communicating effect in 128 (box)
    placement and framing on cards 126–128, *127*
    planning for punchouts 153–157, *154, 155, 157*
ascenders 10
Ascending Empires 241
Atlantic Robot League 20, *182, 190*, 190–191, *227*, 229

B

Bang! 43
Bargain Basement Bathysphere 230, *231, 265*, 266
Baskerville URW font *9*
Bequest 236
Bimodal cards *138*, 139
Bird Bucks 110, 111
black and white design 50–53, *51, 52*
blister packs 256–259
Blob Party 109, *110*, 265
board
    size 191–193, *192*
    text 193–195, *194*
borders and frames on cards 128–130, *129*, 130 (box)
box sleeves 238–239
boxes and packaging
    age testing 267 (box)
    anatomy of cover 245–248, *246*
    basic specs 243–245, *243–244*
    box base 251–254, *252*
    common packages 256–262
    component trays 262–264, *263*
    cover 234–235, *236*
    game title design 268–273, *269, 272*
    language 239 (box)
    side panel 248–251, *249*
    stat blocks 264–268, *265*
    summary 273–274
    title placement 250 (box)
    trade dress 248 (box)
    user 237–240, *238*
    visual trends 240–242, *241*
    writing a summary 254–256
break apart sandwiches 203
brevity, card design principle 108
Bricker, Bill 12, 208, 222, 254, 278, 279
Buckendorf, Kirk W. 2, 78, 122, 128, 135, 156, 178, 226, 235, 251, 278, 279
Building Blocks of Game Design 93, *94*

C

card backs 139–142, *141*
card displays on game board 203–205, *204*
cardboard trays 264
cards
    art placement and framing 126–128, *127*
    backs 139–142, *141*
    borders and frames 128–130, *129*,
      130 (box)
    corners and edges 133–135, *134*
    design for distance *131*, 131–133
    layers 119–122, *120*
    multi-purpose 135–137, *137*
    orientation 137–139, *138*, 142 (box)
    production errors *116*, 116–119,
      117, *118*
    purpose of 109–112
    sizing 112–116, *114*
    spreadsheets 142–148, *143*, *146*,
      147–148 (box)
    summary 148–149
    text placement *122*, 122–125, *123*,
      124, *125*
    three principles of design 106–109
career path/progression 276–278
chess 44, *45*, 47 (box)
"Chop Suey" fonts 30 (box)
Clash of Cultures 160, *161*
Clash of Cultures: Monumental Edition 48,
    124, *141*, *158*, *199*, *219*, *235*, *236*
cloth bags 260
color accessibility 56–58, *57*
colorblindness 56, *57*
Colosseum 99, *99*, *100*
Colosseum: Emperor's Edition 220–222, *221*
columns 33–35, *34*
    alternate width 35 (box)
"comics" layout 226 (box)
commodity cards 111
conditional and optional steps in diagrams
    96–101, *98*, *99*, *100*
conserving space 14–16, *15*
consistent terminology 41 (box)
constructible components *173*, 173–178,
    174, *176*, *177*, *178*
contrast, 5–8, *6*, *7*
cool down hot spots 201

costs and rewards 132 (box)
counter-spaces 8–10
Crooked Mayor 95
cultural typography 28–31
custom boards 165–168, *166*, 168 (box)

D

DaFont 12 (box)
Daviau, Lindsay 8, 18, 23, 28, 58, 119, 148,
    168, 225, 242, 278, 282
debossing 272–273
depicting movement in diagrams 85–88,
    86, *87*, *88*
descenders 10
Detective Rummy 161, 162
diagrams
    alphanumeric characters in 78–80, *80*
    conditional and optional steps 96–101,
      98, *99*, *100*
    depicting movement 85–88, *86*, *87*,
      88
    frames in 74–78, *75*, *76*, *77*
    in-game actions 88–93, *89*, *91*, *92*
    introduction 68–70
    player aids 101–104, *102*
    players in 93–96, *94*, *96*
    punctuation 80–83, *82*
    purpose of 71–74
    summary 104–105
    theme in 83–85, *84*
Diamonds 91, *91*
Dice Conquest 123, *238*, 239
display fonts 26–28, *27*
distance, design on cards *131*, 131–133
distributors 237
double-coding colors 59–61, *60*
double-spacing 22 (box)
double-spacing after sentences 22 (box)
drop shadows 8 (box)

E

embossing 272
Empire Builder 197
Ettin 20, *107*, *108*, *110*, 111
expansions and special indicators
    119 (box)
external card slots 205

F

Fantasy Realms: Deluxe Edition 246,
    249, 252
feedback 279–280
figurative window diagram *76*, 78
font creation tools 64 (box)
fonts 8–12
    logo design 271 (box)
    reliable sources 12 (box)
    samples *9*
FontSelfMaker 64 (box)
FontSpace 12 (box)
frames in diagrams 74–78, *75, 76, 77*
Free Radicals 141, 158, 179, 209, *210,*
    226

G

game boards
    action spaces 205–208, *206*
    card displays 203–205, *204*
    interaction points 201–203, *202*
    introduction 187–189
    map adaptation 195–198, *196*
    noise vs quiet 189–191, *190*
    rule book used as 229–232, *231*
    size 191–193, *192*
    summary 211–212
    terrain art 198–201, *199, 200*
    text 193–195, *194*
    tracks 208–209, *210*
Garamond Premier Pro font *9*
Gates of Mara 55, *55, 155,* 156, *157, 158,*
    165, 180
geometric typefaces 10
Get Bit 83
Gloomhaven: Jaws of the Lion 229
Google Fonts 12 (box)
grayscale 52 (box)
Greece Lightning 161, 162, *170, 265*
grids, typography 31–33, *32*
groups of icons 53–55, *54, 55*
grunge text 28 (box)
Günther, Heiko 14, 41, 148, 152, 172, 191,
    193, 232, 240, 278
Gustafsson, Stephanie 35, 53, 62, 116, 198,
    205, 273, 277, 278

H

headers 16–18, *18*
hierarchy, card design principle 106–110
holo foil 271
Horizontal cards 137–139, *138*
humanist typefaces 10

I

I Can't Even With These Monsters 122
IcoMoon 64 (box)
iconography
    abstraction 44–47, *45, 46*
    black and white design 50–53, *51, 52*
    case study *(Trickster: Champions of*
        Time) 64–66
    color accessibility 56–58, *57*
    double-coding colors 59–61, *60*
    groups 53–56, *54, 55*
    hybrid approach to icons 43 (box)
    keyword ligatures 62–64, *63*
    summary 66–67
    symbols 41–44, *42*
    use of icons 47–50, *48*
    visual languages 39–41, *40*
illustrated icons 55, 55 (box)
in-game actions in diagrams 88–93,
    89, 91, 92
Indelicato, Brigette 74, 80, 101, 112, 133,
    181, 195, 216, 268, 277, 279
indents 21 (box)
interaction points 201–203, *202*
intersection, standee 164
irregular sized cards 116 (box)
ISS Vanguard 229

J

Jokkmokk 42, 151, 204, 235, 236, 265
Junk Orbit 72, 73, 259, *260, 263*

K

Kardashev Scale 178
keyword ligatures 62–64, *63*
knowledge for novice designers 278–279
Kodama: the Tree Spirits 238, 239
Kokoro: Avenue of the Kodama. 268, *269,* 270
Krosmaster Arena 229

L

layers, card design 119–122, *120*
Light Rail 161, 162
line spacing 22, *23*
lists 18–21, *20*
Love Letter 10–12, *11*
LYNX 194

M

Markowitz, Mike 83, 198, 201, 209, 264
Martian Dice 259
Marvel: Age of Heroes 171
Mastrangeli, Tony 31, 53, 125, 130, 137,
    218, 256, 278, 279
metallic stamps 271
Minion font *9*
Misjudged 95
Mr. Burns, a Post-Electric Play 37–38
Muldoon, Rory 4, 16, 33, 47, 55, 163, 220,
    245, 277, 279, 282
multi-purpose cards 135–137, *137*

N

noise vs quiet 189–191, *190*
non-hand cards 135 (box)
non-temporal diagram *77*, 78
Norsker, Jeppe 271, 277
notation 47 (box)

O

O'Connor, Jacoby 21, 64, 93, 173, 184, 189,
    248, 262, 280, 282
oldstyle figures 26 (box)
ongoing cards 111
orientation of cards 137–139, *138*
    backs 142 (box)
outdents 21 (box)
owner of game 237

P

page numbers 33 (box)
Pandemic 197
papercraft constructibles 178 (box)
paragraph cards 109–111
paragraph spacing 22, *23*
passive voice, use in rulebook 217 (box)

personal setup 229 (box)
phase structure diagram 75–78, *76*
pickup grooves 205
plastic base, standee 164–165
player aids in diagrams 1–104, *102*
players in diagrams 93–96, *94*, *96*
playing cards 109
point size 12, *13*
Princes of Florence 102, *209*, 209
problem characters 24–26, *25*
production errors, cards *116*, 116–119,
    117, *118*
Publish or Perish: Wiñay Kawsay 102, 140,
    141, *176*, *202*, 265
publishers 237
punch components, blending with wood/
    plastic 172 (box)
punchouts
    constructible components *173*, 173–178,
        174, *176*, *177*, *178*
    custom boards 165–168, *166*, 168 (box)
    designing sheets *179*, 178–181
    file prep 181–184
    interlocking components *169*, 168–172,
        170, *171*, *172*
    introduction 150–152, *151*
    planning art 153–157, *154*, *155*, *157*
    standees *163*, 163–165
    summary 184–186
    tiles 160–163, *161*
    tokens *158*, 158–160
punctuation in diagrams 80–83, *80*

R

ragged edges and rivers 14 (box)
Rainy Day Fund 95
Ratzlaff, Torben 23, 50, 85, 104, 160, 229,
    277, 280, 283
representation 44–47, *45*, *46*
retailers 237
Roboto font *9*
Rodriguez, Estefania 26, 44, 74, 88, 95, 142,
    165, 203, 262, 273, 277
Rolling America 197
Rotating cards *138*, 139
rulebooks
    avoid forward referencing 225 (box)

components section 223–225, *224*
examples 220–222, *221*, 222 (box)
flow of book *214*, 214–216, 216 (box)
introduction 213–214
"keep" options 220 (box)
merging sections 228–229, *228*
page size vs book length 216–218, *217*
passive voice 217 (box)
setup 225–226, *227*
summary 232–233
tightly bound games 232 (box)
topic spread 218–220, *219*
used as game board 229–232, *231*

S

Sagrada Artisans 229–230
Sanders, Todd 139, 216, 267, 277, 280, 283
Sea Glass 169
Seastead 20, 40, 82, *141*, *158*, 165–167, *166*, *224*, *238*, 239
Senators 91, *92*
serifs 8, 16 (box)
Shapers of Gaia *110*, 111, *200*
Shogunate 84–85, *84*
Sidereal Confluence: Remastered Edition 177
silhouette 4
skirts, standee 165
Sleeping Gods 229
sleeves 204
spreadsheets, used for card design 142–148, *143*, *146*, 147–148 (box)
standees *163*, 163–165
stat blocks 264–268, *265*
stickers on shrinkwrap 237–238
strokes and outlines 18 (box)
Stuffed Fables 229
Sundae Split 263
Super-Skill Pinball 53, *54*, 253
System Gateway project 112 (box)

T

"tabular lining" 26 (box)
tags 121 (box)
Tales of the Arthurian Knights *110*, 111, *196*
targeted panels 239
team collaboration 280–283
terrain art 198–201, *199*, *200*

text
    game board 193–195, *194*
    placement on cards *122*, 122–125, *123*, *124*, *125*
The Duke 44–47, *46*, 72, 73
The Making of the President 197
theme in diagrams 83–85, *84*
Ticket to Ride 111, 197
tiles, 160–163, *161*
Timeline 260
tins 259
title placement on cards 125 (box)
tokens *158*, 158–160
    extremely small 160 (box)
tracks on game board 208–209, *210*
trade dress 248 (box)
Trade Gothic Next LT Pro
    Condensed font 9
TransAmerica 197
translucent materials 58 (box)
Trickster: Champions of Time 64–66, *65*
Trickster: Fantasy, Trickster: Symbiosis, Trickster: Starship 60
tubes 259
tuckboxes 256
turn order diagram 75, *75*
"two alphabets" rule 12–13
two-part boxes 256
typography
    "Chop Suey" fonts 30 (box)
    columns 33–35
    conserving space 14–16, *15*
    contrast 5–8, *6*, *7*
    cultural typography 28–30, *29*
    display fonts 26–28, *27*
    double-spacing 22 (box)
    drop shadow 8 (box)
    fonts 8–12, *9*, *11*
    grids 31–33, *32*
    grunge text 28 (box)
    headers 16–18, *18*
    introduction to 3–4
    line spacing 22, *23*
    lists 18–21, *20*
    problem characters 24–26, *25*
    serifs 8, 16 (box)
    summary 35–36
    "two alphabets" rule 12–13

U

UV coating 271

V

vacuform 262–264
vector file formats 50 (box)
visibility, card design principle 106
visual languages 39–41, *40*

W

warm up cold spots 201

While The Cat's Away 95
Wingspan 173
WizKids 239, *241*, *243–244*, 247, *257*,
   258, *259*, 266, 276
Wonderland 260, *261*
word cards 109
worker placement spaces 203

Z

Zeppelin Attack! 124
Zombie Dice 259

For Product Safety Concerns and Information please contact our EU
representative GPSR@taylorandfrancis.com Taylor & Francis Verlag GmbH,
Kaufingerstraße 24, 80331 München, Germany

Printed and bound by CPI Group (UK) Ltd, Croydon, CR0 4YY

08/06/2025

01896985-0003